3 ★ All-Star

Linda Lee ★ Kristin Sherman
Grace Tanaka ★ Shirley Velasco

Second Edition

McGraw Hill

Connect
Learn
Succeed™

Connect
Learn
Succeed™

ALL-STAR 3 STUDENT BOOK

Published by McGraw-Hill, a business unit of The McGraw-Hill Companies, Inc., 1221 Avenue of the Americas, New York, NY, 10020. Copyright © 2011, 2006 by The McGraw-Hill Companies, Inc. All rights reserved. No part of this publication may be reproduced or distributed in any form or by any means, or stored in a database or retrieval system, without the prior written consent of The McGraw-Hill Companies, Inc., including, but not limited to, in any network or other electronic storage or transmission, or broadcast for distance learning.

Some ancillaries, including electronic and print components, may not be available to customers outside the United States.

This book is printed on acid-free paper.

1 2 3 4 5 6 7 8 9 0 WDQ/WDQ 1 0 9 8 7 6 5 4 3 2 1 0

ISBN   978-0-07-719712-4

MHID   0-07-719712-7

ISE ISBN 978-0-07-131384-1

ISE MHID 0-07-131384-2

Vice president/Editor in chief: *Elizabeth Haefele*
Vice president/Director of marketing: *John E. Biernat*
Director of Sales and Marketing, ESL: *Pierre Montagano*
Director of development: *Valerie Kelemen*
Developmental editor: Maya Lazarus, Laura LeDrean, Nancy Jordan
Marketing manager: *Kelly Curran*
Lead digital product manager: *Damian Moshak*
Digital developmental editor: *Kevin White*
Director, Editing/Design/Production: *Jess Ann Kosic*
Lead project manager: *Susan Trentacosti*
Senior production supervisor: *Debra R. Sylvester*
Designer: *Srdjan Savanovic*
Senior photo research coordinator: *Lori Kramer*
Photo researcher: *Allison Grimes*
Digital production coordinator: *Cathy Tepper*
Illustrators: *Alyta Adams, Burgundy Beam, Jerry Gonzalez, Mike Hortens, Andrew Lange, Bot Roda,
        Daniel Rubenstein, Rich Stergulz, Carlotta Tormey, Laserwords*
Typeface: *11.5/12.5 Frutiger LT Std 45 Light*
Compositor: *Laserwords Private Limited*
Printer: *Worldcolor*
Cover credit: *Andrew Lange*
Credits: *The credits section for this book begins on page 232 and is considered an extension of the copyright page.*

The Internet addresses listed in the text were accurate at the time of publication. The inclusion of a Web site does not indicate an endorsement by the authors or McGraw-Hill, and McGraw-Hill does not guarantee the accuracy of the information presented at these sites.

www.mhhe.com

ACKNOWLEDGMENTS

The authors and publisher would like to thank the following individuals who reviewed *All-Star Second Edition* at various stages of development and whose comments, reviews, and field-testing were instrumental in helping us shape the second edition of the series:

Carlos Alcazar, Newport-Mesa USD Adult School, Costa Mesa, CA ★ Isabel V. Anderson, The English Center, Miami, FL ★ Carol Antunano, The English Center, Miami, FL ★ Ted Anderson ★ Josefina Aucar, Miami Beach Adult and Community Education Center, Miami, FL ★ Veronica Pavon-Baker, Miami Dade County Public Schools, Miami, FL ★ Barry Bakin, Pacoima Skills Center, Pacoima, CA ★ Michael Blackman, Reseda Community Adult School, Reseda, CA ★ Taylor H. Blakely, Newport-Mesa USD Adult School, Costa Mesa, CA ★ Marge Bock, Sweetwater USD Adult Education, Chula Vista, CA ★ Lusine Bokhikyan ★ Rothwell H Bouillon, Pacoima Skills Center, Pacoima, CA ★ Ian Brailsford, South Piedmont Community College, Monroe, NC ★ Roy Carl Brungardt, Riverside Adult School, Riverside, CA ★ Paul Buczko, Pacoima Skills Center, Pacoima, CA ★ Gemma S Burns, Riverside Adult School, Riverside, CA ★ Kathleen Bywater, Riverside Adult School, Riverside, CA ★ Helen Canellos, Milwaukee Area Technical College, Milwaukee, WI ★ Richard H Capet, Pimmit Hills Adult Education Center, Falls Church, VA ★ Waldo Cardenas, Miami Dade County Public Schools, Miami, FL ★ Gemma Santos Catire, Miami Beach Adult and Community Education Center, Miami, FL ★ Julio Chow, Pacoima Skills Center, Pacoima, CA ★ Claire Cirolia, Fairfax County Adult ESL Program, Fairfax, VA ★ Sabine Cooke, Riverside Adult School, Riverside, CA ★ Jeffrey R Corrigan, Newport-Mesa USD Adult School, Costa Mesa, CA ★ Don Curtis, Oakland USD Adult Education, Neighborhood Centers, Oakland, CA ★ Angela DeRocco, Sweetwater USD Adult Education, Chula Vista, CA ★ Jorge de la Paz, Miami Sunset Adult Center, Miami, FL ★ Deborah Ebersold, Pacoima Skills Center, Pacoima, CA ★ Fernando Egea, Miami Sunset Adult Center, Miami, FL ★ Marilyn Farrell, Riverside Adult School, Riverside, CA ★ Lora Finch, Newport-Mesa USD Adult School, Costa Mesa, CA ★ Pat Fox, Montgomery College, Rockville, MD ★ Antoinette Galaviz, Reseda Community Adult School, Reseda, CA ★ Elizabeth Gellatly, Newport-Mesa USD Adult School, Costa Mesa, CA ★ Dennys Gonzalez, Miami Dade College, Miami, FL ★ Amber G Goodall, South Piedmont Community College, Monroe, NC ★ Amy Grodzienski, Reseda Community Adult School, Reseda, CA ★ Ana Guadayol, Miami-Dade College VESOL, Miami, FL ★ Diane Helvig, Sweetwater USD Adult Education, Chula Vista, CA ★ Kristine Hoffman, Newport-Mesa USD Adult School, Costa Mesa, CA ★ Dr. Coral Horton, Miami-Dade College, Miami, FL ★ Valerie Johnson, Reseda Community Adult School, Reseda, CA ★ Ali Kiani, Reseda Community Adult School, Reseda, CA ★ Donna Kihara, Reseda Community Adult School, Reseda, CA ★ Angela Kosmas, Wilbur Wright College, Chicago, IL ★ Alida Labiosa, Newport-Mesa USD Adult School, Costa Mesa, CA ★ Lourdes A. Laguilles, Reseda Community Adult School, Reseda, CA ★ Holly Lawyer, Elgin Community College, Elgin, Illinois ★ Lia Lerner, Burbank Adult School, Burbank, CA ★ Mae F Liu, Chinese American Planning Council, New York, NY ★ Levia Loftus, College of Lake County, Grayslake, IL ★ Nancy Magathan, Reseda Community Adult School, Reseda, CA ★ Monica Manero-Cohen, Miami Beach Adult and Community Education Center, Miami, FL ★ Matilda Martinez, Miami Beach Adult and Community Education Center, Miami, FL ★ Suzette Mascarenas, Newport-Mesa USD Adult School Costa Mesa, CA ★ Sara McKinnon, College of Marin, Kentfield, CA ★ Ibis Medina, Miami Sunset Adult Center, Miami, FL ★ Alice-Ann Menjivar, Carlos Rosario International Public Charter School, Washington, DC ★ Kathleen Miller, Reseda Community Adult School, Reseda, CA ★ Kent Minault, Pacoima Skills Center, Pacoima, CA ★ Pedro Monteagudo, Miami Beach Adult and Community Education Center, Miami, FL ★ Jose Montes, The English Center, Miami, FL ★ Ilene Mountain, Newport-Mesa USD Adult School Costa Mesa, CA ★ Mary Murphy-Clagett, Sweetwater USD Adult Education, Chula Vista, CA ★ Fransisco Narciso, Reseda Community Adult School, Reseda, CA ★ Anita Nodarse, Miami Dade College, Miami, FL ★ Zoila Ortiz, Miami Sunset Adult Center, Miami, FL ★ Phil Oslin, Sweetwater USD, Adult Education, Chula Vista, CA ★ Nancy Pakdel, Newport-Mesa USD Adult School, Costa Mesa, CA ★ Eduardo Paredes-Ferro, Miami Sunset Adult Center, Miami, FL ★ Virginia Parra, Miami Dade College, Interamerican Campus, Miami, FL ★ Elaine S Paris, Chinese American Planning Council, New York, NY ★ Ellen R. Purcell, Public Schools/Pimmit Hills, Falls Church, VA ★ Michelle R Quiter, Austin Community College, Austin, TX ★ Sandra Ramirez, Pacoima Skills Center, Pacoima, CA ★ Corinne Rennie, Newport-Mesa USD Adult School, Costa Mesa, CA ★ Barbara Rinsler ★ Ray Rivera, South Dade Adult Education Center, Homestead, FL ★ Abdali Safaei, Reseda Community Adult School, Reseda, CA ★ Bernard Sapir, Reseda Community Adult School, Reseda, CA ★ Amy Schneider, Pacoima Skills Center, Pacoima, CA ★ Delisa Sexton, Pacoima Skills Center, Pacoima, CA ★ Norma S Smith, Pacoima Skills Center, Pacoima, CA ★ Mandi M Spottsville, Newport-Mesa USD Adult School ★ Helen G Stein, Miami Dade College, Miami, FL ★ Jennifer C Storm, College of Lake County, Grayslake, IL ★ Terri L Stralow, South Piedmont Community College, Monroe, NC ★ Dina P Tarrab, Reseda Community Adult School, Reseda, CA ★ Maliheh Vafai, East Side Adult Education, San Jose, CA ★ Rosanne Verani, Riverside Adult School, Riverside, CA ★ Kermey Wang, Riverside Adult School, Riverside, CA ★ Cynthia Whisner, Riverside Adult School, Riverside, CA ★ Duane Wong, Newport-Mesa USD Adult School, Costa Mesa, CA

SCOPE AND SEQUENCE

LIFE SKILLS

UNIT	Listening and Speaking	Reading and Writing	Critical Thinking	Vocabulary	Grammar
Pre-Unit **Getting Started** *page 2*	• Express your opinions • Introduce yourself • Interview your classmates	• Write about your classmates • Preview the text	• Evaluate	• Introductions • Information questions	
1 **Setting Goals** *page 4*	• Talk about daily routines • Talk about family responsibilities • Talk about goals • Listen to conversations about goals • Ask for focused repetition • Discuss success • **Pron:** Stress in repetition questions • **WB:** Talk to your child's teacher	• Write long- and short-term goals • Preview • Read about goals • Write about personal goals • Take notes on conversations • Read a success story • **Use prewriting strategies:** brainstorm, make a cluster diagram • **WB:** Read about communicating with your child's school • **WB:** Read about how to get the most from your job • Use context to guess meaning	• Make inferences • Apply knowledge • Draw conclusions • Predict • Summarize	• Strategies to reach goals • Family responsibilities • Goals	• Simple present, review • *Want, need,* and *would like* • Future with *will*, review • Simple past, review
2 **Housing** *page 18*	• Talk about houses • Describe different types of housing • Report housing problems • Describe a house • Evaluate a house for sale • Role-play phone conversations with real estate agents • Listen to and role-play phone conversations between tenants and landlords • Ask for a more specific time • Talk about tenants' and landlords' responsibilities • Talk about the Fair Housing Act	• Read housing ads • Read a floor plan • Take notes on telephone conversations • Read and take notes on a rental application • Read the Fair Housing Act • Preview a webpage • Identify a purpose for writing; read and write letters of complaint • **WB:** Read an article about a consumer hero • **WB:** Read about childproofing your home	• Make decisions • Evaluate • Interpret • Apply knowledge to new situations • Predict • Give opinions	• Parts of a house • Words and abbreviations used in housing ads • Vocabulary used in rental applications • Childproofing equipment	• Quantifiers • Gerunds after prepositions • Simple present vs. present continuous

Civics Concepts	Math Skills	CASAS Life Skills Competencies	SCANS Competencies (Workplace)	EFF Content Standards	Florida	LAUSD
		• 0.1.4	• Decision making • Sociability • Knowing how to learn	• Speak so others can understand • Reflect and evaluate	• 4.01.01, 4.01.02, 4.01.03	• 1, 3
• Identify educational responsibilities and research education/ training requirements to achieve personal goals • **WB:** Prepare for a parent-teacher conference		• **1:** 7.2.2, 7.2.4, 8.2.2, 8.2.3 • **2:** 4.4.5, 7.1.1 • **3:** 0.1.6, 4.4.5, 7.1.1 • **4:** 5.3.6 • **5:** 7.2.4 • **6:** 7.2.3, 7.2.6 • **WB:** 0.1.2, 0.1.5, 2.5.5, 7.3.1, 7.3.2	• Reasoning • See things in the mind's eye • Know how to learn • Organize and maintain information • Problem solving • Self-management • Decision making • Creative thinking	• Cooperate with others • Plan • Learn through research • Reflect and evaluate • Speak so others can understand • Observe critically • Take responsibility for learning	• **1:** 4.01.05 • **2:** 4.02.07, 4.02.08, 4.03.13 • **3:** 4.03.13, • **WB:** 4.03.05, 4.03.12	• **1:** 50 • **2:** 48 • **3:** 7 (b), 13, 48, 51, G3 • **4:** 1, G5a • **5:** 50 • **6:** 51 • **WB:** 12, 59, 60a
• Understand how to look for housing • Understand the Fair Housing Act	• Calculate housing costs	• **1:** 1.4.1 • **2:** 1.4.2 • **3:** 1.4.7 • **4:** 1.4.3 • **5:** 1.4.5, 7.2.4 • **6:** 0.2.3, 7.2.4	• Decision making • Reasoning • Acquire and evaluate information • See things in the mind's eye • Know how to learn • Organize and maintain information • Creative thinking • Integrity and honesty	• Reflect and evaluate • Speak so others can understand • Cooperate with others • Convey ideas in writing • Observe critically	• **3:** 4.04.04 • **6:** 4.04.05 • **WB:** 4.01.08	• **1:** 52, G 24 • **2:** 26, G19b • **3:** 4a, G2a and b • **4:** 2 • **5:** 53 • **6:** 9 • **WB:** 27

CASAS, Florida, and LAUSD standards: Numbers in bold indicate lesson numbers. • **G:** Grammar • **WB:** Workbook • **RC:** Online Teacher Resource Center

v

SCOPE AND SEQUENCE

LIFE SKILLS

UNIT	Listening and Speaking	Reading and Writing	Critical Thinking	Vocabulary	
3 **Healthy Living** *page 32*	• Talk about healthy and unhealthy behavior • Listen to conversations between patients and doctors • Role-play conversations between patients and doctors • Give opinions about healthy and unhealthy behavior • Give health advice	• Read a health history questionnaire • Read a bar graph • Take notes on conversations • Write about a health problem • Read about hotlines and emergency services • Read information in a telephone directory • Skim and scan; read prescription labels • Use compound sentences; write about your healthy or unhealthy behavior as a child	• Classify • Interpret • Evaluate	• Healthy and unhealthy activities • Words used on health forms • Words used on medicine labels • Ways to give suggestions and advice • Hotlines; emergency services	• Present perfect • Simple past vs. present perfect • Present perfect with *for* and *since* • *Used to*
4 **Money and Consumerism** *page 46*	• Offer polite disagreement • Listen to and role-play conversations between customers and car salespeople • Talk about opinions • **WB:** Talk about common car problems and car maintenance procedures	• Read warranties • Read a glossary of banking terms • Write about a purchase you made • Read about ways to shop • Write a letter requesting a refund • Find the main idea • **WB:** Read about different types of financial institutions • **WB:** Read a return policy • **WB:** Read store ads • **WB:** Read about car maintenance procedures • **WB:** Complete a check • **WB:** Complete a checking account application	• Synthesize • Use content • Interpret • Evaluate • Choose the best alternative • Solve problems	• Activities at a car dealership • Words associated with automobiles • Ways to disagree politely • Words used in warranties and guarantees • Banking terms • Shopping terms	• Gerunds as subjects • Gerunds as objects of verbs • Comparative and superlative adjectives; *as* adjective *as*
5 **Accidents and Emergencies** *page 60*	• Talk about work injuries • Talk about personal injuries • Listen to and role-play conversations between employers and employees • Talk about safety procedures • Talk about health hazards • Talk about first aid • **Pron:** Intonation in clauses	• Fill out accident reports • Take notes on conversations • Read and take notes on a first aid guide • Read about safety and rights on the job • Write about job preferences • Use the SQ3R strategy (survey, question, read, recite, and review) • Make a Venn diagram; write a paragraph from a Venn diagram	• Interpret • Analyze • Make decisions • Evaluate	• Health hazards • Types of injuries • Types of emergencies • Ways to apologize • Basic first aid terms • **WB:** Workplace safety equipment	• Past continuous, statements • Past continuous with time clauses • Simple past vs. past continuous • Real conditionals

Civics Concepts	Math Skills	CASAS Life Skills Competencies	SCANS Competencies (Workplace)	EFF Content Standards	Florida	LAUSD
• Understand prescription labels • Identify telephone numbers for emergency health services	• Convert units of measurement	• **1:** 3.4.2, 3.5.9 • **2:** 3.1.1, 3.2.1, 3.6.3 • **3:** 0.1.3, 3.6.4 • **4:** 2.1.1, 7.5.4, 7.5.5 • **5:** 3.3.2, 3.3.4, 3.6.4, 7.2.1 • **6:** 3.5.9, 7.2.2	• Decision making • See things in the mind's eye • Self-management • Integrity and honesty • Acquire and evaluate information • Organize and maintain information • Know how to learn • Reasoning • Work well with others • Creative thinking • Problem solving • Use resources wisely	• Cooperate with others • Speak so others can understand • Reflect and evaluate • Learn through research • Guide others • Observe critically	• **1:** 4.05.02, 4.07.01 • **2:** 4.05.01 • **4:** 4.01.10 • **5:** 4.05.04 • **6:** 4.05.02 • **WB:** 4.05.05, 4.06.05 • **RC:** 4.05.03, 4.05.06	• **1:** G7b-d • **2:** 38, 36, G7a, 41 • **3:** 5d, 37 • **6:** G5b • **RC:** 31, 40
• Understand automobile terms • **WB:** Identify common car problems • **WB:** Understand car maintenance procedures		• **1:** 0.1.2, 1.3.1, WB: 1.2.1, 1.2.2 • **2:** 1.3.3, 1.6.4 • **3:** 1.9.5 • **4:** 1.6.7, 1.8.1, 1.8.3 • **5:** 1.3.1, 1.5.2, 7.2.1 • **6:** 1.3.3 • **WB:** 1.8.1, 1.8.2	• Decision making • See things in the mind's eye • Know how to learn • Reasoning • Acquire and evaluate information • Organize and maintain information • Problem solving • Use resources wisely • Understand how systems work • Work within the system • Integrity and honesty • Teach others new skills • Act as leader	• Cooperate with others • Reflect and evaluate • Speak so others can understand • Learn through research • Observe critically	• **1:** 4.04.02 • **4:** 4.04.07 • **5:** 4.01.03, 4.04.09 • **6:** 4.04.05 • **WB:** 4.04.02, 4.04.08, 4.06.05 • **RC:** 4.01.09, 4.04.01, 4.04.06	• **1:** 6 • **2:** 30, G19a • **3:** 24, G32a and b • **4:** 25 • **5:** 25 (d) • **6:** 51 • **WB:** 23, 25a-b, 28, 29
• Identify health hazards • Understand basic first aid • Understand safety procedures • Understand safety rights on the job • **WB:** Understand safety signs • **WB:** Prepare for an emergency • **WB:** Understand an evacuation plan		• **1:** 3.4.2, 4.3.2, 4.3.3 • **3:** 0.1.4, 4.3.4 • **4:** 2.1.2, 3.4.3 • **5:** 4.2.6, 4.3.2, 7.2.4 • **6:** 6.6.5, 7.2.3, 7.2.7	• See things in the mind's eye • Reasoning • Know how to learn • Analyze and communicate information • Creative thinking • Decision making • Acquire and evaluate information • Organize and maintain information • Problem solving	• Cooperate with others • Solve problems and make decisions • Speak so others can understand • Observe critically • Use math to solve problems and communicate	• **1:** 4.07.01 • **3:** 4.03.08, 4.03.07 • **5:** 4.07.01 • **WB:** 4.02.05, 4.06.04	• **1:** G6a • **2:** G6b • **3:** 4 (b), 47(c), G6 a and b • **4:** 52, G4 • **6:** 50, 51 • **RC:** 34

CASAS, Florida, and LAUSD standards: Numbers in bold indicate lesson numbers.   •   **G:** Grammar   •   **WB:** Workbook   •   **RC:** Online Teacher Resource Center

SCOPE AND SEQUENCE

LIFE SKILLS

UNIT	Listening and Speaking	Reading and Writing	Critical Thinking	Vocabulary	Grammar
6 **Community** *page 74*	• Talk about community • Talk about rules in the community • Listen to and role-play conversations between citizens and authorities • Accept criticism • Talk about your opinion • **Pron:** Reductions with *to* • **WB:** Offer excuses	• Read a crime report • Rewrite a paragraph in your own words (paraphrase) • Write a summary of an article • **WB:** Write a paragraph giving your opinion • **WB:** Read about trash disposal and recycling procedures • **WB:** Read an article about disciplining children	• Use context • Classify • Interpret • Analyze	• Necessary documents • Community rules and consequences • Ways to accept criticism	• Infinitives after verbs • *Be allowed, be permitted,* and *be illegal* • Infinitives after nouns or object pronouns
7 **Getting a Job** *page 88*	• Ask questions about a position • Talk about qualities of the workplace • Talk about benefits • Talk about ways to find a job • Listen to and role-play conversations between receptionists and applicants • **WB:** Inquire about job requirements and application procedures	• Read about workplace benefits • Read a résumé • Read a cover letter • Write a cover letter • Write a résumé • Make inferences • **WB:** Fill out a job application • **WB:** Read about the Family and Medical Leave Act (FMLA) • **WB:** Read about Federal Equal Employment Opportunity Laws (EEOC)	• Make inferences • Apply knowledge • Evaluate • Reason • Classify • Make associations • Analyze • Use context	• Qualities of the workplace • Benefits • Ways to ask polite questions • Parts of a résumé • Parts of a cover letter • Types of jobs	• Verbs followed by gerund or infinitive • *Prefer, would prefer,* and *would rather* for preference • *Be able to*
8 **Communi-cation** *page 102*	• Talk about the ways people communicate • Listen to conversations of people communicating • Role-play conversations • Check for understanding • **Pron:** Using stress for emphasis • **WB:** Thank someone • **WB:** Apologize and make excuses • **WB:** Communicate with school personnel • **WB:** Ask favors politely	• Preview a text • Read articles about communication • Read persuasive paragraphs • Write a persuasive paragraph • Distinguish fact from opinion • Give examples; support your ideas • **WB:** Read and write short work-related emails • **WB:** Write a note to a child's teacher • **WB:** Read a performance evaluation	• Interpret • Evaluate • Analyze • Use context	• Ways of communicating • Communication skills	• Indefinite pronouns • *Will* and *would* for requests • *May* and *might* for possibility; *must* for conclusion

Civics Concepts	Math Skills	CASAS Life Skills Competencies	SCANS Competencies (Workplace)	EFF Content Standards	Florida	LAUSD
• Identify common laws and ordinances • Interpret and identify legal response to regulations • Understand community rules • Understand how to interact with law enforcement • Learn how to report a crime • **WB:** Understand trash disposal and recycling procedures • **WB:** Identify U.S. federal holidays • **WB:** Understand customs regarding child discipline in the U.S.		• **1:** 2.7.3 • **2:** 5.3.1, 5.6.1 • **3:** 0.1.4, 5.3.7, 5.5.6 • **4:** 5.3.8 • **5:** 5.3.1, 5.6.5, 7.2.1 • **6:** 5.6.5	• Know how to learn • Creative thinking • Analyze and communicate information • Decision making • Responsibility • Integrity and honesty • Self-management • See things in the mind's eye • Organize and maintain information • Problem solving • Work well with others • Use resources wisely • Select the right technology for the task	• Cooperate with others • Solve problems and make decisions • Reflect and evaluate • Use information and communications technology • Speak so others can understand • Observe critically	• **3:** 4.01.01, 4.03.07, 4.06.02 • **4:** 4.07.02 • **5:** 4.02.02 • **6:** 4.02.02 • **RC:** 4.06.01, 4.06.03	• **1:** G20b • **2:** 52, G16 • **3:** 4 (b), G20e • **4:** 35, 53 • **6:** 21 • **RC:** 20, 22
• Locate, analyze, and describe job requirements • Understand work benefits • Understand how to look for a job • **WB:** Understand the Family and Medical Leave Act (FMLA) • **WB:** Understand Federal Equal Employment Opportunity Laws (EEOC)	• Understand payroll deductions	• **1:** 4.1.8 • **2:** 3.1.6, 3.2.3, 4.2.5 • **3:** 2.1.8, 4.1.3, 4.1.6 • **4:** 4.1.2, 4.2.1 • **5:** 7.2.2, 7.2.4 • **6:** 4.1.2 • **WB:** 4.1.2, 4.1.3, 4.1.5	• Decision making • See things in the mind's eye • Reasoning • Work well with others • Know how to learn • Acquire and evaluate information • Organize and maintain information • Self-management • Creative thinking • Use resources wisely • Self esteem	• Cooperate with others • Plan • Reflect and evaluate • Observe critically	• **1:** 4.01.03, 4.03.06 • **3:** 4.01.06, 4.03.01, 4.03.02 • **4:** 4.03.03 • **WB:** 4.03.04	• **1:** G20b • **2:** 6, 49 • **3:** 42,G15 • **5:** 50 • **6:** 46, 51, 52 • **4: WB:** 44, 42, 45 • **RC:** G19d
• **WB:** Communicate with school personnel • **WB:** Understand cell phone etiquette • **WB:** Understand job performance evaluations		• **1:** 0.1.1 • **2:** 0.1.2, 0.1.4, 0.1.7, 7.5.6 • **3:** 0.1.2, 0.1.7 • **4:** 7.4.2, 7.4.3, 7.5.6 • **5:** 7.2.3 • **6:** 0.1.3 • **Review:** 2.1.8 • **WB:** 0.1.2, 0.1.4, 2.5.5, 4.9.3, 7.3.2	• See things in the mind's eye • Creative thinking • Acquire and evaluate information • Know how to learn • Reasoning • Problem solving • Analyze and communicate information • Organize and maintain information • Understand how systems work	• Cooperate with others • Speak so others can understand • Reflect and evaluate • Convey ideas in writing • Observe critically • Learn through research	• **1:** 4.01.04 • **2:** 4.01.01, 4.01.04 • **3:** 4.01.01, **WB:** 4.03.07 • **4:** 4.01.04 • **6:** 4.07.01 • **WB:** 4.03.03, 4.03.14 • **RC:** 4.03.14	• **1:** 52, G25d • **2:** 4 (c), 5 (a, c, d), 6, G14 • **3:** 5 (a, c), G17-18 • **5:** G21a • **6:** 6 • **WB:** 4b, 5c, 12, 16 • **RC:** 8, 14, 15, G21b

CASAS, Florida, and LAUSD standards: Numbers in bold indicate lesson numbers. • **G:** Grammar • **WB:** Workbook • **RC:** Online Teacher Resource Center

SCOPE AND SEQUENCE

LIFE SKILLS

UNIT	Listening and Speaking	Reading and Writing	Critical Thinking	Vocabulary	Grammar
9 **Government** *page 116*	• Compare governments between two countries • Listen for dates and origins of holidays • Role-play conversations about holiday plans • Decline an invitation • Listen to conversations about voting	• Read about the U.S. Congress • Read and interpret a diagram of the three branches of the U.S. federal government • Read a website about voter registration • Read a biography • Read a persuasive letter • Write a persuasive letter to your representative • Use a dictionary • **WB:** Read about two presidents • **WB:** Read an article about unemployment insurance	• Analyze • Evaluate • Classify • Apply knowledge	• Government terms • Major national holidays • **WB:** Phrasal verbs	• Phrasal verbs • *Must, have to,* and *have got to* for necessity and prohibition • *Should* and *why don't* for advice
10 **On the Job** *page 130*	• Listen to conversations about taking time off from work • Ask for a message on the telephone • Talk about advantages and disadvantages of working on a team	• Read and interpret a work schedule • Write down a telephone message • Read and interpret a pay stub • Read an article about teamwork • Read and analyze a professional email • Understand pronoun reference • Write professional emails	• Analyze • Evaluate • Use context • Apply knowledge • Make inferences	• Types of jobs • Work equipment • Types of work leave • Tax-related terms	• Possessive and reflexive pronouns • *Because* and *since* for reasons • Present perfect continuous

Civics Concepts	Math Skills	CASAS Life Skills Competencies	SCANS Competencies (Workplace)	EFF Content Standards	Florida	LAUSD
• Understand the U.S. federal government • Understand major U.S. national holidays • Understand how to register to vote • **WB:** Understand how to file for unemployment • **WB:** Write to your representative		• **1:** 5.1.4, 5.1.6, 5.5.2, 5.5.9 • **2:** 5.2.2, 5.5.2, 5.5.3, 5.5.4, 5.5.9 • **3:** 0.1.4, 2.7.1 • **4:** 5.1.1 • **5:** 7.4.5 • **6:** 0.1.3, 5.1.7 • **WB:** 2.5.4, 2.5.5	• Acquire and evaluate information • See things in the mind's eye • Interpret and communicate information • Know how to learn • Reasoning • Problem solving • Exercise leadership	• Speak so others can understand • Read with understanding • Learn through research	• **3:** 4.01.01, 4.02.03 • **4:** 4.02.04 • **6:** 4.01.01 • **WB:** 4.02.08 • **RC:** 4.02.01	• **2:** 32, G10a-c • **3:** 4 (b), 33 • **4:** 52, 53, G12-13 • **5:** 50 • **6:** 6, 51 • **WB:** 10, 11
• Interpret information about W-2 forms and taxes • **WB:** Identify the functions of the Department of Labor		• **1:** 4.5.1 • **2:** 4.4.3 • **3:** 2.1.7 • **4:** 4.2.1, 5.4.1 • **5:** 4.4.1 • **6:** 4.6.2 • **WB:** 0.2.2, 4.1.5	• Acquire and evaluate information • Interpret and communicate information • Reasoning • Problem solving • Creative thinking	• Convey ideas in writing	• **1:** 4.03.15 • **2:** 4.03.09 • **3:** 4.01.01, 4.01.07 • **4:** 4.02.04 • **5:** 4.03.10 • **RC:** 4.03.12	• **1:** G25 a and c • **2:** 47 (d), G22a • **3:** 17, 18, 19, G8 a and b • **5:** 52, WB: 3 • **6:** 51, 53 • **WB:** 43 • **RC:** 47 (a, b)

CASAS, Florida, and LAUSD standards: Numbers in bold indicate lesson numbers. • **G**: Grammar • **WB**: Workbook • **RC**: Online Teacher Resource Center

TO THE TEACHER

All-Star Second Edition is a four-level, standards-based series for English learners featuring a picture-dictionary approach to vocabulary building. "Big picture" scenes in each unit provide springboards to a wealth of activities developing all of the language skills.

An accessible and predictable sequence of lessons in each unit systematically builds language and critical thinking skills around life-skill topics. *All-Star* presents family, work, and community topics in each unit and provides alternate application lessons in its workbooks, giving teachers the flexibility to customize the series for a variety of student needs and curricular objectives. *All-Star* is tightly correlated to all of the updated major national and state standards for adult instruction.

New to the Second Edition

- **Updated content** provides full coverage of all major *revised* standards including CASAS, Florida, LAUSD, EFF, and Texas.
- **NEW comprehensive, carefully sequenced grammar program** connects target grammar to the content to enrich learning and provide full coverage of grammar standards.
- **NEW robust listening program** addresses the latest CASAS standards and prepares students for the types of listening items on CASAS tests.
- **NEW Work-Out CD-ROM with complete student audio** provides a fun, rich interactive environment with over 25 hours of learning and the entire *All-Star Second Edition* student audio program in downloadable MP3 files.
- **NEW Teacher Resource Center** offers downloadable and printable Study Guides and Learner Persistence Worksheets, EZ-Tests, Big Picture PowerPoint Slides, full Teacher Audio for Tests in downloadable MP3 files, and other materials to support teaching.
- **NEW Interactive Correlations Chart** allows teachers to easily cross-reference standards with Student Book, Workbook, and Study Guide pages.

Hallmark *All-Star* Features

- Dynamic Big Picture scenes present life-skills vocabulary and provide lively contexts for activities and discussions that promote all-skills language development.
- Predictable sequence of seven two-page lessons in each unit reduces prep time for teachers and helps students get comfortable with the format of each lesson.
- Flexible structure, with application lessons addressing family, work, and community topics in both the Student Book and Workbook, allows teachers to customize each unit to meet a variety of student needs and curricular objectives.
- Comprehensive coverage of key standards, such as CASAS, Florida, LAUSD, EFF, and Texas, prepares students to master a broad range of critical competencies.

- Multiple assessment measures like CASAS-style tests and performance-based assessment offer a variety of options for monitoring and assessing learner progress.

The Complete *All-Star* Program

- The **Student Book** features ten 14-page units that integrate listening, speaking, reading, writing, grammar, math, and pronunciation skills with life-skills topics, critical thinking activities, and civics concepts.
- The **Student Work-Out CD-ROM with full student audio** extends the learning goals of each Student Book unit with an interactive set of activities that build vocabulary, listening, reading, writing, and test-taking skills. The CD-ROM also includes the full Student Book audio program.
- The **Teacher's Edition with Tests** includes:
  - Step-by-step procedural notes for each Student Book activity
  - Notes on teaching the Target Grammar Pages
  - Expansion activities addressing multi-level classes, literacy, and students that need to be challenged
  - Culture, Grammar, and Pronunciation Notes
  - Two-page written test for each unit (Note: Listening passages for the tests are available on the Teacher Audio with Testing CD and on the Online Teacher Resource Center)
  - Audio scripts for all audio program materials
  - Answer keys for Student Book, Workbook, and Tests
- The **Workbook** includes supplementary practice activities correlated to the Student Book. As a bonus feature, the Workbook also includes two alternate application lessons per unit that address the learner's role as a worker, family member, and/or community member. These lessons may be used in addition to, or as substitutes for, the application lessons found in Lesson 4 of each Student Book unit.
- The **Teacher Audio with Testing CD** contains recordings for all listening activities in the Student Book as well as the listening passages for each unit test.
- The **Online Teacher Resource Center** provides teachers with the tools to set goals for students, customize classroom teaching, and better measure student success. It includes:
  - EZ-Tests that allow teachers to create customized online tests
  - An Interactive Correlations Chart that allows teachers to easily cross-reference standards with Student Book, Workbook, and Study Guide pages
  - Big Picture PowerPoint slides that present the Student Book Big Picture scenes
  - A Learner Persistence Kit that sets and tracks student achievement goals
  - A Post-Testing Study Guide that moves students toward mastery and tracks their progress using the reproducible Study Guide Worksheets
  - Downloadable MP3 files for the Testing audio programs

Overview of the *All-Star Second Edition* Program

UNIT STRUCTURE

The *Welcome to All-Star Second Edition* guide on pages xvi–xxi offers teachers and administrators a visual tour of one Student Book unit and highlights the exciting new features of the Second Edition.

All-Star Second Edition is designed to maximize flexibility. Each unit has the following sequence of seven two-page lessons:

- Lesson 1: Talk about It
- Lesson 2: Vocabulary in Context
- Lesson 3: Listening and Speaking
- Lesson 4: Application
- Lesson 5: Reading Strategy
- Lesson 6: Writing Skill
- Lesson 7: Review and Assessment

Each unit introduces several grammar points. A Target Grammar icon

⊙ **Target Grammar**
Expressing preferences   page xxx

in the lessons refers teachers and students to the Target Grammar Pages at the back of the book where they can find explanations of the grammar points and contextualized practice.

SPECIAL FEATURES OF EACH UNIT

- **Target Grammar Pages:** Throughout each unit, students are directed to the Target Grammar Pages in the back of the book, where the grammar point they have been exposed to in the lesson is presented and practiced in manageable chunks. Students learn the target grammar structure with clear charts, meaningful examples, and abundant practice activities.

  This approach gives teachers the flexibility to introduce grammar in any of several ways:
  - At the beginning of a lesson
  - At the point in the lesson where the grammar appears in context
  - As a follow-up to the lesson

- **CASAS Listening:** Each unit has at least two activities that simulate the CASAS listening experience.

- **Window on Pronunciation.** This special feature , which appears in the Listening/Speaking lesson, addresses issues of stress, rhythm, and intonation so that the students' spoken English becomes more comprehensible.

- **Window on Math.** Learning basic math skills is critically important for success in school, on the job, and at home. As such, national and state standards for adult education mandate instruction in basic math skills. Across the book, an orange box called Window on Math is dedicated to helping students develop the functional numeracy skills they need for basic math work.

TWO-PAGE LESSON FORMAT

The lessons in *All-Star* are designed as two-page spreads. Lessons 1–3 follow an innovative format with a list of activities on the left-hand page of the spread and picture dictionary visuals supporting these activities on the right hand page. The list of activities, entitled Things to Do, allows student and teachers to take full advantage of the visuals in each lesson, enabling students to achieve a variety of learning goals.

"BIG PICTURE" SCENES

Each unit includes one "big picture". This scene is the visual centerpiece of each unit, and serves as a springboard to a variety of activities in the Student Book, Teacher's Edition, and Work-Out CD-ROM. In the Student Book, the "big picture" scene introduces the topic and serves as a prompt for classroom discussion. The scenes feature characters with distinct personalities for students to enjoy, respond to, and talk about. There are also surprising and fun elements for students to discover in each scene.

The Teacher's Edition includes a variety of all-skills "Big Picture Expansion" activities that are tied to the Student Book scenes. For each unit, these expansion activities address listening, speaking, reading, writing, and grammar skills development, and allow teachers to customize their instruction to meet the language learning needs of each group of students.

CIVICS CONCEPTS

Many institutions focus direct attention on the importance of civics instruction for English language learners. Civics instruction encourages students to become active and informed community members. Throughout each *All-Star* unit, students and teachers will encounter activities that introduce civics concepts and encourage community involvement. In addition, Application lessons provide activities that help students develop in their roles as workers, parents, and citizens. Those lessons targeting the students' role as citizen encourage learners to become more active and informed members of their communities.

CASAS, SCANS, EFF, FLORIDA, TEXAS, LAUSD, AND OTHER STANDARDS

Teachers and administrators benchmark student progress against national and/or state standards for adult instruction. With this in mind, *All-Star* carefully integrates instructional elements from a wide range of revised standards including CASAS, SCANS, EFF, LAUSD, Texas, and the Florida Adult ESOL Standards. Unit-by-unit correlations of these standards appear in the scope and sequence. Here is a brief overview of our approach to meeting the key national, state, and district standards.

- **CASAS.** Many U.S. states, including California, tie funding for adult education programs to student performance on the Comprehensive Adult Student Assessment System (CASAS). The CASAS (www.casas.org) competencies identify more than 300 essential skills that adults need in order to succeed in the classroom, workplace, and community. Examples of these skills include identifying or using appropriate nonverbal behavior

in a variety of settings, responding appropriately to common personal information questions, and comparing price or quality to determine the best buys. *All-Star* comprehensively integrates all of the CASAS Life Skill Competencies throughout the four levels of the series.

- **SCANS.** Developed by the United States Department of Labor, SCANS is an acronym for the Secretary's Commission on Achieving Necessary Skills (wdr.doleta.gov/SCANS/). SCANS competencies are workplace skills that help people compete more effectively in today's global economy. The following are examples of SCANS competencies: works well with others, acquires and evaluates information, and teaches others new skills. A variety of SCANS competencies is threaded throughout the activities in each unit of *All-Star*. The incorporation of these competencies recognizes both the intrinsic importance of teaching workplace skills and the fact that many adult students are already working members of their communities.

- **EFF.** Equipped for the Future (EFF) is a set of standards for adult literacy and lifelong learning developed by The National Institute for Literacy (www.nifl.gov). The organizing principle of EFF is that adults assume responsibilities in three major areas of life—as workers, as parents, and as citizens. These three areas of focus are called "role maps" in the EFF documentation. In the parent role map, for example, EFF highlights these and other responsibilities: participating in children's formal education and forming and maintaining supportive family relationships. *All-Star* addresses all three of the EFF role maps in its *Application* lessons.

NUMBER OF HOURS OF INSTRUCTION

The *All-Star* program has been designed to accommodate the needs of adult classes with 70–180 hours of classroom instruction. Here are three recommended ways in which various components in the *All-Star* program can be combined to meet student and teacher needs.

- **70–100 hours.** Teachers are encouraged to work through all of the Student Book materials. Teachers should also look to the Teacher's Edition for teaching suggestions and testing materials as necessary. Students are encouraged to "Plug in and practice" at home with the Work-Out CD-ROM for each unit. *Time per unit: 7–10 hours*

- **100–140 hours.** In addition to working through all of the Student Book materials, teachers are encouraged to incorporate the Workbook and Work-Out CD-ROM activities for supplementary practice. Students are encouraged to "Plug in and practice" at home with the Work-Out CD-ROM for each unit. *Time per unit: 10–14 hours*

- **140–180 hours.** Teachers and students working in an intensive instructional setting can take advantage of the wealth of expansion activities threaded through the Teacher's Edition to supplement the Student Book, Workbook, and Work-Out CD-ROM materials. Students are encouraged to "Plug in and practice" at home with the Work-Out CD-ROM for each unit. *Time per unit: 14–18 hours.*

ASSESSMENT

The *All-Star* program offers teachers, students and administrators the following wealth of resources for monitoring and assessing student progress and achievement:

- **Standardized testing formats.** *All-Star* is correlated to the CASAS competencies and many other national and state standards for adult learning. Students have the opportunity to practice answering CASAS-style listening questions in Lesson 7 of each unit. Students practice with the same item types and bubble-in answer sheets they encounter on CASAS and other standardized tests. Student also practice CASAS-style listening items in the Work-Out CD-ROM Listening and Practice Test sections.

- **Achievement tests.** The *All-Star Teacher's Edition* includes end-of-unit tests. These paper-and-pencil tests help students demonstrate how well they have learned the instructional content of the unit. Adult learners often show incremental increases in learning that are not always measured on the standardized tests. The achievement tests may demonstrate learning even in a short amount of instructional time. Twenty percent of each test includes questions that encourage students to apply more academic skills such as determining meaning from context, making inferences, and understanding main ideas. Practice with these question types will help prepare students who may want to enroll in academic classes.

- **EZ Test Online.** *All-Star's* online test generator provides a databank of assessment items from which instructors can create customized tests within minutes. The EZ Test Online assessment materials are available at www.eztestonline.com. For EZ Test tutorials, go to http://mpss.mhhe.com/eztest/eztotutorials.php.

- **Performance-based assessment.** *All-Star* provides several ways to measure students' performance on productive tasks. In addition, the Teacher's Edition suggests writing and speaking prompts that teachers can use for performance-based assessment. These prompts derive from the "big picture" scene in each unit and provide rich visual input as the basis for the speaking and writing tasks asked of the students.

- **Portfolio assessment.** A portfolio is a collection of student work that can be used to show progress. Examples of work that the instructor or the student may submit in the portfolio include writing samples, audio and video recordings, or projects. Every Student Book unit includes several activities that require critical thinking and small-group project work. These can be included in a student's portfolio. The Teacher's Edition identifies activities that may be used as documentation for the secondary standards defined by the National Reporting System.

- **Self-assessment.** Self-assessment is an important part of the overall assessment picture, as it promotes student involvement and commitment to the learning process. When encouraged to assess themselves, students take more control of their learning and are better able to connect the instructional content with

their own goals. The Student Book includes *Learning Logs* at the end of each unit, which allow students to check off the vocabulary they have learned and the skills they feel they have acquired. In the Workbook, students complete the Practice Test Performance Record on the inside back cover.

- **Other linguistic and nonlinguistic outcomes.** Traditional testing often does not account for the progress made by adult learners with limited educational experience or low literacy levels. Such learners tend to take longer to make smaller language gains, so the gains they make in other areas are often more significant. These gains may be in areas such as self-esteem, goal clarification, learning skills, access to employment, community involvement and further academic studies. The SCANS and EFF standards identify areas of student growth that are not necessarily language based. *All-Star* is correlated with both SCANS and EFF standards. Like the Student Book, the Workbook includes activities that provide documentation that can be added to a student portfolio.

About the author and series consultants

Linda Lee is lead author on the *All-Star* series. Linda has taught ESL/ELT in the United States, Iran, and China, and has authored or co-authored a variety of successful textbook series for English learners. As a classroom instructor, Linda's most satisfying teaching experiences have been with adult ESL students at Roxbury Community College in Boston, Massachusetts.

Grace Tanaka is professor and coordinator of ESL at the Santa Ana College School of Continuing Education in Santa Ana, California, which serves more than 20,000 students per year. She is also a textbook co-author and series consultant. Grace has 25 years of teaching experience in both credit and non-credit ESL programs.

Shirley Velasco is principal at Miami Beach Adult and Community Education Center in Miami Beach, Florida. She has been a classroom instructor and administrator for the past 28 years. Shirley has created a large adult ESL program based on a curriculum she helped develop to implement state/national ESL standards.

Welcome to *All-Star*
Second Edition

All-Star is a four-level series featuring a "big picture" approach to meeting adult standards that systematically builds language and math skills around life-skill topics.

Complete Standards Coverage Using the "Big Picture" Approach

ACCESSIBLE, TWO-PAGE LESSON FORMAT follows an innovative layout with a list of activities labeled "Things to Do" on the left and picture-dictionary visuals on the right.

COMPREHENSIVE COVERAGE OF REVISED KEY STANDARDS, such as CASAS, Florida, Texas, LAUSD, and EFF prepares students to master critical competencies.

PREDICTABLE UNIT STRUCTURE includes the same logical sequence of seven two-page lessons in each unit.

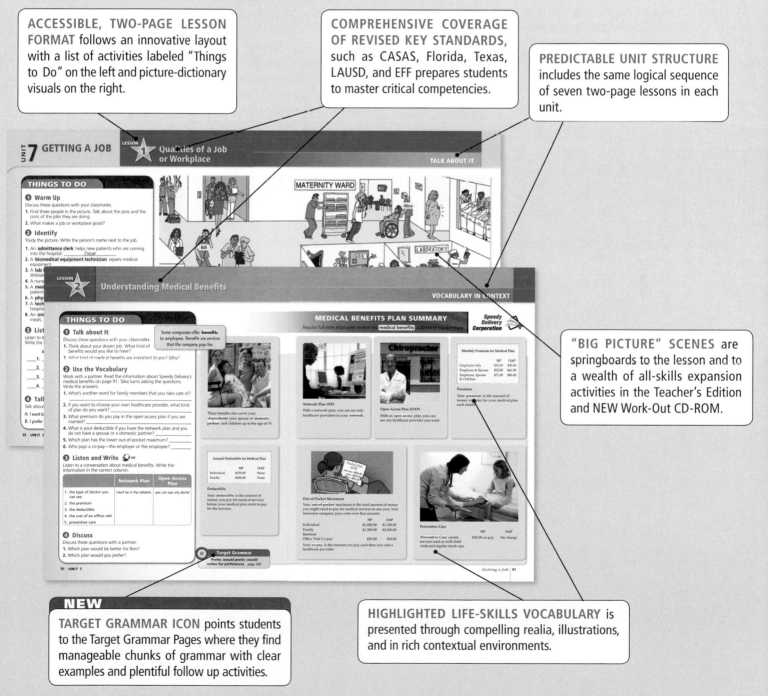

"BIG PICTURE" SCENES are springboards to the lesson and to a wealth of all-skills expansion activities in the Teacher's Edition and NEW Work-Out CD-ROM.

HIGHLIGHTED LIFE-SKILLS VOCABULARY is presented through compelling realia, illustrations, and in rich contextual environments.

NEW
TARGET GRAMMAR ICON points students to the Target Grammar Pages where they find manageable chunks of grammar with clear examples and plentiful follow up activities.

NEW Comprehensive Grammar Program

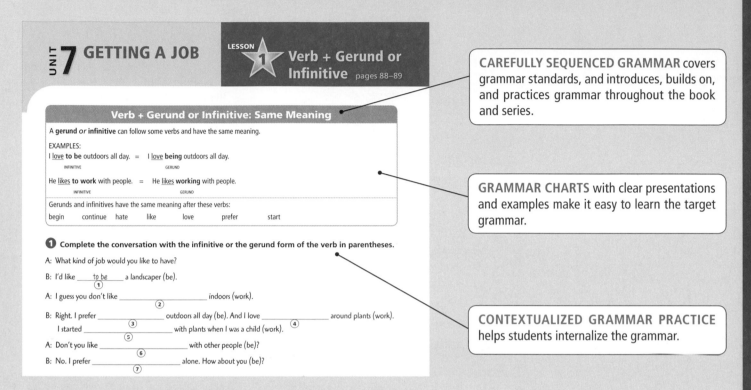

CAREFULLY SEQUENCED GRAMMAR covers grammar standards, and introduces, builds on, and practices grammar throughout the book and series.

GRAMMAR CHARTS with clear presentations and examples make it easy to learn the target grammar.

CONTEXTUALIZED GRAMMAR PRACTICE helps students internalize the grammar.

NEW Work-Out CD-ROM with Interactive Activities and Complete Student Audio

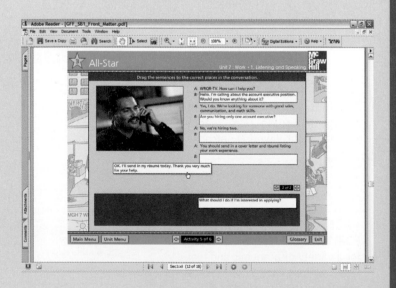

- Over 25 hours of listening, reading, writing, and grammar activities

- Voice record activities

- Entire student audio program MP3s for download

Integrated Skills with Enhanced Listening

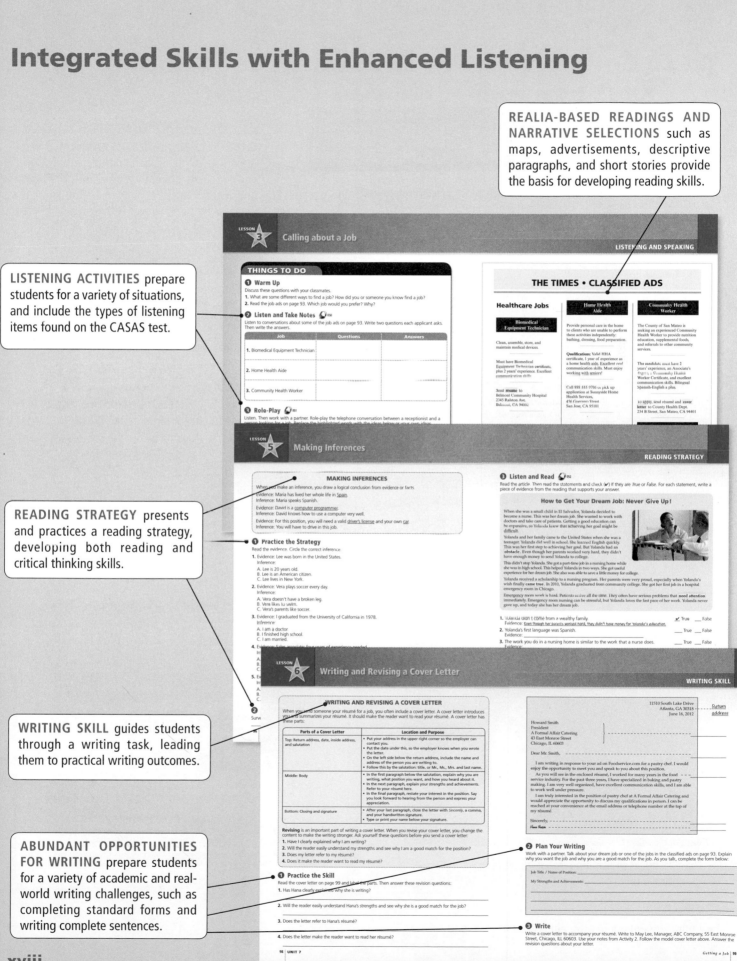

REALIA-BASED READINGS AND NARRATIVE SELECTIONS such as maps, advertisements, descriptive paragraphs, and short stories provide the basis for developing reading skills.

LISTENING ACTIVITIES prepare students for a variety of situations, and include the types of listening items found on the CASAS test.

READING STRATEGY presents and practices a reading strategy, developing both reading and critical thinking skills.

WRITING SKILL guides students through a writing task, leading them to practical writing outcomes.

ABUNDANT OPPORTUNITIES FOR WRITING prepare students for a variety of academic and real-world writing challenges, such as completing standard forms and writing complete sentences.

Real World Applications

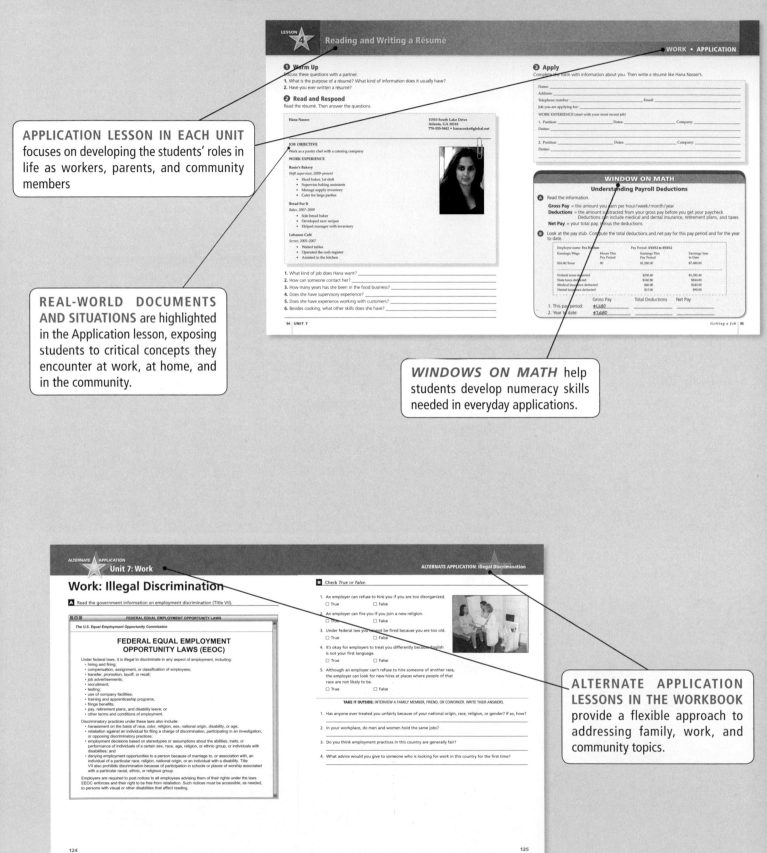

APPLICATION LESSON IN EACH UNIT focuses on developing the students' roles in life as workers, parents, and community members

REAL-WORLD DOCUMENTS AND SITUATIONS are highlighted in the Application lesson, exposing students to critical concepts they encounter at work, at home, and in the community.

WINDOWS ON MATH help students develop numeracy skills needed in everyday applications.

ALTERNATE APPLICATION LESSONS IN THE WORKBOOK provide a flexible approach to addressing family, work, and community topics.

Multiple Opportunities for Assessment

> **GRAMMAR REVIEW** provides an opportunity to review and assess the unit grammar point.

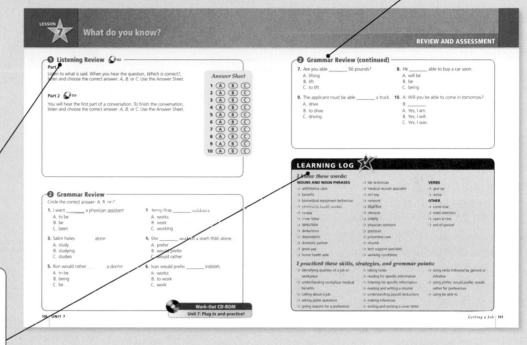

> **NEW**
>
> **CASAS LISTENING REVIEW** helps teachers assess listening comprehension, while giving students practice with the item types and answer sheets they encounter on standardized tests.

> **LEARNING LOGS** ask students to catalog the vocabulary, grammar, and life skills they have learned, and determine which areas they need to review.

> **WORKBOOK AND WORK-OUT CD-ROM PRACTICE TESTS** provide additional practice.

UNIT TEST in the Teacher's Edition rounds out the assessment program.

NEW Online Teacher Resource Center

- EZ Test Online bank of 500+ test questions for teachers to create customized tests.

- Study Guide reproducible worksheets support a portfolio-based approach to assessment.

- Persistence Kit includes reproducible worksheets that promote student goal setting and achievement.

- Interactive Correlations Chart allows teachers easy and immediate access to standards coverage in the *All-Star Second Edition* program.

GETTING STARTED

❶ Decide

What is the best response to these introductions and greetings? Check (✔) your answers.

1

How do you do? I'm Charles Wilson.

- ❑ Hi, Charles. I'm Donald.
- ❑ Nice to meet you, Mr. Wilson. I'm Donald Turner.
- ❑ Hey, Charles. How are you doing?

2

Hi. I'm Suzy.

- ❑ How do you do, Suzy? Are you a student here?
- ❑ Hi. Nice to meet you.
- ❑ Nice to meet you. My name is Sam.

3

Hi. My name is Roberto.

- ❑ Hi. Are you a student here?
- ❑ Hi, Roberto. I'm Hector. What do you think of this class?
- ❑ Hi, I'm Hector.

4

I'd like you to meet my friend Yuko. She's from Japan.

- ❑ Nice to meet you, Yuko.
- ❑ Nice to meet you, Yuko. Where in Japan are you from?
- ❑ Hi, Yuko.

What do you like and dislike about each response? Share ideas with your classmates.

Example: *The first response in #1 seems very informal.*
Charles gave his full name, but Donald only gave his first name.

❷ Get Together

Introduce yourself to three classmates. Then ask three questions to learn more about each person. Write their information below.

Sample Questions
- Where are you from?
- When did you move here?
- Does your family live here, too?
- What sports do you like?
- What do you do for fun?

EXAMPLE:

A: Hello. My name is Nina.

B: Nice to meet you, Nina. I'm Antonio.

A: Nice to meet you, Antonio. Where are you from?

B: I'm from Argentina. How about you?

Classmate #1	Classmate #2	Classmate #3
Name: _____	Name: _____	Name: _____
Information: _____	Information: _____	Information: _____
_____	_____	_____
_____	_____	_____
_____	_____	_____
_____	_____	_____

Tell the class what you learned about each person.

❸ Look It Over

What's in this book? Complete the sentences below.

1. The topic of Unit 1 is ___*Setting Goals*_____.

2. There is a health history questionnaire in Unit 3 on page _____.

3. The topic of Unit 5 is _____.

4. You can learn about banking terms in Unit _____.

5. A vocabulary list begins on page _____.

6. There is an article about a literacy volunteer in Unit 6 on page _____.

7. There is a complaint letter in Unit 2 on page _____.

8. Unit _____ and Unit _____ are about jobs.

9. There are pictures of _____ on pages 116-117 in Unit 9.

10. There is _____ on pages 144-202.

THINGS TO DO

❶ Warm Up

Discuss these questions with your classmates.

1. What are five things that are happening in the picture?

2. What do you know about Laura and Ed from the picture? What are some of their responsibilities?

3. What are eight things that you do every day?

❷ Listen and Match 🎧 002

Listen to the conversations. Match the conversation to the responsibility. Listen again and check your answers.

Conversation	Responsibility
1. _c_	**a.** clean the kitchen
2. ___	**b.** pay the bills
3. ___	**c.** buy food
4. ___	**d.** go to a meeting
5. ___	**e.** cook dinner
6. ___	**f.** do homework

❸ Interview

Work with a partner. Ask questions about the responsibilities in the chart above.

Example: *A: Do you clean the house?*
       B: Yes, I do.
       A: When?
       B: On the weekends.

❹ Give Your Opinion

Complete the sentences using information in the picture and your own ideas. Then discuss with a partner.

1. I think Laura (has/doesn't have) a job because <u>she is dressed for work and she is wearing a name tag</u>.

2. I think education (is/isn't) very important to this family because. . .

3. I think the parents (have/don't have) enough time to do everything because. . .

4. I think Laura and Ed (are/aren't) good parents because . . .

Target Grammar

Simple present, review   *page 144*

Work-Out CD-ROM

Unit 1: Plug in and practice!

Long- and Short-Term Goals

THINGS TO DO

❶ Warm Up

Discuss these questions with your classmates.

1. What is one of your goals? What will you do to reach this goal?

2. What is the difference between a **long-term goal** and a **short-term goal**? Give one example of each kind.

❷ Complete the Chart

Read about the people and their goals on page 7. Complete the chart. Then compare your notes with a partner.

Name	What is the long-term goal?	What is a short-term goal?
Kilim	get better grades	spend less time watching TV
Leila		see an academic counselor
Mauricio	start own company	
Tracy	pay off debts	
Mike		
David		

❸ Read and Match

Match the words with their definitions.

Word	Definition
1. _c_ debt	**a.** work without pay
2. ____ financial aid	**b.** deal with in order of importance
3. ____ pay off	**c.** amount of money owed
4. ____ prepare	**d.** decrease
5. ____ prioritize	**e.** teacher who helps students one-on-one
6. ____ reduce	**f.** money to pay for education
7. ____ tutor	**g.** give back money that is owed
8. ____ volunteer	**h.** get ready

❹ Talk about It

Write your goals. Then talk to your partner about them.

Write one of your long-term goals:

I want to _____.

Write two short-term goals that will help you reach your long-term goal:

I need to _____ and _____.

> **Target Grammar**
>
> *Want, need,* and
> *would like*   page 146

Kilim

I need to get better grades. I have so much homework, but I have to **prioritize** . I'm going to spend less time watching TV. This is the first thing I plan to do.

Leila

I want to attend college. I don't know what to study and I don't have enough money, so first I need to see an **academic counselor** . Then I'm going to fill out an application for **financial aid** .

Mauricio

I want to start my own painting company. I can't read very well, so first I need to take some **continuing education** classes. Then I'm going to take some business courses.

Tracy

I want to **pay off** my **debts** . I plan to save $100 a month. How? I'm going to **reduce my expenses** !

Mike

I want to be more involved in my children's education. I want to change my work schedule so I can go to the **parent-teacher conferences** and **volunteer** in the classroom.

David

I would like to become a U.S. citizen. I'm working with a **tutor** twice a week. She's helping me **prepare** for the interview. I need to learn a lot about American government and history.

THINGS TO DO

❶ Warm Up

Discuss these questions with your classmates.

1. Where are the people in each picture?
2. What do you think they are saying to each other?
3. What is one of your goals? Who could you go to for advice about reaching that goal?

❷ Listen and Take Notes 🎧 003

Listen to the conversations and write the person's long-term goal. Listen again and write the suggested short-term goal.

	What is the person's long-term goal?	What is the suggested short-term goal?
1.	become a medical technician	
2.		
3.		
4.		

❸ Role-Play 🎧 004

Listen. Then work with a partner. Role-play a conversation between a student and a counselor. Replace the highlighted words with the information below. Use the communication strategy.

A: What can I do for you?

B: Hi. I'd like to attend college.

A: Well, you'll need to get a high school diploma or a GED certificate first.

B: What's a GED certificate?

A: It's a certificate that you get when you pass the General Education Development exam.

B: Sounds great.

Long-Term Goal	Short-Term Goal / Suggestion	Definition
start my own business	get an **SBA loan**	Small Business Administration loan
send my children to college	open a **CD account**	certificate of deposit account

COMMUNICATION STRATEGY

Asking for a Definition

When you don't understand a particular word or phrase, ask for a definition.

A: You could take the GED.

B: The *GED*? What's *that*?

A: You could apply for financial aid.

B: What's *financial aid*?

A: You should take some continuing education classes.

B: Can you tell me what *continuing education* is?

🅞 Target Grammar

Future with *will*, review   *page 147*

WINDOW ON PRONUNCIATION

Stress When Asking for a Definition 🎧 005

When you ask for a definition of a word or phrase, you give that word or phrase more stress than the other words in your question.

A Listen to the questions. Then listen and repeat.

The <u>GED</u>? What's <u>financial aid</u>?

B Read the questions. Draw a line under the word(s) that gets the most stress. Then listen and check your answers.

1. A certificate? What is that?

2. What's a grant?

3. Can you tell me what English for Parents is?

C Work with a partner. Practice the role plays in Activity 3 again. Pay special attention to words and phrases that need stress.

Becoming a Citizen

❶ Warm Up

Answer the questions about yourself. Then discuss your answers with your classmates.

1. Where were you born? _____

2. When did you move to this country? _____

3. How long will you live here? _____

4. Do you like the United States? _____

5. If you are a citizen: When did you become a citizen? _____

   _____

6. If you aren't a citizen: Would you like to become a citizen? _____

   Why or why not? _____

   _____

❷ Read and Match

Read the information about becoming a U.S. citizen.

USCIS Home Page

Home | Contact Us | Site Map | FAQ

U.S. Citizenship and Immigration Services

Search [GO]

Services and Benefits   Immigration Forms   Laws & Regulations   About USCIS   Education & Resources   Press Room

MORE INFORMATION:

Permanent Resident
(Green Card)

Citizenship

Employment Authorization

Humanitarian Benefits

"How Do I?" Guides

Field Offices

Finding Legal Advice

Naturalization

Welcome to the **naturalization** home page. Naturalization is the process by which U.S. citizenship is conferred upon a foreign citizen or national after he or she fulfills the requirements established by Congress in the Immigration and Nationality Act (INA). The general requirements for naturalization include:

- a period of continuous residence or physical presence in the United States;
- residence in a particular USCIS District prior to filing;
- an ability to read, write and speak English;
- a knowledge and understanding of U.S. history and government;
- good moral character;
- attachment to the principles of the U.S. Constitution; and,
- favorable disposition toward the United States.

Match the phrases to the meanings.

Phrase

1. __d__ a period of continuous residence and physical presence in the United States
2. _____ a knowledge and understanding of U.S. history and government
3. _____ good moral character
4. _____ attachment to the principles of the U.S. Constitution
5. _____ favorable disposition toward the United States

Meaning

a. liking the United States
b. knowing about U.S. history and government
c. being a good citizen
d. living in the United States for a certain period of time
e. believing in U.S. laws

❸ Write

Answer the questions about the USCIS Web page. Then compare your answers with a partner.

1. What is *naturalization*? _____

_____

_____

2. What kind of person do you need to be if you want to become a U.S. citizen? _____

_____

_____

3. What kind of feelings do you need to have about the United States if you want to become a U.S. citizen?

_____

_____

4. What English skills do you need to become a citizen? _____

_____

_____

❹ Listen and Circle 🎧 006

Listen to a conversation about citizenship. Then circle *True* or *False*.

If you want to become a citizen:

1. you need to memorize the U.S. Constitution.	True	False
2. you need to follow U.S. laws.	True	False
3. you need to have a lot of money in the bank.	True	False
4. you need to marry an American.	True	False
5. you need to live in the United States for at least three to five years.	True	False

Target Grammar

Simple past, review   *page 148*

Using Context to Guess Meaning

USING CONTEXT TO GUESS MEANING

You can use the words around a new word to understand its meaning. This is called *context*.
The context can help in a number of ways. It can provide:

a definition
A successful student can **prioritize**—do jobs in order of importance.

a synonym
Jane needs to **reduce**, or cut back, her expenses.

a cause and effect relationship
I applied for **financial aid** because I needed to borrow money for school.

an example
One of his goals was to become a **volunteer**. Now he helps in his son's classroom one day a month
and he teaches the parents' English class one night a week.

a description
My goal this year is to pay off all my **debts**. I'm going to pay the money I owe on my credit card and
student loan.

---

❶ Practice the Strategy

Use context to choose the correct meaning of the words in bold.

1. I didn't reach my goals this year because I **wasted time** playing video games and watching TV.
   a. used time well   **b.** used time poorly   **c.** didn't have time

2. To prepare for the citizenship interview, Magda is learning about **Congress**, the branch of the
government that makes the country's laws.
   a. a kind of business   **b.** English grammar   **c.** part of the government

3. Binh is a real **entrepreneur**. He had a great idea for making money, and now he owns a very successful
business.
   a. a person who graduates   **b.** a person who starts a   **c.** a person who makes a
       from college   new business   scientific discovery

4. Walt is proud of the things he **accomplished** this year. He graduated from college, got married,
and got a promotion at work.
   a. completed   **b.** started   **c.** continued

5. If you **focus**, or center your attention, it's not hard to learn a new instrument.
   a. practice   **b.** exercise   **c.** pay attention

❷ Listen and Read 🎧 007

Read the article. Use context to guess the meaning of new words. Match the terms and definitions below.

Term	Definition
1. _____ open doors	**a.** to ask others to do a job
2. _____ advance	**b.** to speak and understand two languages
3. _____ be in charge of	**c.** to give opportunities
4. _____ delegate	**d.** to move up
5. _____ bilingual	**e.** to be responsible for

Person of the Week:

Homero E. Zayas

1 Homero E. Zayas is an executive with a major communications company. Mr. Zayas has used his education and his ability to communicate well in English and Spanish to become one of the youngest managers at his company.

2 Mr. Zayas's father taught him what goals are and helped him achieve them. The most important goal was to get a good education. Mr. Zayas's father knew that a good education would **open** many **doors** for his son in the future. His father was right. Mr. Zayas had many opportunities in life because of his education. In high school, he studied hard and got excellent grades. He attended and later graduated from the University of Denver.

3 Mr. Zayas knew that he needed to be ready to move to different parts of the country to **advance** in his career. For example, he moved to New Jersey for training. As a result, he got a much better job. In his new job, he designed a new computer system that would take care of eighty million customer accounts. This was a great responsibility.

4 After six months of testing the computer system, he moved again. Now he is an operations manager **in charge of** the International Communications Service Center. Many office managers report to him. He supervises about 175 people in his department. He makes sure that everything runs smoothly.

5 Mr. Zayas is a good manager because he knows how to **delegate**. He can choose the right people to help him get the job done. He is also able to communicate with people very well. He is **bilingual**—he can speak and write both Spanish and English. In addition to these skills, Mr. Zayas also feels that his strong personality has helped him be a successful executive. He says, "Anyone can be a success if they are secure with themselves, ready to move, and work hard to be an achiever."

❸ Understand the Reading

Answer the questions about the article.

1. What was Mr. Zayas's most important goal? _____

2. What happened when Mr. Zayas moved to New Jersey for training? _____

_____

3. What does Mr. Zayas do at the International Communications Service Center? _____

_____

4. Why is Mr. Zayas a good manager? _____

_____

5. In Mr. Zayas's opinion, what has helped him to be a successful executive? _____

_____

Brainstorming and Making a Cluster Diagram

PREWRITING: BRAINSTORMING

Brainstorming is a prewriting activity. When you brainstorm:

- write down as many ideas as you can.
- write quickly. Don't think much about the ideas.

Before you brainstorm, set a goal of a certain number of ideas — think of 10, 15, or 20 ideas before you stop your list.

EXAMPLE:
Writing topic: How to save money

Brainstorming ideas:

eat at home	use coupons	buy on sale
cut own hair	take the bus	turn down the thermostat
use the library	buy a used computer	pay bills on time

---

❶ Practice the Skill

Choose one of the topics below and brainstorm ten ideas. Write your ideas on the lines.

TOPICS

be a good community member	become a citizen	get a better job
be a good student	start a business	meet new people

1. _____   6. _____

2. _____   7. _____

3. _____   8. _____

4. _____   9. _____

5. _____   10. _____

Share your ideas with a classmate.

❷ Write Sentences

Choose two or three of your ideas and write sentences about the topic.

Example: *There are many ways to save money. You can eat at home instead of at a restaurant. You can buy things when they are on sale.*

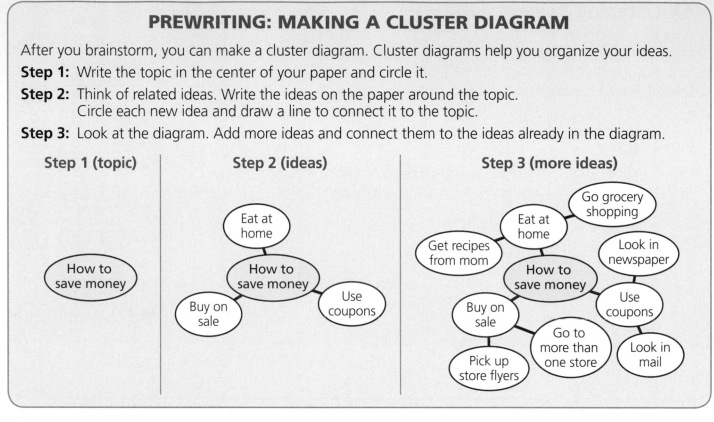

PREWRITING: MAKING A CLUSTER DIAGRAM

After you brainstorm, you can make a cluster diagram. Cluster diagrams help you organize your ideas.

Step 1: Write the topic in the center of your paper and circle it.

Step 2: Think of related ideas. Write the ideas on the paper around the topic.
Circle each new idea and draw a line to connect it to the topic.

Step 3: Look at the diagram. Add more ideas and connect them to the ideas already in the diagram.

❸ Plan Your Writing

Look again at the topics in Activity 1. Keep the same topic or choose a different topic.
Create a cluster diagram below for your ideas.

❹ Write

Write a paragraph about the topic using your ideas in Activity 3.

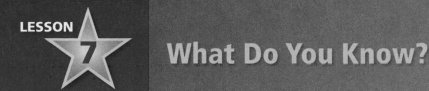

What Do You Know?

① Listening Review 🎧 008

Part 1

First, you will hear a question. Next, listen carefully to what is said. You will hear the question again. Then choose the correct answer: *A*, *B*, or *C*. Use the Answer Sheet.

Part 2 🎧 009

Listen to what is said. When you hear the question, *Which is correct?*, listen and choose the correct answer: *A*, *B*, or *C*. Use the Answer Sheet.

Answer Sheet

1 Ⓐ Ⓑ Ⓒ
2 Ⓐ Ⓑ Ⓒ
3 Ⓐ Ⓑ Ⓒ
4 Ⓐ Ⓑ Ⓒ
5 Ⓐ Ⓑ Ⓒ
6 Ⓐ Ⓑ Ⓒ
7 Ⓐ Ⓑ Ⓒ
8 Ⓐ Ⓑ Ⓒ
9 Ⓐ Ⓑ Ⓒ
10 Ⓐ Ⓑ Ⓒ

② Grammar Review

Circle the correct answer: *A*, *B*, or *C*.

1. Rob _____ food on Thursdays.

A. buy
B. buys
C. buying

2. Sam _____ homework every night.

A. does
B. doing
C. do

3. José and Marta _____ to the PTA meeting once a month.

A. go
B. goes
C. going

4. Bob wants _____ his own company.

A. start
B. starting
C. to start

5. Wei _____ to become a U.S. citizen.

A. would
B. like
C. would like

6. You'll _____ to take a placement test.

A. needs
B. needing
C. need

② Grammar Review (continued)

7. This information packet will ___ your questions.

   A. answered
   B. answer
   C. to answer

8. He _____ his degree next year.

   A. 'll get
   B. got
   C. will gets

9. Lara _____ to the United States in 2005.

   A. move
   B. moved
   C. moving

10. When _____ you become a citizen?

   A. did
   B. doing
   C. does

LEARNING LOG

I know these words:

NOUNS AND NOUN PHRASES

- ○ academic counselor
- ○ certificate
- ○ Congress
- ○ continuing education
- ○ debt
- ○ entrepreneur
- ○ expenses
- ○ financial aid
- ○ GED
- ○ long-term goal
- ○ naturalization

- ○ parent-teacher conference
- ○ PTA meeting
- ○ responsibilities
- ○ short-term goal
- ○ tutor
- ○ volunteer

VERBS

- ○ accomplish
- ○ advance
- ○ be in charge of
- ○ delegate

- ○ focus
- ○ pay off
- ○ prepare
- ○ prioritize
- ○ reduce
- ○ volunteer

ADJECTIVES

- ○ bilingual

OTHER

- ○ open doors
- ○ waste time

I practiced these skills, strategies, and grammar points:

- ○ making short- and long-term goals
- ○ listening for specific information
- ○ making inferences
- ○ interviewing classmates
- ○ asking for definitions
- ○ finding out about citizenship

- ○ using context to guess meaning
- ○ brainstorming
- ○ making a cluster diagram
- ○ reviewing the simple present
- ○ using *want*, *need*, and *would like*
- ○ reviewing the future with *will*
- ○ reviewing the simple past

Work-Out CD-ROM

Unit 1: Plug in and practice!

UNIT 2 HOUSING

THINGS TO DO

❶ Warm Up

Discuss these questions with your classmates.

1. Do you live in a house or an apartment? Do you like living there?
2. Who are the people in the picture? What are their jobs?
3. What is your opinion of the house in the picture?

❷ Identify

Look at the picture and the floor plan. Write the number of the item next to each word. Then compare answers with a partner.

_____ a porch		_____ a 2-car garage
_____ a dining room		_____ a bathroom
_____ windows		_____ a bedroom
_____ a deck		_____ tree
_____ a chimney		_____ front yard
_____ a driveway		_____ tomato plants
_____ a roof		_____ a crack

❸ Listen and Check 🎧 010

Look at the picture and listen to the conversation. Check *True* or *False*.

	True	False
1. They want a house with two bedrooms.	○	○
2. There isn't a problem with the plumbing	○	○
3. The crack will be fixed.	○	○
4. The man doesn't like the windows.	○	○
5. They are going to call Ida later.	○	○

❹ Talk about It

Talk with a partner about the house in the picture. Talk about the pros (the things you like about the house) and the cons (the things you don't like).

The Pros	The Cons
There are a lot of windows.	

Would you buy this house? Why or why not?

Target Grammar

Quantifiers   *page 150*

Floor Plan

deck

br 1

br 2

2-car garage

bath

kitchen

living room

bath

m br

din rm

IDA FRANKS

FOR SALE

BEST ROOFERS

Work-Out CD-ROM

Unit 2: Plug in and practice!

LESSON 2

Understanding Housing Ads

THINGS TO DO

❶ Use the Vocabulary

Work with a partner. Ask and answer the questions below the pictures. Talk about your own house or apartment.

❷ Find the Abbreviation

Read the classified ads on page 21 and find an abbreviation for each word.

1. air conditioning _____AC_____
2. utilities _____
3. parking _____
4. location _____
5. available _____
6. immediately _____

7. elevator _____
8. bedroom _____
9. neighborhood _____
10. bathroom _____
11. large _____
12. washer and dryer hookup _____

a. Does the apartment have **air conditioning**?

e. Is it in a safe **neighborhood**?

❸ Listen and Match 🎧 011

Listen to the conversation. Match the conversation with the ad. Write the letter.

Conversation	Ad	Conversation	Ad
1	G	3	
2		4	

❹ Role-Play 🎧 012

Listen. Then work with a partner. Role-play the conversation. Then make new conversations about the ads on page 21.

A: Hi, I'm calling about the apartment for rent.

B: Oh, great. Which one are you interested in renting?

A: I'm interested in the one-bedroom apartment on Lake Avenue. Are pets allowed?

B: Cats are okay, but not dogs.

A: Okay. Are utilities included?

B: Yes, they are.

A: Is there a garage?

B: Yes, there is. So, would you like to see the place?

A: Yes, I would.

Target Grammar

Gerunds after prepositions
page 152

b. Is there an **elevator** in the building?

c. Is there a **laundry room** in the building?

d. Is there a **washer-dryer hookup** in the apartment?

f. Does the building have 24-hour **security**?

g. Are **utilities** included in the rent?

h. Is **heat** included in the rent?

CLASSIFIEDS

Homes   Apartments

Houses for Rent

A SO. MAIN STREET
Bright & sunny 3 BR, 1 ba
ranch, 2 car gar., lg front
yd., $1500 + utils. No
pets/smkrs. 555-8897

B LAKE AVE 3 bedroom,
1 bath home, W/D hookup,
pets o.k., street prkg.,
$900.00 plus utilities,
security, references. Call
555-4583

Apartments for Rent

C LAKE AVE, 14th Floor,
1 BR, $600, incl. utils.
Elev., view. Garage. No
dogs. 555-4493

D CANAL STREET, 3rd
flr, 3BR, w/d hkup, porch,
on-street prkg, yd.
$850/mo. No pets. Hot
water & elec. extra. Avail
4/1. 555-9947

Apartments for Rent

E NORTH STREET
2nd flr., 2BR, clean, quiet,
prkg. & utils incl., no pets,
$800 mo., 555-4556

F BELMONT STREET
Branch River Apartments.
Lg. modern two & three
bedroom units, garage &
outside parking, AC,
balcony, laundry & pool on
site, gas ht., $795-$950.
Plus utils. Good credit
required. Sorry, no dogs.
Call 555-4983

Apartments for Rent

G NORTH STREET
2BR apt. avail immed, 1
car gar., no dogs; cats OK,
good loc., $1200/mo. Utils
incl. 555-4887

H BELMONT ST. 3 bdrm
1.5 ba duplex, gar, lg yard,
fm. nghbd, no smokers,
pets OK, $1375/mo + first
and last months' rent.
555-9986

Reporting Housing Problems

THINGS TO DO

❶ Warm Up

Discuss these questions with your classmates.

1. What are some common problems people have with their houses or apartments?

2. What problems do you think the people in the pictures are having?

❷ Listen and Take Notes 🎧 013

Listen to the telephone conversations. For each conversation, write the tenant's problem. Then listen again and write the landlord's response. Match each conversation to the correct picture.

	Tenant's Problem	Landlord's Response	Picture
1.	The air conditioner isn't working.		B
2.			
3.			
4.			

❸ Role-Play 🎧 014

Listen. Then work with a partner. Role-play the conversation. Then make new conversations with your own ideas. Use the problems you discussed in Activity 1 and the Communication Strategy questions.

A: Hello.

B: Hi. This is your tenant in Apartment 16. I'm calling because I have a problem in my apartment.

A: Yes. What can I do for you?

B: Well, the bathroom ceiling is leaking. Can you come and fix it?

A: Oh, I'm sorry about that. I'll be over some time tomorrow.

B: Do you know what time? I usually work from 9 to 1.

A: I can probably be there between 3 and 6.

B: Great. Thanks. I'll see you then.

COMMUNICATION STRATEGY

Asking for a More Specific Time

Here are some ways you can ask for a more specific time if someone gives you a general time:

Do you know what time?

How soon can you get here?

Can you give me a rough time?

Will that be today?

Target Grammar

Simple present vs. present continuous *page 153*

WINDOW ON MATH

Calculating Housing Costs

When moving into an apartment, renters often have to pay the first and last months' rent plus a security deposit. Here is how you can calculate it.

$$\text{monthly rent} \times 2 + \text{security deposit} = \text{amount to move in}$$
$$\$700 \times 2 + \$700 = \$2,100$$

1. Pilar found a great apartment to rent. She has to pay the first and last months' rent plus a security deposit of one month's rent. If the rent for the apartment is $600 a month, how much money must she give the landlord before she can move in? _____

2. When Bruce and Sylvia moved into their rented house in June, they paid the landlord $2,400 for the first and last months' rent and the security deposit. If the monthly rent is $750, how much was the security deposit?

_____

Filling Out a Rental Application

❶ Warm Up

1. Do you rent an apartment or a house? If you are a renter, did you fill out a rental application? What kind of information was on the application?

2. What kind of information does a landlord need to know about a renter? Why?

❷ Read and Respond

Read the rental application. Then review your answer to Question 2, above.

RENTAL APPLICATION

Renter's Information

Name: _Susan Smith_   Social Security Number: _000-35-9805_   Date of Birth: _2/11/1982_

Present Address: _476 Pine Street, San Diego, CA 92102_   Phone Number: _619-555-9786_

Previous Address: _670 Oak Street, Chicago, IL 60608_

Dates: _December 2009_   to _Present_

Manager's Name: _Amy Vu_   Manager's Phone Number: _312-555-7869_

Reason for Leaving: _Moved to San Diego_

Other Occupants:

Name: _Olivia Smith_   Date of Birth: _9/9/2003_

Name: _____   Date of Birth: _____

Employment Information

Present Employer: _Green Restaurant Group_   Dates: _July 2011_   to _Present_

Address: _345 3rd Street, San Diego, CA 92102_

Position: _Assistant Manager_   Monthly Salary: _$3,100_

Supervisor's Name: _Richard Alaya_   **Supervisor's** Phone Number: _619-555-3678_

Previous Employer: _Park Street Inn_   Dates: _January 2009_   to _June 2011_

Address: _896 Park Street, Chicago, IL 60608_

Position: _Assistant Manager_   Monthly Salary: _$2,800_

Supervisor's Name: _Linda Larkin_   Supervisor's Phone Number: _312-555-4536_

Credit History

Checking Account   Bank Name: _Chester Bank_   Balance: _$1,500_

Savings Account   Bank Name: _Chester Bank_   Balance: _$5,000_

Credit Card   Bank Name: _Chester Bank_   Amount Owed: _$0_

Auto Loan   Bank Name: _None_   Amount Owed: _$0_

Match the term with its meaning.

Term	Meaning
1. _____ credit history	**a.** the address you have now
2. _____ occupants	**b.** the person you work for
3. _____ position	**c.** information about money you have and money you owe
4. _____ present address	**d.** people who live in a place
5. _____ previous address	**e.** the address you had before
6. _____ supervisor	**f.** your job title

❸ Read and Write

Read about Alan Wong. Complete his rental application.

Alan Wong lives at 5694 Oak Drive, Granada Hills, California, 91344. From June 2008 to July 2010, he lived at 19000 Tulsa Avenue in Granada Hills. He's married to Jane Jones and has one son named Sam Wong. Sam was born July 5, 2009. Jane Jones was born Sept. 16, 1979. Alan works at Sunrise Healthcare. He's an accountant. His previous job was at Greenville Community Hospital. He was an accountant there, too. His supervisor at Greenville Community Hospital was Ana Martinez. Alan has an auto loan with Greenville Bank and he owes $8,569 on that loan.

RENTAL APPLICATION

Renter's Information

Name: _Alan Wong_   Social Security Number: _000-00-0000_   Date of Birth: _5/4/1979_

Present Address: _____   Phone Number: _818-555-6789_

Previous Address: _____

Dates: _____ to _____

Manager's Name: _Wendy Murtha_   Manager's Phone Number: _818-555-7968_

Other Occupants:

Name: _____   Date of Birth: _____

Name: _____   Date of Birth: _____

Employment Information

Present Employer: _____   Dates: _June 2008_ to _Present_

Address: _345 3rd Street, Simi Valley, CA 93062_

Position: _____   Monthly Salary: _$4,500_

Supervisor's Name: _Jason Richards_   Supervisor's Phone Number: _805-555-7830_

Previous Employer: _____   Dates: _January 2003_ to _June 2008_

Address: _34589 Central Street, Los Angeles, CA 90071_

Position: _____   Monthly Salary: _$3,800_

Supervisor's Name: _____   Supervisor's Phone Number: _213-555-3486_

Credit History

Checking Account	Bank Name: _Simi Bank_	Balance: _$3,210_
Savings Account	Bank Name: _Simi Bank_	Balance: _$10,043_
Credit Card	Bank Name: _Credit of America_	Amount Owed: _$867.90_
Auto Loan	Bank Name: _____	Amount Owed: _____

PREVIEWING

The word *preview* means to look before. When you preview an article or a Web page, you look over the reading quickly before you read it carefully. Previewing helps you to understand the reading better.

Here are some ways to preview an article or a Web page:

- Look at the title. Guess what the reading is going to be about.
- Read the headings. Headings are like titles—they tell what the sections of the reading are about.
- Ask yourself what you already know about the topic of the reading.

❶ Practice the Strategy

Read the title and headings from a Web article. Guess what the reading is about. Then guess what kind of information might be in each section of the article. Write your guesses on the lines.

Title: How to Keep Your Home Safe

Heading 1: Safety in the Bathroom: _____

Heading 2: Safety in the Kitchen: _____

Heading 3: Safety in the Bedroom: _____

❷ Preview

Look at the title of the Web page on page 27. What do you think it is going to be about?

_____

_____

_____

_____

Now read each heading. Check (✔) the predictions you agree with.

I think this Web page is about:

Predictions

- ○ how to get an apartment in the United States
- ○ an organization that helps people get fair housing
- ○ a law that helps people get fair housing
- ○ actions that are against the law for landlords
- ○ how to advertise housing to special groups of people

Write two things that you already know about this topic.

_____

_____

_____

❸ Read

Read the Web page and check your answers in Activity 2. Were your predictions correct?

EQUAL HOUSING OPPORTUNITY

Office of Fair Housing and Equal Opportunity

Who We Are

The Office of Fair Housing and Equal Opportunity (FHEO) is a government agency. It makes sure that all persons living in the United States have equal housing opportunities.

What We Do

FHEO enforces laws that make it illegal to discriminate in housing on the basis of race, color, religion, gender, national origin, disability, and familial status. The FHEO makes sure that landlords follow the Fair Housing Act.

The Fair Housing Act

Under the Fair Housing Act, it is illegal for anyone to take the following actions based on the factors listed below.

Factors
- Race or color
- National origin
- Religion
- Gender
- Familial status
  (including families with children)
- Disability

Actions
- Refuse to rent to you or sell you housing
- Tell you housing is unavailable when in fact it is available
- Show you apartments or homes in certain neighborhoods only
- Advertise housing to preferred groups of people only

---

❹ Understand the Reading

Answer the questions. Then discuss them with your classmates.

1. How does the Office of Fair Housing and Equal Opportunity (FHEO) help people?

_____

2. What is the purpose of the Fair Housing Act?

_____

3. What are three factors that landlords can't use to refuse to rent to you?

_____

4. Karen owes a lot of money on her credit card. She is not making payments and now she has bad credit. She is trying to rent an apartment, but the landlord won't rent the apartment to her because of her bad credit.

Can the landlord legally refuse to rent to Karen? Why or why not?

_____

Writing a Complaint Letter

IDENTIFYING A PURPOSE FOR WRITING

People write letters for many different purposes:

to thank	to inform	to request something
to complain	to invite	to congratulate

❶ Practice the Skill

Match each sentence to a purpose for writing.

1. Thank you so much for the beautiful flowers. _____ to thank _____

2. I called three times last week, but no one returned my call. _____

3. This is to remind you that your appointment is on June 5th. _____

4. Congratulations on your new job. _____

5. I'm writing to see if you'd like to have dinner on Friday. _____

6. I am writing to request a copy of your brochure #352 called *Against Discrimination*.

_____

❷ Read and Respond

Read the letter on page 29 and answer these questions.

1. Who wrote the letter? _____ Rachel Lewis _____

2. When did she write the letter? _____

3. Who is the letter addressed to? _____

4. What is the relationship between the letter writer and the recipient of the letter? _____

_____

5. What is the writer's purpose for writing this letter? _____

6. What information does the writer include in her letter? _____

_____

7. Do you think this is an effective letter? Why or why not? _____

_____

❸ Brainstorm

Think of three problems you would like to complain about. To whom would you write a letter of complaint?

I would like to complain about...	I would write a letter to...

5532 Bigelow Street
Apartment 125
Chicago, IL 60086

November 12, 2012

Ms. Carol Jawkowsky
Jefferson Point Apartments
5532 Bigelow Street
Chicago, IL 60086

Dear Ms. Jawkowsky:

I am writing to tell you that I have a problem in my apartment. The bathroom sink is leaking. I called maintenance three times about this problem, but no one came to fix it. I've had a bucket under my sink for a month now. I would like to call a plumber to fix the leak. I will pay the plumber, and I'll deduct the amount of the bill from my next rent check. If you have a problem with this, please contact me as soon as possible.

Sincerely,

Rachel Lewis

4 Write

Choose one problem from Activity 3. Write a short letter of complaint. Use the letter above as a model.

_____

_____

_____

_____

_____

_____

_____

_____

_____

_____

_____

_____

_____

_____

Sincerely,

_____

❶ Listening Review  015

Part 1

Listen to what is said. When you hear the question, *Which is correct?*, listen and choose the correct answer: *A, B,* or *C.* Use the Answer Sheet.

Part 2 🎧 016

You will hear the first part of a conversation. To finish the conversation, listen and choose the correct answer: *A, B,* or *C.* Use the Answer Sheet.

Answer Sheet

1	Ⓐ	Ⓑ	Ⓒ
2	Ⓐ	Ⓑ	Ⓒ
3	Ⓐ	Ⓑ	Ⓒ
4	Ⓐ	Ⓑ	Ⓒ
5	Ⓐ	Ⓑ	Ⓒ
6	Ⓐ	Ⓑ	Ⓒ
7	Ⓐ	Ⓑ	Ⓒ
8	Ⓐ	Ⓑ	Ⓒ
9	Ⓐ	Ⓑ	Ⓒ
10	Ⓐ	Ⓑ	Ⓒ

❷ Grammar Review

Circle the correct answer: *A, B,* or *C.*

1. There isn't _____ space for a garden.

   A. many
   B. much
   C. little

2. There are _____ houses for rent in my neighborhood.

   A. a little
   B. a few
   C. a lot

3. There aren't _____ trees in the yard.

   A. a lot
   B. a little
   C. any

4. I'm interested in _____ the apartment on State Street.

   A. rent
   B. renting
   C. rents

5. We're planning on _____ a new apartment.

   A. getting
   B. get
   C. to get

6. Sue is thinking _____ a cat.

   A. about getting
   B. on getting
   C. in getting

❷ Grammar Review (continued)

7. I _____ about the broken air conditioner.
A. calling
B. am calling
C. call

8. The refrigerator usually _____ very well.
A. working
B. is working
C. works

9. The air conditioner _____ right now.
A. aren't working
B. isn't working
C. not work

10. The bathroom ceiling _____ now.
A. is leaking
B. not leak
C. leaking

LEARNING LOG ✔

I know these words:

NOUNS AND NOUN PHRASES
○ air conditioning
○ credit history
○ elevator
○ equal opportunity
○ fair housing
○ heat

○ laundry room
○ location
○ neighborhood
○ occupants
○ position
○ security
○ supervisor

○ rental application
○ utilities
○ washer and dryer hookup

ADJECTIVES
○ available
○ present
○ previous

ADVERB
○ immediately

VERBS
○ complain
○ congratulate
○ inform
○ request
○ thank

I practiced these skills, strategies, and grammar points:

○ expressing and supporting an opinion
○ taking notes
○ reading for specific information
○ listening for specific information
○ asking for a more specific time
○ discussing pros and cons
○ describing a house
○ filling out a rental application
○ calculating housing costs
○ using abbreviations

○ understanding housing ads
○ reporting housing problems
○ previewing information
○ identifying a purpose for writing
○ writing a letter of complaint
○ using quantifiers
○ using gerunds after prepositions
○ contrasting the present continuous and the simple present

Work-Out CD-ROM

Unit 2: Plug in and practice!

THINGS TO DO

❶ Warm Up

Discuss these questions with your classmates.

1. What do you like to do to relax?

2. What do you do to stay healthy?

3. What do you see people in the picture doing? Which of these things do you do?

❷ Find and Classify

Find someone in the picture doing each of the activities. Write the name. Then decide if the activity is healthy or unhealthy.

1. _____ wearing a hat

2. _____ sunbathing

3. _____ exercising

4. _____ putting on **sunblock**

5. _____ wearing a **life vest** in a boat

6. _____ drinking soda

7. _____ eating fruit

8. _____ smoking

9. _____ relaxing

10. _____ sitting in the shade

What other examples of healthy and unhealthy behavior do you see in the picture? Tell your classmates.

❸ Find Someone Who

Read the list of activities Add another idea from the picture. Talk to your classmates. Find someone who answers *yes* or *no* to each question.

Example: *A: Have you used sunblock today?*
B: Yes, I have. / No, I haven't.

Have you _____?	Name	Yes	No
1. used sunblock today	_____	○	○
2. eaten junk food today	_____	○	○
3. been sick this month	_____	○	○
4. had a check-up this year	_____	○	○
5. done something relaxing today	_____	○	○
6. exercised today	_____	○	○
7. smoked today	_____	○	○
8. _____	_____	○	○

Work-Out CD-ROM

Unit 3: Plug in and practice!

Bob

Dave

Fred

Cara

Ali

Charcoal

MILK

CHIPS

NO LITTERING

Target Grammar

Present perfect   *page 155*

Healthy Living | 33

Understanding Medical Terms

THINGS TO DO

❶ Talk about It

1. Study the pictures and the health questionnaire on page 35. What do you know about Gisela Lozano? Share ideas with your classmates.

Example: *She doesn't drink alcohol. She takes supplements.*

❷ Expand Your Vocabulary

Write the missing word forms. Then complete the questions with the correct form of a word from the chart.

Noun Form	Verb Form	Adjective Form
a. _____	✗	surgical
b. supplement	_____	supplemental
c. _____	prescribe	✗
d. _____	✗	nutritional
e. _____	✗	allergic
f. _____	provide	✗
g. operation	_____	operative

1. Did you have _____ *surgery* _____ last year?

2. Are you _____ to cats?

3. Vitamin C is a kind of _____.

4. What _____ supplements do you take?

5. You fill a _____ at a drugstore.

6. I am going to have an _____ on my feet this year.

7. What is the name of your healthcare _____?

❸ Listen and Write 🎧 017

Listen to a conversation between Gisela and a healthcare provider. Complete Gisela's health questionnaire with the missing information.

a. Gisela has **allergies**.

e. Gisela has had two ear **infections** this year.

Target Grammar

Simple past vs. present perfect *page 158*

b. Gisela's doctor gave her a **prescription** for allergy medication.

c. Gisela sees **healthcare providers** regularly. She gets a **check-up** each year.

d. Gisela's brother has **asthma**.

f. Gisela takes **nutritional supplements**.

g. Gisela hasn't had many **surgeries**, but she had an **operation** 5 years ago.

h. Gisela doesn't drink **alcohol** and she has a **low-fat diet**.

Health History Questionnaire

Date: 5 / 2 / 2012   **Name:** Gisela Lozano   **DOB:** 7 / 4/ 75

Medical problems	Year started	Surgeries	Date	Prescriptions, medications and supplements/ How long have you taken them?
ear infections	1998	appendectomy	2007	nasal spray / since 2009
nasal allergies	_____			vitamin ___ / since 2007
				calcium / since _____

Healthcare Providers: Dr. Benton, family doctor, & Doctor Wilson, dentist

Do you smoke? ○ Yes ○ No

How much alcohol do you drink each week? ○ None ○ 1 drink ○ 2 drinks ○ 3 or more drinks

Do you use illegal drugs? ○ Yes ⊗ No

Please mark the behaviors you follow:

⊗ Wear a seatbelt ⊗ Keep a smoke detector in house ⊗ Exercise more than 3 times per week

○ Eat a low-fat diet ○ Have annual check-ups

Please mark if you have a family history of any of the following:

○ Heart disease ○ Skin cancer ○ High cholesterol ○ Asthma

THINGS TO DO

❶ Warm Up

Discuss these questions with your classmates.

1. When was the last time you got sick? What was the problem? What did you do?

2. According to the bar graph on page 37, what are the three most common reasons people see a doctor?

❷ Listen and Take Notes 🎧 018

Listen to conversation #1 and write the person's reason for visiting the doctor and when the problem started. Listen a second time and write the doctor's advice. Repeat with conversation #2.

	Reason for Visiting the Doctor	When It Started	Doctor's Advice
1.	trouble sleeping		
2.			

❸ Role-Play 🎧 019

Listen. Then work with a partner. Role-play the conversation between a doctor and a patient. Replace the underlined words with the problems in the bar graph on page 37 and your own ideas.

Doctor: What seems to be the problem?

Patient: <u>I have a stomachache.</u>

Doctor: How long have you had it?

Patient: <u>Since Tuesday.</u>

Doctor: When did it start?

Patient: <u>It started in the evening.</u>

Doctor: I suggest that you <u>try to improve your diet.</u>
Why don't you <u>try a low-fat diet?</u>

Patient: I guess I could try that.

COMMUNICATION STRATEGY

Giving Advice

Here are some common ways that people give suggestions and advice:

I think that you should . . .

I suggest that you . . .

Why don't you . . .?

You could . . .

⦿ Target Grammar

Present perfect with *for* and *since*   *page 160*

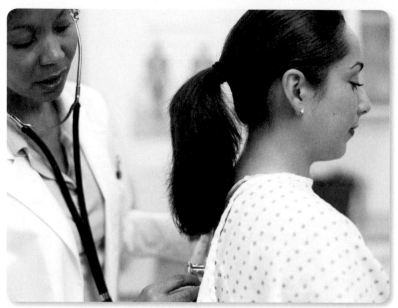

Top 10 Reasons for Doctor's Office Visits

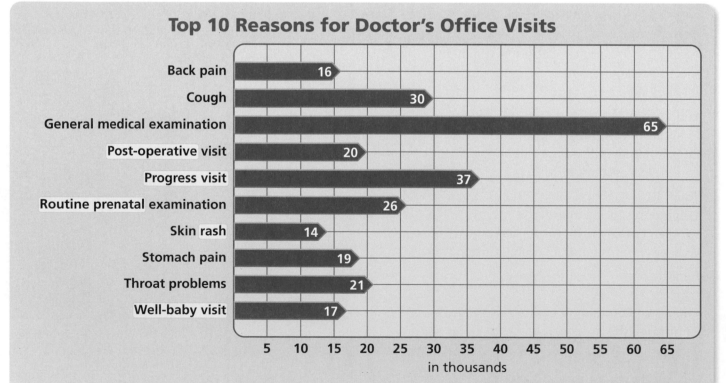

Reason	in thousands
Back pain	16
Cough	30
General medical examination	65
Post-operative visit	20
Progress visit	37
Routine prenatal examination	26
Skin rash	14
Stomach pain	19
Throat problems	21
Well-baby visit	17

in thousands

Source: National Center for Health Statistics.

Finding Help

❶ Warm Up

Discuss these questions with a partner.

1. What kind of health information can you find in a telephone book?

2. What other kinds of help can you find in a telephone book?

3. What is a telephone hotline?

❷ Read and Respond

Read this telephone directory.

EMERGENCY SERVICES

Police, Fire, Ambulance
9-1-1

Poison Control
800-222-1222

COMMUNITY SERVICES

Abuse, Assault & Domestic Violence
National Domestic Violence **Hotline** 800-555-3999
Women's **Crisis** Center Hotline 555-1212

AIDS
AIDS Hotline 555-4877

Alcohol and Drug Abuse
Al-Anon/Alateen 555-6443
Alcohol Abuse and Drug 24-Hour Helpline 555-2900
Alcoholics **Anonymous** 555-2233
Alcohol and Drug Treatment Referral 555-8805

Child Abuse and/or Neglect
Child-at-Risk Hotline 800-555-4539
International Child Abuse Network 800-555-3387
Parental Stress Line 800-555-5499

Food
Community Food Bank 555-6758
Supplemental Nutrition and Assistance Program (SNAP) 800-555-2200
Women, Infants, and Children Program (WIC) 800-555-3999

Health Care
Cancer Care. 555-6830
Council of Community Clinics 555-5702
Family Health Center. 555-2079

Volunteer answers calls at Domestic Violence Hotline.

Community clinics offer free and **reduced-cost** healthcare to people without insurance.

Discuss these questions with your classmates.

1. What is the difference between emergency services and community services?

2. What do you think Alcoholics Anonymous might be?

3. Why do you think people would call the Parental Stress Line?

4. What do you think the Supplemental Nutrition and Assistance Program provides?

5. If you wanted to help someone with a drug problem, what numbers could you call?

6. If someone in your family had cancer, what number could you call?

❸ Listen and Write 🎧 020

Listen to phone conversations between callers and community volunteers. Write the reason for each call.

Call	Reason for the Call
1	baby won't stop crying
2	
3	
4	

❹ Apply

Look in your local telephone directory to find a telephone number for each category below. Write the telephone number. Then add the name and number for two more community services.

1. Alcohol Abuse: _____

2. Drug Abuse: _____

3. Domestic Violence: _____

4. Child Abuse: _____

5. _____

6. _____

Skimming and Scanning

SKIMMING AND SCANNING

Skimming means to look quickly over a passage to find the topic or main idea. To skim, look at the title and any pictures, and read the first sentence of each paragraph.

Scanning means to look quickly for specific information. To scan, move your eyes quickly across the words. Don't read every word. For example, just look for names and numbers.

---

❶ Practice the Strategy

Read the questions. Then scan the labels to find the answers.

1. What is one example of a reason to use "Pain Away"?

_____

2. How long can you take "Pain Away"?

_____

3. How many "Pain Away" tablets can you take in 4 hours?

_____

4. What is the prescription medication used for?

_____

5. Who wrote the prescription?

_____

6. How often should the patient take the prescription medicine?

_____

Over-the-counter (OTC) medication

❷ Preview

Skim the reading on page 41 and identify the topic. Then scan it to find specific answers to the questions below.

Topic

1. What is the reading about?

_____

Specific Information

2. What organization wrote the information?

_____

3. What kind of operation did the patient have?

_____

4. What kind of exercise can the patient do?

_____

5. How long does the patient have to keep the dressings on?

_____

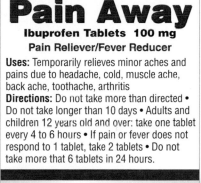

Prescription medication

❸ Listen and Read 🎧 021

Read the instructions. Then check your answers in Activity 2.

The Community Clinic

123 Green Street, Boston, MA 02114 • (888-555-3248)

The Community Clinic

Post-Operative Instructions for Appendectomy Patients

After you leave the hospital, follow these instructions. They will help you recover quickly from your recent operation.

- You may eat and drink normally. You do not have to follow a special diet.
- Do not do heavy exercise or lift objects over 15 pounds. However, light exercise, such as walking, will help you recover faster.
- Keep your dressings dry. You can remove them 3 days after surgery. Take sponge baths until you remove the dressings.
- If you become nauseated or start vomiting, have diarrhea, or have a fever, call your doctor immediately.
- For moderate pain, take ibuprofen.
- For severe pain, take the prescription pain medication.
- You can drive as long as you do not take the prescription pain medication.

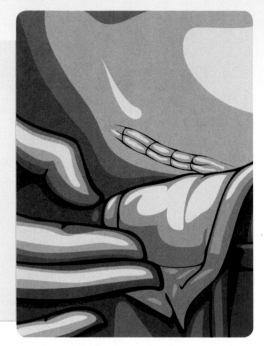

Keep your dressings dry.

❹ Understand the Reading

Answer the questions about different people. They have each had an appendectomy.

1. Mark still has his dressings on, but he wants to take a bath. What should he do? _____

2. Leila has a fever. What should she do? _____

3. José needs to go to work, but he's in a little pain. Which medication should he take? _____

4. Alex is in severe pain. He can't sleep. Which medication should he take? _____

WINDOW ON MATH

Converting Units of Measurement

Use the chart to answer the questions.

When you know	You can find	If you multiply by
grams	milligrams	1000
pounds	kilograms	0.45
kilograms	pounds	2.2

1. Amal takes .5 grams of medication every morning. How many milligrams is that? _____

2. Wen weighs 136 pounds. How many kilos is that? _____

3. Franco weighs 70 kilos. How many pounds is that? _____

Compound Sentences

COMPOUND SENTENCES

A compound sentence is two or more simple sentences joined together. You can join the simple sentences with a comma (,) and a coordinating conjunction (*and*, *but*).

Simple Sentences	Compound Sentence
I eat a low-fat diet. I always feel healthy.	I eat a low-fat diet, and I always feel healthy.
Marta seems to be in good health. She doesn't like to exercise.	Marta seems to be in good health, but she doesn't like to exercise.

❶ Practice the Skill

Combine each pair of simple sentences to make a compound sentence. Use a comma with *and* or *but*.

1. He always wears a hat outside. He never wears sunblock.

He always wears a hat outside, but he never wears sunblock.

2. They ride bicycles on the weekend. They play soccer, too.

_____

3. She has nasal allergies. She has never had asthma.

_____

4. They have a smoke detector in their house. They don't have a fire extinguisher.

_____

5. My brother hurt his back. It's still not better.

_____

6. He eats a low-fat diet. He doesn't drink much coffee.

_____

USED TO

We use *used to* + verb to write about things in the past that are no longer true.
I <u>used to eat</u> a lot of junk food, but now I eat a healthy diet.
I <u>used to ride</u> my bike to work, but now I take the bus.

Target Grammar

Used to   *page 161*

❷ Read and Write

Read the story below. Find and underline any *used to* + verb combinations. Then identify each sentence as simple (S) or compound (C). Write your answers on the lines to the right.

My Hat and I

(1) I was an odd child. (2) I used to wear a hat everywhere I went. (3) I was afraid of the sun, and I didn't want to get skin cancer. (4) We lived in a very sunny place, and adults used to talk all the time about staying out of the sun. (5) I think that made me afraid of the sun. (6) I know it sounds silly, but I never took my hat off. (7) I wore it in the bathtub. (8) I used to wear it at the movies. (9) I also wore it to school. (10) I even tried to wear it in the classroom, but the teacher made me take it off. (11) Now, I don't wear a hat everywhere, but I do wear one whenever I go outside. (12) My doctor says I have very healthy skin. (13) It's also smooth and clear. (14) I was an odd child, but today I'm a very healthy adult!

1. ___S___	8. _____
2. _____	9. _____
3. _____	10. _____
4. _____	11. _____
5. _____	12. _____
6. _____	13. _____
7. _____	14. _____

❸ Plan Your Writing

Think about a healthy or unhealthy behavior that you had when you were a child, or any time in the past. Write it here:

_____

Now write three examples of the behavior:

Example 1: _____

Example 2: _____

Example 3: _____

Is your behavior different now? Explain: Now, I _____

❹ Write

Now write a paragraph about something you did in the past. Use your notes from Activity 3. Remember to use simple and compound sentences in your writing. Give your paragraph a title.

❶ Listening Review 🎧 022

Part 1

You will hear the first part of a conversation. To finish the conversation, listen and choose the correct answer: *A*, *B*, or *C*. Use the Answer Sheet.

Part 2 🎧 023

First you will hear a question. Next, listen carefully to what is said. You will hear the question again. Then choose the correct answer: *A*, *B*, or *C*. Use the Answer Sheet.

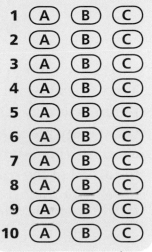

Answer Sheet

	A	B	C
1	Ⓐ	Ⓑ	Ⓒ
2	Ⓐ	Ⓑ	Ⓒ
3	Ⓐ	Ⓑ	Ⓒ
4	Ⓐ	Ⓑ	Ⓒ
5	Ⓐ	Ⓑ	Ⓒ
6	Ⓐ	Ⓑ	Ⓒ
7	Ⓐ	Ⓑ	Ⓒ
8	Ⓐ	Ⓑ	Ⓒ
9	Ⓐ	Ⓑ	Ⓒ
10	Ⓐ	Ⓑ	Ⓒ

❷ Grammar Review

Circle the correct answer: *A, B,* or *C.*

1. I have _____ two ear infections this year.

  A. have
  B. having
  C. had

2. _____ Rafael had a check-up this year?

  A. Have
  B. Has
  C. Did

3. A: Have you used sunblock today?
  B. No, I _____.

  A. hasn't
  B. am not
  C. haven't

4. Linda has taken supplements
  since _____.

  A. 2009
  B. three years ago
  C. two years

5. I have been allergic to cats for _____.

  A. 20 years
  B. I was a child
  C. 20 years ago

6. Franco has eaten a low-fat diet for _____.

  A. 2003
  B. 8 years
  C. last year

Work-Out CD-ROM

Unit 3: Plug in and practice!

❷ Grammar Review (continued)

7. A: When did it start?
   B: It started _____.

   A. yesterday
   B. 24 hours
   C. a day

8. When did Gisela _____ her medication?

   A. taken
   B. take
   C. took

9. A: How long have you had allergies?
   B: I _____ allergies for 5 years.

   A. have
   B. having
   C. have had

10. I _____ eat a lot of junk food.

   A. use
   B. used to
   C. use to

LEARNING LOG

I know these words:

NOUNS AND NOUN PHRASES				ADJECTIVES
○ abuse	○ cholesterol	○ nutrition	○ vitamin	○ allergic
○ alcohol	○ crisis	○ operation	○ well-baby visit	○ anonymous
○ allergy	○ diet	○ prescription	**VERBS**	○ low-fat
○ appendectomy	○ domestic violence	○ progress visit	○ infect	○ nutritional
○ assault	○ drug abuse	○ provider	○ operate	○ post-operative
○ asthma	○ healthcare provider	○ rash	○ prescribe	○ prenatal
○ calcium	○ hotline	○ referral	○ prohibit	○ reduced-cost
○ cancer	○ infection	○ sunblock	○ provide	○ routine
○ check-up	○ life vest	○ supplement	○ supply	○ surgical
	○ medication	○ surgery		
	○ neglect	○ treatment		

I practiced these skills, strategies, and grammar points:

○ classifying types of activities
○ listening for specific information
○ taking notes
○ reading for specific information
○ reading labels
○ learning word forms
○ giving examples
○ giving advice
○ asking about time

○ converting units of measurement
○ interpreting a bar graph
○ skimming and scanning
○ using compound sentences
○ using the present prefect
○ using the present perfect with *for* and *since*
○ using the simple past and present perfect
○ using *used to*
○ filling out a health history questionnaire
○ reading a telephone directory

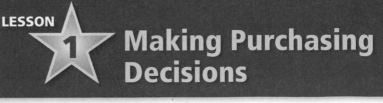

UNIT 4 MONEY AND CONSUMERISM

LESSON 1 Making Purchasing Decisions

THINGS TO DO

❶ Warm Up

Discuss these questions with your classmates.

1. What was the last thing you bought? Where did you buy it?

2. Do you buy things on sale? What things are on sale in the picture?

3. What are different ways to pay for things in a department store?

❷ Write and Find

Write the verb that goes with each activity. (You'll use some verbs more than once.) Then find someone in the picture doing each of the activities.

buying	paying	waiting

	Activity	Person
1.	_paying_ by credit	_Tina_
2.	_____ something on sale	_____
3.	_____ by check	_____
4.	_____ shoes	_____
5.	_____ in line	_____

❸ Listen and Circle 🎧 024

Listen to the conversations. Circle *True* or *False*.

1. The man is paying by credit.   True   False

2. Pants are on sale.   True   False

3. The man is paying with cash.   True   False

4. They're going to pay with a check.   True   False

❹ Talk about It

Read the statements. Circle *Agree* or *Disagree*. Then explain your answers to a partner.

1. Using a debit card is a bad idea.   Agree   Disagree

2. Buying everything in one place is best.   Agree   Disagree

3. Paying with cash is a good idea.   Agree   Disagree

4. Getting things on sale always saves money.   Agree   Disagree

5. Using a credit card is a good idea.   Agree   Disagree

Target Grammar
Gerunds as subjects *page 162*

Warranties and Return Policies

THINGS TO DO

❶ Talk about It

Discuss these questions with your classmates.

1. What products do you see in each picture?

2. Have you ever returned a product to a store? If yes, what happened?

3. A **warranty** is a promise that a product is good; if not, the company will take care of the problem. How important is a warranty when you buy a cell phone? A computer?

❷ Use Context

Study the pictures and read the information. Choose the best meaning for each of the words below.

defect	refund	replacement
valid	~~void~~	workmanship

1. not good or legal anymore: _____ void _____

2. money you get back: _____

3. mistake or problem: _____

4. how well something is made: _____

5. good; legal: _____

6. new product in exchange for the original: _____

❸ Role-Play 🎧 025

Listen. Then work with a partner. Role-play the conversation between a customer and a salesperson. Replace the highlighted words with the items below.

A: I'd like to return this laptop computer.

B: Certainly. Do you have the receipt?

A: Yes. Here it is.

B: It looks like it's still under warranty. What's the problem?

A: It stopped working.

B: Do you want a refund or a replacement?

A: A replacement, please.

DVD player / It quit working. / I'll take it somewhere else.

the warranty isn't valid / to repair it here or somewhere else

This warranty covers **defects** in materials and *workmanship*

The warranty does not cover **damage** due to scratches, cuts, or accidents.

Target Grammar

Gerunds as objects of verbs
page 163

2

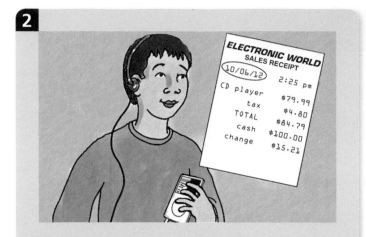

The **period of coverage** of this warranty is for one year from the date of purchase.

3

You may return the product to the store for a **refund** or a **replacement**.

5

Return Policy: Clothing must be **unworn**. DVDs must be in **unopened** packages. Appliances must be **unused**.

6

Improper care and cleaning will **void** the warranty

7

You must present the **original receipt**.

8

This warranty is **valid** for 6 months from the date of purchase if accompanied by the receipt.

Selecting a Car

THINGS TO DO

❶ Warm Up

Discuss these questions with your classmates.

1. Who are the people in the picture? What do you think they are talking about?

2. What is a **pre-owned** car?

3. What should a good car warranty include? Is the warranty on this page a good warranty? Why or why not?

❷ Listen and Take Notes 🎧 026

Listen to two conversations. Write the missing information in the chart below.

	Car 1 **Make:** KMC **Model :** Via	Car 2 **Make:** Tanaka **Model:** Cargo
What's the **mileage**? (How many miles are on it?)		
What's the **gas mileage**? (How many miles does it get per gallon?)	City: Highway:	City: Highway: 28 mpg
What year is it?		
What's the price?	$8,998	

Work with a partner. Ask and answer questions about the cars.

❸ Role-Play 🎧 027

Listen. Then work with a partner. Role-play the conversation between a customer and a salesperson. Replace the underlined words with the information in the chart above. Use the communication strategy.

A: How can I help you today?

B: I'm thinking about buying a pre-owned car.

A: Sure. How about one of these?

B: Which one is better?

A: <u>The KMC Via has less mileage than the Tanaka Cargo.</u>

B: How much is the <u>KMC</u>?

A: <u>It's only $8,998</u>.

B: I'm afraid that's <u>too expensive</u>.

Vehicle Warranty

This chart summarizes the warranty coverage on your pre-owned car.

Type of coverage	Years/Miles
Car body parts	2/24,000
Rust	2/24,000
Engine	3/30,000
Seat belts	3/30,000

The coverage is for whatever comes first. For example, if you drive 24,000 miles before you reach 2 years, you are covered up to 24,000 miles.

Your dealer will repair or replace any defective parts during that period of coverage.

COMMUNICATION STRATEGY

Disagreeing Politely

Here are some ways to disagree politely:

I'm afraid that. . .

I'm sorry, but. . .

Thanks, but. . .

⊙ Target Grammar

Comparative and superlative adjectives, *as adjective as* *page 165*

WINDOW ON PRONUNCIATION

Linking Words 🎧 028

We often link a consonant sound at the end of one word to the vowel at the beginning of the next word.

A Listen to the words. Then listen and repeat.

it's as   (sounds like *it zaz*)

isn't as   (sounds like *izn taz*)

price is   (sounds like *pri siz*)

B Draw marks to predict the linking in the sentences below. Then listen and check.

1. It's in better shape than yours is.
2. The Tanaka isn't as expensive as the KMC.
3. The price is lower.
4. It's as nice as the other one.
5. How many miles are on it?

C Work with a partner. Practice the role play in Activity 3 again. Pay special attention to linking words.

Bank Services and Problems

❶ Warm Up

Discuss these questions with a partner.

1. What bank services do you use now?
2. What other banking services do you know about?
3. Do you know anyone who pays bills online?

❷ Read and Discuss

Read the glossary on page 53 and discuss these questions in small groups.

1. How can you prevent bounced checks?
2. What is the difference between a credit card and a debit card?
3. What are two ways that you can pay for a costly item such as a car?
4. What bank service can you use when the bank is closed?
5. Why should you keep your PIN a secret?

❸ Listen and Check 🎧 029

Listen to a conversation between a banker and a customer. Check (✔) the services the customer gets.

_____ checking account   _____ check card

_____ savings account   _____ a PIN

_____ loan   _____ direct deposit

_____ credit card   _____ overdraft protection

❹ Apply

Work with a partner. Use the glossary to solve these problems.

1. Katy just opened a new checking account. She works full-time and she doesn't have a car, so it's hard for her to get to the bank to deposit her paycheck. What service does she need?

2. Paul has a big family, so he does a lot of shopping each week. He doesn't like to carry a lot of money in his wallet. He doesn't want to use a credit card because he doesn't want to get into debt. What should he use for shopping?

3. Luisa wants to buy a used car. The car dealer won't take a check from her checking account. What bank service does Luisa need?

4. On May 17th, Alex had $27 in his checking account. He wrote a check for $35 to pay for his parking permit. His bank charged him a fee. What was the problem?

At an ATM

Swiping a credit card

Paying bills online

Seattle Central Bank   ⊟ ⊞ ☒

Seattle Central Bank

Home | Contact Us | Site Map | FAQ | Account Login

Search   (GO)

- HOME
- POLICIES
- ACCOUNTS
- GLOSSARY
- CONTACT

Glossary of Banking Terms

Account balance: The amount of money you have in your account. You can access your account balance online, at a branch, by phone, or at an ATM. (automatic teller machine).

Bounced check: A check that the bank will not pay because you do not have enough money in your account to cover it.

Cashier's check: A check that a bank writes. It promises to pay the amount that is on it. You can use it for large purchases such as a car.

Check card: See *Debit card.*

Checking account: A bank account where you can keep money. You can write checks or withdraw money from an ATM with this account.

Credit card: A small plastic card that lets you buy things now and pay for them later. You can get a credit card through Seattle Central Bank.

Debit: Any withdrawal from your account.

Debit card or check card: A bank card you can use at an ATM or a store to purchase goods and services. It takes money directly from your bank account.

Direct deposit: A method of deposit where money goes electronically into your account (usually a paycheck).

Insufficient funds: A situation in which you do not have enough money in your bank account to cover a check or debit. This situation can cause a check to bounce (see Bounced check).

Interest: Money the bank pays you while they are using your money. Also the amount you have to pay when you borrow money.

Loan: Money you can borrow from the bank for different needs. Seattle Central Bank offers auto loans, personal loans, home mortgage loans, and student loans.

Online banking: A service that allows you to access your account balance, transfer funds, and pay bills online. Seattle Central Bank offers this service.

Overdraft: A situation in which you write a check for more money than you have in your account. Seattle Central Bank offers overdraft protection for a fee. With overdraft protection, the bank automatically transfers money from your savings account or your credit card to cover an overdraft.

PIN: Personal Identification Number. A code that you use to access your account at an ATM or bank branch. Remember to keep your PIN private. Do not share it with anyone.

Savings account: Savings accounts are like checking accounts, but they usually offer higher interest and they have certain conditions. For example, you cannot write checks on some savings accounts.

Service charge: The monthly fee Seattle Central Bank charges for handling your checking account.

Statement: A list of your banking transactions for a period of time.

FINDING THE MAIN IDEA

The *topic* is what a reading is about. The *main idea* is the important idea that the writer expresses about the topic. A reading as a whole can have a main idea, and each paragraph in a reading can have a main idea, too. You can express a topic as a word or a phrase. You express a main idea as a complete sentence.

Sometimes, a writer expresses the main idea directly. Look at this example:

> Debit cards have advantages and disadvantages. With a debit card, you don't have to carry a lot of cash around with you. Also, you can use a debit card just about anywhere. You can even use it like a credit card for shopping online. Debit cards have a few disadvantages, though. For example, you must keep track of your debit card use; otherwise, you might overdraw on your account. Also, some ATM machines charge a fee when you use your debit card to get cash.

Topic: debit cards

Main idea: Debit cards have advantages and disadvantages.

Sometimes, the writer doesn't state the main idea directly. To find it, you can:

- ask yourself, "What is the writer telling me?"
- notice if the ideas are related in some way.
- think of a sentence that describes the message of the paragraph or the whole reading.

❶ Practice the Strategy

Read the paragraphs. Write a sentence about each paragraph that expresses the main idea.

1. Many families want to own homes. Before buying, families should consider several things. First, they should make sure they have enough money for the down payment and can still pay their other bills. Second, families may want to wait if the interest rates on mortgages are too high. Another thing to consider is the type of mortgage that may be best. Sometimes a mortgage that offers a low interest rate now may require a much higher interest rate in a few years.

Main idea: _____

2. Do you keep your cash at home under the bed or in a box somewhere? It may be a better idea to use a bank or credit union. Both banks and credit unions offer checking accounts and savings accounts. These are generally safe places to keep your money. By using a bank or credit union, you can save time and avoid theft. Many credit unions make it easy for immigrants to open accounts.

Main idea: _____

❷ Preview

Skim the reading on page 55 to identify the topic. Look at the title and the picture.

Topic: _____

❸ Listen and Read 🎧 030

Read the article. What are the main ideas of paragraphs 2, 3, and 4? Write a sentence for each one.

Paragraph 2: _____

Paragraph 3: _____

Paragraph 4: _____

Ways to Shop

1   You want to buy some new furniture. Should you buy it in a store, online, or by phone? There are several ways to make a major purchase, and each way has its own advantages and disadvantages. Let's take a closer look at different ways to buy things.

2   One way to buy something such as furniture is to go to a store, look at everything, and make a choice. With in-store buying, you can see and feel the items yourself. You can try them out and compare them up close. In addition, with this method, you can pay by cash, credit, or by check. However, if you don't have a lot of free time to shop or if you live far from a shopping area, in-store shopping can be time consuming. Although it has some disadvantages, buying in a store lets you see items up close and offers more payment options.

In-store shopping

3   Online shopping is another way to make a purchase. Online shopping lets you shop from home or from work. You don't have to worry about using gas or parking your car. It's an easy way to compare prices, because you can look at the same item in many stores with a few clicks of the mouse. Of course, you can't see or feel something before you buy it. Also, with an online purchase, you can't pay with cash. You can usually pay by credit. Paying by credit online can be dangerous because your credit card information isn't always private. So, buying online can save you time and money, but it has limited payment options and certain risks.

4   Buying over the phone through a catalog company is similar to shopping online, and it has some of the same advantages and disadvantages. It can save you time and money, and has the same payment options. One of the main benefits of catalog shopping is that a catalog picture sometimes gives you a better idea of your purchase than an online image. With catalog buying, you can sometimes also pay by check. Mailing the company a check is safer than using a credit card, but it takes more time.

5   So, the next time you need to make a purchase, ask yourself: How much time do I have? How far away is the store? How do I want to pay for my purchase? The answers to these questions will help you choose the best way to shop.

❹ Understand the Reading

Discuss these questions with your classmates.

1. Which way to shop do you like best—in-store, online, or by catalog? Why do you like to shop this way?

2. What are the advantages of each way to shop? What are the disadvantages?

Writing a Letter to Return Merchandise

STATING REASONS

When you write a letter to return something, you should state the purpose in the first sentence. This is the main idea sentence. It includes the cause or the reason for the return.

Example: *I am returning this coffeemaker because it's defective.*

Here are some reasons for returns:

a. It's defective.

b. It doesn't match the picture.

c. It's not as advertised.

d. It's the wrong color / size / type / model.

e. It's poor quality.

f. I don't like it. / I've changed my mind.

❶ Practice the Skill

Match each problem with a reason for return from the box above.

_____C_____ **1.** Marta bought a bottle of sunblock. The ad for the product said that it was waterproof. Marta used the sunblock and then went swimming. She got a bad burn on her back.

_____ **2.** Jack bought a shirt that he found on the Internet. He washed it once, and the material started to come apart.

_____ **3.** Lin bought her son a toy truck on the Internet. When it arrived, it was much smaller than it appeared on the website.

_____ **4.** Mark bought a sweater from a catalog. He ordered a size Large. The company sent him a size Small.

_____ **5.** Anna bought a lamp. She plugged it in. It didn't work.

_____ **6.** Luis bought a laptop computer on the Internet. Just before it arrived, Luis's mother gave her old laptop to him. Now he doesn't need the new laptop.

USING LOGICAL CONNECTORS

The body, or main part, of a return letter contains details and examples that explain the reason for the return. Writers connect details and examples with logical connectors. Logical connectors list ideas and show how they are related.

Example: *I am returning this toaster because it isn't as advertised. <u>First of all</u>, it doesn't work properly.*

Some logical connectors are:

First of all,
Secondly,
Another . . .
In addition, . .
Finally, . . .

❷ Read and Write

Read the letter. Underline the main idea sentence and the logical connectors.

5532 Bigelow Street
Apartment 223
Chicago, IL 60086

February 12, 2012

Sunshade Products
Customer Relations
4538 Corporate Way, Suite 879
Oakland, CA 94621

To Whom It May Concern:

I am returning the enclosed sunblock because it isn't as advertised. First of all, it's very difficult to apply. It's sticky and doesn't cover the skin well. Secondly, it's supposed to be waterproof, but it came off as soon as I got into the swimming pool. In addition, the ad says that it lasts for 5 hours, but it obviously doesn't, especially if you use it in water. Finally, it has a terrible smell.

Please send my refund to the address above. Thank you.

Sincerely,

Marta Taylor

❸ Plan Your Writing

Think about a product you bought recently that had a problem. What are your reasons for returning it? Write the information here:

Product: _____.

Reason for returning it: _____

Detail / Example 1: _____

Detail / Example 2: _____

Detail / Example 3: _____

❹ Write

Now write a return letter. Use your notes from Activity 3. Start with a main idea sentence that explains the purpose of your letter. Use logical connectors to connect the details and examples.

❶ Listening Review 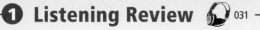 031

Part 1

First, you will hear a question. Next, listen carefully to what is said. You will hear the question again. Then choose the correct answer: *A*, *B*, or *C*. Use the Answer Sheet.

Part 2 032

Listen to what is said. When you hear the question, *Which is correct?*, listen and choose the correct answer: *A*, *B*, or *C*. Use the Answer Sheet.

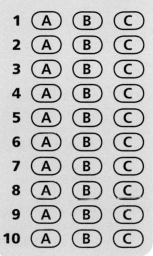

Answer Sheet

1 Ⓐ Ⓑ Ⓒ
2 Ⓐ Ⓑ Ⓒ
3 Ⓐ Ⓑ Ⓒ
4 Ⓐ Ⓑ Ⓒ
5 Ⓐ Ⓑ Ⓒ
6 Ⓐ Ⓑ Ⓒ
7 Ⓐ Ⓑ Ⓒ
8 Ⓐ Ⓑ Ⓒ
9 Ⓐ Ⓑ Ⓒ
10 Ⓐ Ⓑ Ⓒ

❷ Grammar Review

Circle the correct answer: *A*, *B*, or *C*.

1. _____ by cash is a good idea.

   A. Pay
   B. Paid
   C. Paying

2. Waiting in line _____ very boring!

   A. is
   B. are
   C. be

3. The MP3 player quit _____.

   A. work
   B. working
   C. to work

4. I don't mind _____ you up.

   A. picking
   B. to pick
   C. pick

5. She keeps _____ the same sweaters.

   A. buy
   B. to buy
   C. buying

6. My new laptop isn't _____ my old one.

   A. as fast
   B. as fast as
   C. faster as

② Grammar Review (continued)

7. The KMC is _____ the Tanaka.

   A. new
   B. newer than
   C. newest

8. The KMC is _____ economical than the America.

   A. more
   B. most
   C. very

9. The Tanaka is _____ deal on the lot.

   A. better than
   B. better
   C. the best

10. The Via gets _____ mileage on the highway than the Cargo.

   A. good
   B. better
   C. the best

LEARNING LOG

I know these words:

NOUNS AND NOUN PHRASES
- account balance
- ATM
- bounced check
- cashier's check
- check card
- checking account
- credit card
- damage
- debit card
- defect

- direct deposit
- gas mileage
- insufficient funds
- interest
- loan
- make (of car)
- mileage
- model (of car)
- online banking
- original receipt
- overdraft
- period of coverage

- PIN
- refund
- replacement
- savings account
- service charge
- statement
- warranty
- workmanship

VERBS
- bounce (a check)
- swipe
- void

ADJECTIVES
- insufficient
- pre-owned
- unopened
- unused
- unworn
- valid
- void

OTHER
- on sale
- pay by (check, credit)

I practiced these skills, strategies, and grammar points:

- comparing ways of paying
- taking notes
- solving banking problems
- comparing information about cars
- identifying and explaining product defects
- understanding warranties
- disagreeing politely
- reading for specific information
- listening for specific information

- understanding basic banking services
- finding the main idea
- writing a return letter
- stating reasons
- using logical connectors
- using gerunds as subjects
- using gerunds as objects of verbs
- using comparative and superlative adjectives
- using as.....as

Work-Out CD-ROM

Unit 4: Plug in and practice!

THINGS TO DO

❶ Warm Up

Discuss these questions with your classmates.

1. Have you ever been hurt at work? What happened?

2. What do you see people doing in the picture?

3. How can people get hurt while working at a **construction site**? In a restaurant?

❷ Find and Discuss

Check (✔) the **hazards** and the **safety equipment** you see in the picture.

Hazards	Safety Equipment
○ a slippery floor	○ a **hard hat**
○ a lot of noise	○ **safety glasses**
○ poor lighting	○ **ear plugs**
○ a hot **surface**	○ a face mask
○ heavy things to lift	○ **scaffolding**
○ **flammable** materials	○ boots
○ chemicals	○ a safety **vest**
○ machinery	

> A **hazard** is anything that can hurt you. **Safety equipment** includes tools, clothing, and other things that keep you safe.

Does this look like a safe place to work? Why or why not? Discuss with a partner.

❸ Listen and Check 🎧 033

Listen to the conversations. Check (✔) *True* or *False*.

	True	False
1. Jake was fixing a hole in the floor when he tripped over a beam.	○	○
2. The driver was talking on her cell phone while she was driving.	○	○
3. Meg tripped over her safety glasses.	○	○
4. The drill hit Bob's head while he was using the hook.	○	○
5. The man with the drill is wearing his ear plugs.	○	○

❹ Talk about It

Discuss these questions with a partner.

1. How can you be safe while driving?

2. How can you be safe while you're at work?

3. How can you be safe while riding a bike?

> **Target Grammar**
>
> Past continuous, statements *page 168*

THINGS TO DO

1 Talk about It

1. Study the pictures. What causes these accidents and emergencies? Share ideas with your classmates.

2. Check (✔) the accidents and emergencies that have happened to you.

2 Use the Vocabulary

Work with a partner. Ask the questions above the pictures. If your partner answers "yes," ask questions to get more information.

Example: A: *Have you ever injured your back?*
B: *Yes, I have.*
A: *When did it happen?*
B: *It happened last year while I was carrying a heavy box.*

3 Listen and Write 🎧 034

Listen to the conversations. Write what actions to take.

Conversation	Actions to Take
1	get the person out of the heat; give water
2	
3	
4	

4 Expand Your Vocabulary

Write the missing forms of some highlighted words in this lesson.

Noun Form	Verb Form	Adjective Form
	injure	
fracture		
exhaustion		
shock		
	rob	✗
explosion		

Target Grammar

Past continuous with time clauses   *page 169*

| **1** | **injured** your back? |

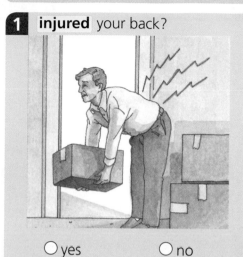

○ yes   ○ no

| **5** | been exposed to **toxic** materials? |

○ yes   ○ no

| **9** | been **robbed**? |

○ yes   ○ no

Have you ever . . .

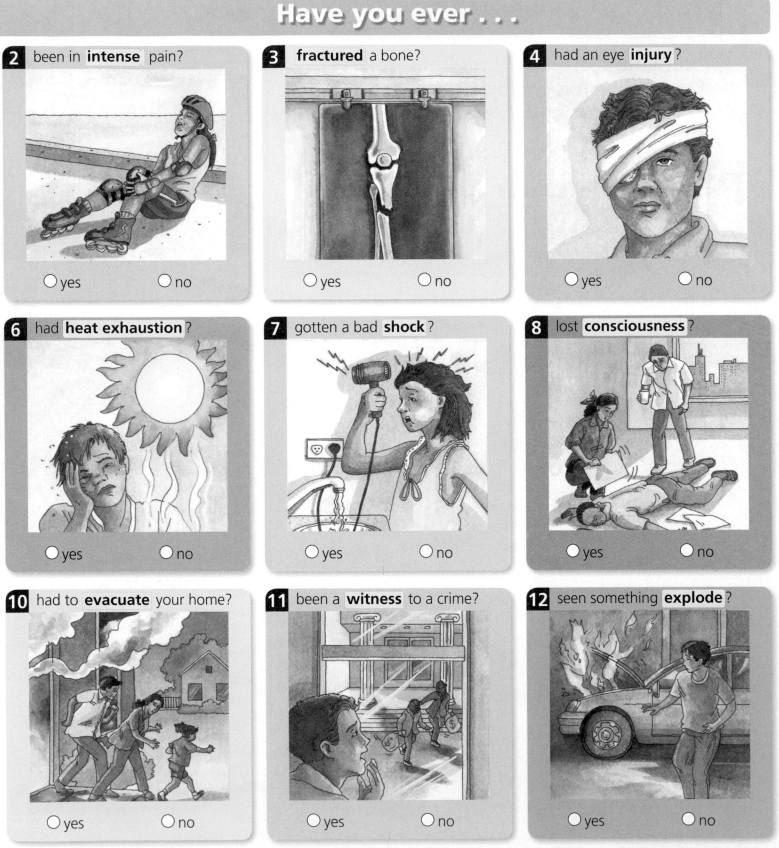

2 been in **intense** pain?

○ yes   ○ no

3 **fractured** a bone?

○ yes   ○ no

4 had an eye **injury**?

○ yes   ○ no

6 had **heat exhaustion**?

○ yes   ○ no

7 gotten a bad **shock**?

○ yes   ○ no

8 lost **consciousness**?

○ yes   ○ no

10 had to **evacuate** your home?

○ yes   ○ no

11 been a **witness** to a crime?

○ yes   ○ no

12 seen something **explode**?

○ yes   ○ no

Accidents and Emergencies | **63**

Reporting Accidents

THINGS TO DO

❶ Warm Up

Discuss these questions with your classmates.

1. Look at the pictures. What do you think happened to each injured person?

2. Who do you think has the most serious injury? Why?

❷ Listen and Take Notes 🎧 035

Listen to each conversation and identify the person's injury. Then listen again for the cause of the injury.

Name	Injury	Cause of Injury
1. Sylvia	got something in her eye	
2. Sandra		
3. Joe		

Compare charts with your classmates. Complete the accident reports #1 and #2 on page 65. Write your own accident report for #3.

❸ Role-Play 🎧 036

Listen. Then work with a partner. Role-play the conversation. Then replace the highlighted words with the cues below.

A: What happened?

B: I burned my hand.

A: What were you doing?

B: I was working near the oven.

A: Were you wearing an oven mitt? You know that's the rule.

B: No, I wasn't. I'm sorry. It won't happen again.

1 hurt my foot	2 hit my head	3 hurt my ears
carry something heavy	walk under a beam	use loud machinery
heavy boots	a hard hat	ear plugs

COMMUNICATION STRATEGY

Apologizing

Here are some common ways that people apologize:

I'm sorry. It won't happen again.

Sorry. I'll be more careful in the future.

My mistake. I won't do it again.

Target Grammar

Simple past vs. past continuous *page 171*

Accident Report #1

1. Employee's name: _Sylvia Hernandez_
2. Part of body affected: _____
   _____
3. Describe accident: _____
   _____
   _____
   _____
   _____
   _____
   _____

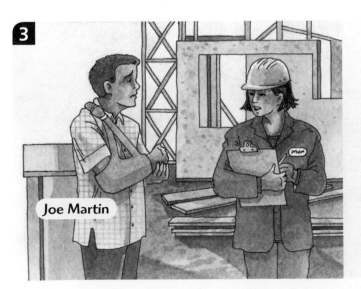

Accident Report #2

1. Employee's name: _Sandra Rochev_
2. Part of body affected: _____
   _____
3. Describe accident: _____
   _____
   _____
   _____
   _____
   _____
   _____

3

Joe Martin

Accidents and Emergencies | **65**

First Aid

① Warm Up

Discuss these questions with your classmates.

1. What first aid equipment do you have at home?
2. What first aid equipment should you have at home?
3. Have you ever given someone first aid? Why? What did you do?

> **First aid** is emergency care you give an injured person until you can get medical help.
>
> To **give first aid** is to care for an injured person in an emergency.

② Read and Respond

Read the first aid instructions on page 67 and take notes in the chart below.

If someone has . . .	You should	You shouldn't
a serious burn	• call 911 immediately	• use any medications • remove the person's clothing
a minor burn		
a sharp object in the eye		
bleeding		
heat exhaustion		

③ Talk about It

Compare charts with a partner. Use complete sentences to explain what you should and shouldn't do.

A: What should you do if someone has a serious burn?   B: If someone has a serious burn, you should call 9-1-1.

④ Apply

Work in a small group to answer these questions. Then share your answers with the class.

1. Sam's five-year-old daughter touched a hot iron and burned her hand slightly. There was a small red spot on her hand but no blisters. Sam immediately called 911. Did Sam do the right thing?
2. Tom stepped on broken glass and got a deep cut in his foot. Tom's brother tried to get the glass out of Tom's foot before taking him to the hospital. Did Tom's brother do the right thing? What would you do?
3. Jasmine got a piece of a stick in her eye. Her friend Tanya covered both eyes with an ice bag and took her to the hospital. Did Tanya do the right thing? What would you do?

Target Grammar

Real conditionals   *page 172*

FIRST AID GUIDE
CALL 911 FOR ANY MEDICAL EMERGENCY

BURNS

- If the burn is serious and the victim is in intense pain, call 911 immediately.
  - ✦ DO NOT apply medications.
  - ✦ DO NOT try to remove the victim's clothing.

- If the burn is **minor**, the skin will appear red and may have small blisters.
  - ✦ **Submerge** the injured area in cold water immediately.
  - ✦ DO NOT break blisters.

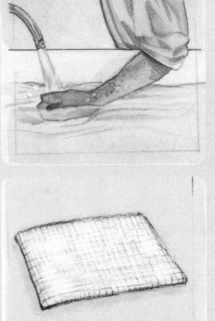

EYE INJURIES

- If there is a sharp object in the eye, call 911 immediately.
  - ✦ DO NOT try to remove the object.
  - ✦ Cover both eyes with eye cups or **gauze pads**. Covering both eyes keeps the injured eye from moving.
  - ✦ DO NOT rub the injured eye or put ice on it.

- If there is something in the eye (not a sharp object), you should use an eye cup to flush the eye with water for 10 minutes.

BLEEDING

- Call 911 for medical assistance. Before providing care, put on protective gloves.
  - ✦ Keep victim lying down.
  - ✦ Apply direct **pressure** using a clean cloth or gauze directly on the wound.
  - ✦ DO NOT take out any object that is lodged in a wound; see a doctor for help in removal.
  - ✦ If there are no signs of a fracture in the injured area, carefully **elevate** the wound above the victim's heart.

HEAT EXHAUSTION

- Move the person to a cool place to rest. Remove as much clothing as possible. Give the person water. Don't allow the person to get chilled. Get medical help.

Using the SQ3R Strategy

THE SQ3R STRATEGY

SQ3R is a five-step strategy that helps you read and understand a passage. SQ3R stands for *Survey, Question, Read, Recite,* and *Review*. Here's what you do at each step:

Step 1: Survey	Step 2: Question	Step 3: Read	Step 4: Recite	Step 5: Review
To survey—or preview—the passage, skim it to get a general idea of the topic. Read the title and the first sentence of each paragraph, and look at any pictures and headings.	Write down five or more questions that you thought of while you were surveying the passage.	Read the passage and look for answers to your questions from Step 2. Underline or take notes on the important ideas in the passage.	After you read, say out loud the most important points in the passage. Try to use your own words.	Look again at your notes and at the points that you underlined. Ask yourself if you understand the important points in the passage.

❶ Practice the Strategy

Follow Step 1: Survey the article on page 69. What's the topic? Write it here.

_____

❷ Preview

Follow Step 2: Read the questions in the chart below. Then write three questions that you thought of while you were surveying the article.

Questions	Answers
• What should you know about safety and health on the job?	
• Why do many workers get hurt on the job?	
•	
•	
•	

❸ Listen and Read 🎧 037

Follow Step 3: Read the article and look for answers to the questions from Step 2. Write the answers in the chart above.

❹ Understand the Reading

Follow Step 4: Say out loud the most important points in the article. Try to use your own words. Then follow Step 5 (Review): Look back at your chart in Step 2. Do you understand the main points of the article?

WHAT YOU SHOULD KNOW ABOUT SAFETY AND HEALTH ON THE JOB

Every year, thousands of workers get hurt badly on the job. Why do these injuries occur? Many workers get hurt due to unsafe equipment and stressful conditions. It's important for all workers to know their rights on the job.

What Are My Rights on the Job?

By law, your employer must provide:

- a safe and healthy workplace.
- safety and health training, including providing information on chemicals that could be harmful to your health.
- for many jobs, payment for medical care if you get hurt or sick because of your job. You may also be entitled to lost wages.

Using safety equipment

You also have a right to:

- report safety problems to OSHA (Occupational Safety and Health Administration).
- refuse to work if the job is immediately dangerous to your life or health.
- join or organize a union.

What Hazards Should I Watch Out For?

Type of Work	Examples of Hazards
Maintenance	• Toxic chemicals in cleaning products • Blood in discarded needles
Food Service	• Slippery floors • Hot cooking equipment • Sharp objects
Retail/Sales	• Violent crimes • Heavy lifting
Office/Clerical	• Stress • Harassment • Poor computer workstation design

Source: www.osha.gov

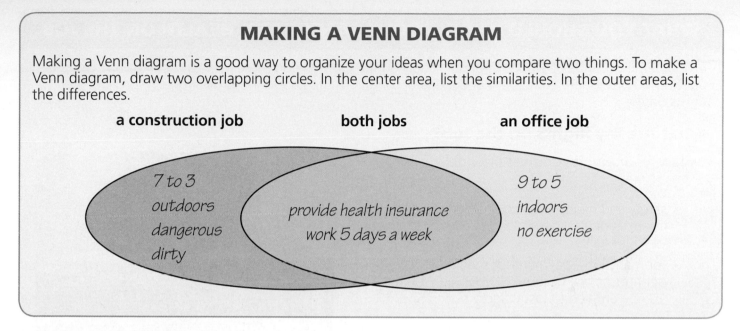

MAKING A VENN DIAGRAM

Making a Venn diagram is a good way to organize your ideas when you compare two things. To make a Venn diagram, draw two overlapping circles. In the center area, list the similarities. In the outer areas, list the differences.

a construction job   **both jobs**   **an office job**

7 to 3
outdoors
dangerous
dirty

provide health insurance
work 5 days a week

9 to 5
indoors
no exercise

❶ Practice the Skill

Read the paragraph on page 71 and take notes in the Venn diagram below.

pilot   **truck driver**

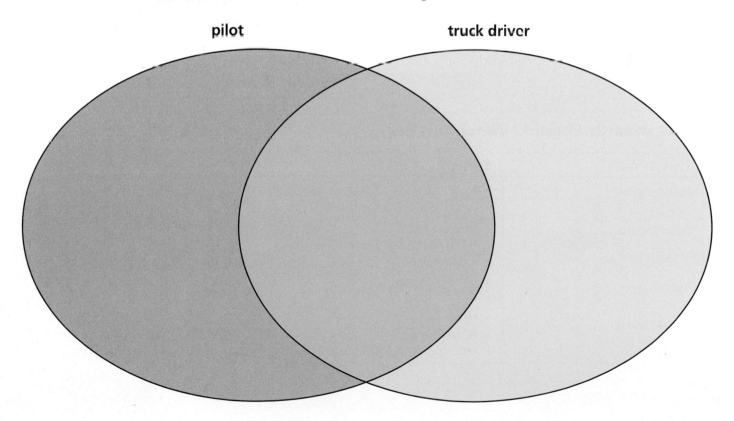

A PILOT OR A TRUCK DRIVER?

Would you rather be a pilot or a truck driver? Both of these jobs are interesting and unpredictable. That is because both a pilot and a truck driver are always on the move. They never stay in the same place for very long. Both a pilot and a truck driver also need to know a lot about engines. In addition, both a pilot and a truck driver need to follow a lot of safety rules so they don't have accidents. One of the biggest differences between a pilot and a truck driver is the training. It takes a long time to learn to fly a plane—much longer than it takes to learn to drive a truck. Another big difference is that many truck drivers own their own truck, but it's unusual for a pilot to own the plane that he or she flies.

❷ Plan Your Writing

Choose two jobs. Make a Venn diagram to compare them.

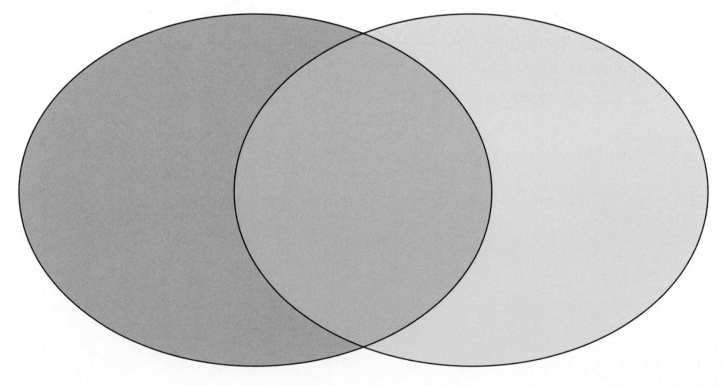

❸ Write

Use your ideas from Activity 2 to write a paragraph comparing two jobs.

What Do You Know?

① Listening Review 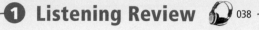 038

Part 1

Listen to what is said. When you hear the question, *Which is correct?*, listen and choose the correct answer: *A*, *B*, or *C*. Use the Answer Sheet.

Part 2 🎧 039

You will hear the first part of a conversation. To finish the conversation, listen and choose the correct answer: *A*, *B*, or *C*. Use the Answer Sheet.

Answer Sheet

1 Ⓐ Ⓑ Ⓒ
2 Ⓐ Ⓑ Ⓒ
3 Ⓐ Ⓑ Ⓒ
4 Ⓐ Ⓑ Ⓒ
5 Ⓐ Ⓑ Ⓒ
6 Ⓐ Ⓑ Ⓒ
7 Ⓐ Ⓑ Ⓒ
8 Ⓐ Ⓑ Ⓒ
9 Ⓐ Ⓑ Ⓒ
10 Ⓐ Ⓑ Ⓒ

② Grammar Review

Circle the correct answer: *A*, *B*, or *C*.

1. Sue _____ a shock while she was drying her hair.

A. getting
B. was getting
C. got

2. He _____ on his cell phone when he drove into a ditch.

A. talk
B. was talking
C. talking

3. I _____ paying attention while I was using the drill.

A. didn't
B. wasn't
C. hadn't

4. Ana was driving 50 miles an hour when she _____ the tree.

A. hitting
B. was hitting
C. hit

5. A: When did it happen?
B: It _____ in 2009.

A. was happening
B. happened
C. happening

6. _____ you wearing your seatbelt?

A. Were
B. Had
C. Did

❷ Grammar Review (continued)

7. A: Was Mark using safety equipment?
   B: No, he _____.

   A. doesn't
   B. isn't
   C. wasn't

8. If someone is bleeding, you shouldn't _____ the object from the wound.

   A. remove
   B. removes
   C. removing

9. If a person _____ heat exhaustion, you should give her some water.

   A. had
   B. having
   C. has

10. You should call 911 if a person _____ consciousness.

   A. lose
   B. loses
   C. losing

LEARNING LOG ✔

I know these words:

NOUNS AND NOUN PHRASES

○ accident
○ bleeding
○ burn
○ consciousness
○ construction site
○ ear plugs
○ emergency
○ first aid
○ gauze pad
○ hard hat
○ hazard

○ heat exhaustion
○ injury
○ pressure
○ safety equipment
○ safety glasses
○ scaffolding
○ shock
○ surface
○ vest
○ witness

VERBS

○ elevate

○ evacuate
○ explode
○ fracture
○ injure
○ rob
○ submerge

ADJECTIVES

○ flammable
○ intense
○ minor
○ toxic

I practiced these skills, strategies, and grammar points:

○ identifying safety hazards
○ identifying safety equipment
○ analyzing hazardous situations
○ identifying causes of accidents and emergencies
○ understanding what to do when accidents and emergencies happen
○ understanding word forms

○ reporting accidents
○ apologizing
○ writing a comparison paragraph
○ evaluating first aid actions
○ using the SQ3R strategy
○ making a Venn diagram
○ using the past continuous
○ using time clauses with the past continuous
○ asking questions with the past continuous
○ using real conditionals

Work-Out CD-ROM

Unit 5: Plug in and practice!

THINGS TO DO

❶ Warm Up

Discuss these questions with your classmates.

1. What are the people in the picture doing?
2. What do you like about your town or city? What do you dislike about it?
3. What makes a community good? Make a list of at least five qualities—for example, good schools.

❷ Identify

Study the picture and read the sentences below. Check (✔) the sentences that are true. Then compare ideas with a partner.

1. No one is entering the **community center**.   ○
2. The police officer is making a **traffic stop**.   ○
3. A **demonstrator** is in front of the town hall.   ○
4. The town hall is across from the **jail**.   ○
5. A woman is walking her pet on a **leash**.   ○
6. The girl on the bicycle is wearing a **helmet**.   ○
7. There are **speed bumps** in front of the school.   ○
8. A man is cleaning **graffiti** off the wall of the museum.   ○

❸ Listen and Write 040

Listen to the conversation. What do the speakers say you *should* do? Which should you *not* do? Write S for *should* and SN for *should not*.

_____ **litter**	_____ wear **seatbelts**
_____ draw graffiti	_____ keep pets on a leash
_____ ride motorcycles	_____ pick up **trash**

❹ Talk about It

Do you agree with the speakers in Activity 3? Compare your ideas with a partner.

Examples: *I think people need to pick up trash because it keeps the community clean and attractive.*

I think pet owners need to keep their pets on leashes so the pets don't bother other people.

Target Grammar
Infinitives after verbs *page 174*

Understanding Community Rules

THINGS TO DO

❶ Talk about It

Discuss these questions with your classmates.

1. What public places are in your community? Which ones do you use?
2. Look at the **prohibited** activities on page 77. Why do you think they are prohibited? Which three are the most serious problems in your community?
3. What are three other problems in your community?

❷ Use the Vocabulary

Work with a partner. Read the information about Mountain Glen Park. Take turns asking the questions. Write the answers.

1. What word means that something is not allowed? _____ *prohibited* _____
2. Who has to wear helmets when riding bicycles? _____
3. Where are you not allowed to park? _____
4. What is an example of **vandalism**? _____
5. What do you need a **license** for? _____
6. If you drive too fast, what are you doing? _____

❸ Decide

Think about the rules at Mountain Glen Park. Write them in the appropriate place in the chart.

Safety	Protection of Property	Politeness to Others
no swimming in posted areas		

❹ Discuss

Work with your classmates. List some rules in your community. Why are they good or not good for the community?

Example: *In my community, children are not allowed to ride their bicycles without helmets.*
I think this is good for the community because it keeps children safe.

> **Target Grammar**
>
> *Be allowed; be permitted; be illegal* page 176

Welcome to **MOUNTAIN GLEN!**

The following are **prohibited**:

- littering
- parking on the grass
- **consumption** of **alcoholic beverages**
- dogs off leash
- children using bicycles or skateboards without proper safety equipment (**helmets** and **pads**)
- **exceeding** the speed limit
- **fishing** without a **license**
- **weapons** or **firearms**
- **trespassing** on private property
- swimming in **posted areas**
- **loitering**
- damage to (**vandalism** of) public or private property

UPCOMING EVENTS

THINGS TO DO

❶ Warm Up

Discuss these questions with your classmates.

1. Look at the pictures. What do you think the problem is in each one?

2. Which problem is the most serious? Why?

3. Have you ever talked to a police officer in your community? When?

❷ Listen and Take Notes 🎧 041

Listen to each conversation and identify the problems. Complete the chart.

	Problems
1.	
2.	
3.	

In the U.S., police officers carry guns.

Now, discuss with a partner: What are the possible consequences of each problem?

❸ Role-Play 🎧 042

Listen. Then work with a partner. Role-play the conversation between a driver and a police officer. Then replace the highlighted words with the ideas below or your own ideas. Use the communication strategy.

A: Did you know you were speeding?

B: No. I'm sorry.

A: I need to see your license and registration.

B: Of course. Right away.

A: I'm going to have to give you a ticket.

B: Yes, officer.

A: I advise you to watch your speed from now on.

B: I will. I'll be very careful.

drove through a red light / stop at red lights

aren't wearing a seat belt / always wear your seat belt

are not allowed to talk on your cell phone while driving / obey cell phone laws

COMMUNICATION STRATEGY

Accepting Criticism

In some situations, especially if you have done something wrong, it's a good idea to respond politely to criticism. Try these phrases:

I'm sorry.

I didn't realize that.

I apologize.

It won't happen again.

⊙ Target Grammar

Verbs followed by object + infinitive *page 178*

CALIFORNIA
DRIVER LICENSE
EXPIRES: 03-02-14   7805067644   CLASS: 2

WILLIAM WATSON
1521 MARKET STREET
SAN FRANCISCO, CA
94821

HAIR: BRN   EYES: BRN
HT: 5'10"   WT: 160 LBS

DOB: 03-02-75

William Watson

Department of Natural Resources Fishing License	**DNR**	
Application		

Date	Official use only:
June 16, 2012	License No. Issued

Name
Sammy Taylor

Street Address
1565 N. Broad St.

City	State	Zip
Lincoln	NE	68522

Date of Birth	Height	Sex (circle one)	Eye color
10/03/1989	5' 11"	(M)/ F	Brown

SS No.	Driver's License No.	Telephone No. (include area code)
000-45-6789	U1200000	402-555-1000

I certify under penalty of law that the statements made herein are true.

Signature of Applicant:
Sammy Taylor

❶ Warm Up

Discuss these questions with a partner.

1. Have you ever seen someone commit a crime? If so, what was it?

2. What can you do if you see someone commit a crime?

3. What problems do you have with crime in your city or town?

❷ Read and Respond

Read the online form.

Greenville Police Department

Home | Contact | Site Map | FAQ | Help

Search [GO]

Greenville Police Department

| HOME |
| CONTACT |
| SAFETY TIPS |
| BE INVOLVED |

Report a Crime

If you have information regarding a crime,
please fill out this form or call (937) 555-4357.

*Name   Lee Trang

*Email Address   Trang257@streetuse.net

*Phone Number   555-7234

Would you like us to contact you?   ○ Yes   ● No

Location of offense   East 15th St. and West Ave.

Please include detailed information about the crime here:

Some kids are loitering at Victory Park every night. They have damaged some park property and play their music really loud. They drink alcohol and bother the people who live near the park.

*You do not have to give your name and personal information.

SUBMIT

DO NOT USE THIS FORM TO REPORT AN EMERGENCY.

Please dial 9-1-1 if you believe someone or something is in danger of harm. Do not use this online form for any violent crime, theft of a firearm, or stolen vehicle.

This form has been developed to allow you to report certain problems such as noise violations, alcohol violations, vandalism, loitering, property loss, trespassing, and suspicious activity. You may also telephone us at (937) 555-4357.

Read the statements. Check (✔) *True* or *False*.

	True	False
1. You can use this form for emergencies.	○	○
2. You can use this form to report a stolen vehicle.	○	○
3. You can use this form to report trespassing.	○	○
4. You should call 9-1-1 if you see a violent crime.	○	○
5. You have to give your name.	○	○
6. You have to click Submit to send the form to the police.	○	○

❸ Listen and Apply 🎧 043

Listen to the conversations about witnessing a crime. Write the crime.
Then check (✔) either Report Online or Call 9-1-1.

	Crime	Report Online	Call 9-1-1
1.		○	○
2.		○	○
3.		○	○
4.		○	○

WINDOW ON PRONUNCIATION

Reductions with *to* 🎧 044

Sometimes we say words quickly and the pronunciation changes. These are reductions. We use reductions in informal speaking situations. We use the full forms in formal speaking situations and in writing.

A Listen to the phrases. Then listen and repeat.

Full form (formal)	Reduction (informal)	Full form (formal)	Reduction (informal)
have to	sounds like *hafta*	used to	sounds like *useta*
want to	sounds like *wanna*	going to	sounds like *gonna*
ought to	sounds like *otta*	has to	sounds like *hasta*

B Listen to the sentences. Write the missing words. Use the full form.

1. I _____ renew my driver's license this month.
2. Sam _____ pay a parking ticket.
3. We _____ do something about all this graffiti!
4. You _____ slow down. You're _____ get a ticket!
5. This community _____ be so nice. I _____ move now.

C Work with a partner. Discuss what the people will do in the situations in Activity 3.
Use *has to*, *ought to*, and *going to*.

PARAPHRASING

Paraphrasing is saying or writing ideas in your own words. When you want to remember what you read, you should practice restating the information either out loud to yourself or to another person.

How to Paraphrase	Examples
Use words that mean the same thing.	TEXT: Please dial 9-1-1 if you believe someone <u>is in danger of harm</u>. PARAPHRASE: If you think someone <u>will get hurt,</u> call 9-1-1.
Use ideas that have an opposite meaning.	TEXT: It is <u>prohibited to let pets off the leash</u> in this park. PARAPHRASE: In this park, you <u>must keep your pets on a leash</u>.
Combine ideas from different sentences.	TEXT: Several <u>teenagers were loitering</u> in Mountain Glen Park on Friday night. Police officers arrived immediately and <u>ordered them to go away</u>. PARAPHRASE: Police officers <u>told several loiterers to leave</u> Mountain Glen Park on Friday night.

❶ Practice the Strategy

Read the sentences below. Circle the letter of the best paraphrase.

1. San Francisco allows bicycle parking in all city-owned garages that rent automobile space to the public.

   A. In San Francisco, you can ride a bicycle.
   B. If a city-owned garage rents parking space for cars, it allows bicycle parking.
   C. If you own a bicycle in San Francisco, you must park it in a garage.

2. No dog is permitted to run loose when not on its owner's property. The fine for not following this rule is $150.

   A. You have to keep your dog on your property or on a leash. If you don't, you will have to pay a $150 fine.
   B. You can buy a dog for $150.
   C. It's okay to let your dog run loose when it's not on your property if you pay $150.

3. Marshville residents are upset about the increase in the number of people who are parking cars on their front lawns.

   A. Marshville residents think it's okay to park on lawns.
   B. A lot of people park their cars on lawns.
   C. More people are parking cars on front lawns and people living in Marshville are upset about it.

4. Use this online form to report a crime, except if it is serious. Then you should call 9-1-1.

   A. Call 9-1-1 to report any crime.
   B. Report a serious crime immediately to 9-1-1. Otherwise, use the online form.
   C. Don't use an online form to report a crime.

Now paraphrase these sentences.

1. Park rules require that all children under the age of 12 wear a helmet when riding a bicycle.

_____

2. The Marshville Community Center offers programs for fun and learning for children, teens, adults, and seniors.

_____

3. People who volunteer in the community not only help their neighbors, but they also learn skills and make new friends.

_____

❷ Preview

Survey the reading below. What is the topic of the reading?

_____

❸ Listen and Read 🎧 045

Read the information below. Rewrite it in your own words. Use a separate piece of paper.

The Greenville Community Center
Services for Immigrants

The Greenville Community Center offers social, educational, and recreational programs for **newcomers** of all ages. Children, teens, adults, and seniors who want to get involved in the community and meet their neighbors will find lots of activities for fun and learning.

In addition, the center provides many services specifically designed for immigrants and their families. Newcomers who would like to become citizens can take citizenship classes at the center. In addition, there are ESOL (English for Speakers of Other Languages) classes for beginning- and intermediate-level students. The community center also offers computer classes, along with interviewing and résumé-writing workshops for job seekers.

SUMMARIZING

When you summarize, you give a short version of the important information in a reading. Follow these steps to write a summary of a reading:

- Identify the topic.
- Find the main idea.
- Read carefully and underline the important ideas
- Break the information into smaller sections.
- Write a sentence that summarizes each section.

---

❶ Practice the Skill

Read each paragraph. Then answer the questions.

Paragraph 1

Hoa was born in Vietnam. She came to the United States to live with her family. When she arrived, she didn't speak any English and her grandchildren didn't speak any Vietnamese. Hoa wanted to help her daughter and take care of her grandchildren, so she had to learn English fast! Her daughter took her to a free English class at the local library. At first, Hoa was nervous, but the teacher looked very kind and there were several other older women in the class. Hoa decided to stay. Today, Hoa reads books to her grandchildren and even helps them with their homework.

Paragraph 2

Many people are surprised to learn about all the services that public libraries offer. Besides books, most public libraries also loan magazines, audiobooks, and DVDs. There are often a lot of activities at the library, too. You can take classes, attend community meetings, and participate in book clubs. Young children can listen to stories. Seniors can learn computer skills. Most libraries also offer Internet access. The public library is a great place to do research, to learn, and to have fun. Most activities and services are free of charge, as well.

What is the topic of Paragraph 1? _____

Write a sentence that summarizes Paragraph 1: _____

_____

What is the topic of Paragraph 2? _____

Write a sentence that summarizes Paragraph 2: _____

_____

❷ Plan Your Writing

Read the following article. Then complete the outline.

Maria Martínez: Literacy Volunteer

Maria Martinez is one of Greenville Community Center's literacy volunteers.

Maria's Early Life

Maria Martínez was born in Peru. She came to the United States as a young child. Her parents worked very hard to give her the best education possible. Maria loved school. After college, she got her teaching credentials and became an elementary school teacher. While she was teaching, Maria became interested in technology, and she went back to school. She studied business information technology, and worked for many years as a senior manager in information technology for a large corporation.

Coming to the Community Center

When Maria retired, she wanted to do something important for the community. She decided to combine her work experience and her interest in helping others. She started volunteering at the community center as a basic skills tutor three years ago. At the beginning, Maria had students of all ages. She helped young children read their first books. She helped older adults with learning disabilities learn to read the newspaper. She made good use of her background as a teacher, and became one of the most popular tutors at the center.

Helping Newcomers

After a while, Maria noticed that the center had many students who were newcomers to Greenville. Maria remembered the difficulties her parents had when they first came to the United States. She especially remembered how they struggled to improve their English so they could get good jobs. As a result, she became interested in the needs of non-English speakers. Today, Maria specializes in workplace English and computer skills for non-native speakers. She has helped many newcomers to Greenville get good jobs.

"This is the best job I have ever had," Maria told us. "It's a good feeling to help someone learn to read a book to a child for the first time or get a job because they can fill out the application."

What is the topic of the article? _____

Write a sentence that summarizes each section of the article:

Section 1: _____

Section 2: _____

Section 3: _____

❸ Write

Now write a summary of the article on a separate piece of paper. Share your summary with a partner.

① Listening Review 🎧 046

Part 1

You will hear the first part of a conversation. To finish the conversation, listen and choose the correct answer: *A*, *B*, or *C*. Use the Answer Sheet.

Part 2 🎧 047

First you will hear a question. Next, listen carefully to what is said. You will hear the question again. Then choose the correct answer: *A*, *B*, or *C*. Use the Answer Sheet.

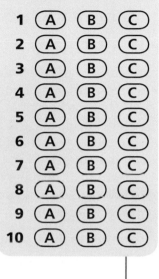

Answer Sheet

1. Ⓐ Ⓑ Ⓒ
2. Ⓐ Ⓑ Ⓒ
3. Ⓐ Ⓑ Ⓒ
4. Ⓐ Ⓑ Ⓒ
5. Ⓐ Ⓑ Ⓒ
6. Ⓐ Ⓑ Ⓒ
7. Ⓐ Ⓑ Ⓒ
8. Ⓐ Ⓑ Ⓒ
9. Ⓐ Ⓑ Ⓒ
10. Ⓐ Ⓑ Ⓒ

② Grammar Review

Circle the correct answer: *A*, *B*, or *C*.

1. People need _____ their pets on a leash.

A. keeping
B. keep
C. to keep

2. He should remember _____ a seatbelt when he drives.

A. to wear
B. wear
C. wears

3. The garbage collector refused _____ the trash.

A. collect
B. to collect
C. collecting

4. It's illegal _____ without a license.

A. to fish
B. fish
C. fishing

5. You're not allowed _____ in this area.

A. to swim
B. swimming
C. swim

6. You're not _____ on the grass.

A. allowed park
B. allowed to park
C. allowed parking

❷ Grammar Review (continued)

7. Tell him _____ the music down.

   A. turn
   B. turning
   C. to turn

8. The officer asked the man _____ his car.

   A. move
   B. to move
   C. moves

9. The officer advised _____ a fishing license.

   A. him to get
   B. him
   C. to get

10. Please tell _____ walk on the grass.

   A. not her to
   B. not to
   C. her not to

LEARNING LOG ✔

I know these words:

NOUNS AND NOUN PHRASES

- alcoholic beverages
- areas
- community center
- consumption
- demonstrator
- disabilities
- firearm
- graffiti
- helmet
- jail
- leash
- license
- newcomers
- knee pads
- seatbelt
- speed bumps
- traffic stop
- trash
- trespassing
- vandalism
- volunteer
- weapons

VERBS

- allow
- exceed
- fish
- litter
- loiter
- permit
- speed
- trespass

ADJECTIVES

- illegal
- posted
- prohibited

I practiced these skills, strategies and grammar points:

- identifying community issues
- understanding community rules
- reporting crimes
- accepting criticism
- taking notes
- listening for specific information
- understanding a website
- analyzing rules
- expressing an opinion
- skimming a reading
- paraphrasing
- summarizing
- using infinitives after verbs
- using *be allowed, be permitted,* and *be illegal*
- using verbs followed by object + infinitive

Work-Out CD-ROM

Unit 6: Plug in and practice!

LESSON 1

Qualities of a Job or Workplace

THINGS TO DO

❶ Warm Up

Discuss these questions with your classmates.

1. Find three people in the picture. Talk about the pros and the cons of the jobs they are doing.

2. What makes a job or workplace good?

❷ Identify

Study the picture. Write the person's name next to the job.

1. An **admittance clerk** helps new patients who are coming into the hospital. _____*Oscar*_____

2. A **biomedical equipment technician** repairs medical equipment. _____

3. A **lab technician** does tests to help doctors diagnose illnesses._____

4. A nurse takes care of patients and assists doctors. _____

5. A **medical records specialist** manages information about patients. _____

6. A **physician assistant** helps doctors treat patients. _____

7. A **tech support specialist** solves computer problems for hospital staff. _____

8. An **orderly** moves equipment and patients and delivers meals. _____

❸ Listen and Write 🎧 048

Listen to the people talking about jobs and **working conditions**. Write the name of the job. Then match the condition with the job.

	Job	Working Conditions
____1.	_____	**a.** alone
____2.	_____	**b.** on a team
____3.	_____	**c.** indoors
____4.	_____	**d.** outdoors

❹ Talk about It

Talk about your dream job with a partner.

A: I want to be a construction worker because I love to be outdoors all day.

B: I prefer working with people. I'd like to be a teacher.

Bill

Sue

Delia's Flowers

Oscar

Lisa

Target Grammar

Verbs followed by gerund or infinitive *page 180*

MATERNITY WARD

Alice

LABORATORY

Ann

Frank

Raul

Sam

BOY

BABY

Understanding Medical Benefits

THINGS TO DO

❶ Talk about It

Discuss these questions with your classmates.

1. Think about your dream job. What kind of benefits would you like to have?
2. What kind of medical benefits are important to you? Why?

> Some companies offer **benefits** to employees. Benefits are services that the company pays for.

❷ Use the Vocabulary

Work with a partner. Read the information about Speedy Delivery's medical benefits on page 91. Take turns asking the questions. Write the answers.

1. What's another word for family members that you take care of?

   _____

2. If you want to choose your own healthcare provider, what kind of plan do you want? _____

3. What premium do you pay in the open access plan if you are married? _____

4. What is your deductible if you have the network plan and you do not have a spouse or a domestic partner? _____

5. Which plan has the lower out-of-pocket maximum? _____

6. Who pays a co-pay—the employer or the employee? _____

These benefits also cover your **dependents**: your spouse or **domestic partner** and children up to the age of 19.

❸ Listen and Write 🎧 049

Listen to a conversation about medical benefits. Write the information in the correct column.

	Network Plan	Open Access Plan
1. the type of doctor you can see	must be in the network	you can see any doctor
2. the premium		
3. the deductible		
4. the cost of an office visit		
5. preventive care		

Annual Deductible for Medical Plan

	NP	OAP
Individual	$150.00	None
Family	$300.00	None

Deductible

Your **deductible** is the amount of money you pay for medical services before your medical plan starts to pay for the services.

❹ Discuss

Discuss these questions with a partner.

1. Which plan would be better for Ron?
2. Which plan would you prefer?

> **Target Grammar**
>
> *Prefer, would prefer, would rather* for preferences   *page 182*

MEDICAL BENEFITS PLAN SUMMARY

Regular full-time employees receive the **medical benefits** outlined in this summary.

Speedy Delivery Corporation

Network Plan (NP)

With a network plan, you can see only healthcare providers in your **network**.

Open Access Plan (OAP)

With an **open access** plan, you can see any healthcare provider you want.

Monthly Premium for Medical Plan

	NP	OAP
Employee only	$28.00	$30.00
Employee & Spouse	$52.00	$65.00
Employee, Spouse & Children	$72.00	$80.00

Premium

Your **premium** is the amount of money you pay for your medical plan each month.

Out-of-Pocket Maximum

Your **out-of-pocket** maximum is the total amount of money you might need to pay for medical services in one year. Your insurance company pays costs over that amount.

	NP	OAP
Individual	$1,000.00	$1,500.00
Family	$1,500.00	$3,000.00
Services		
Office Visit Co-pay	$20.00	$30.00

Your **co-pay** is the amount you pay each time you visit a healthcare provider.

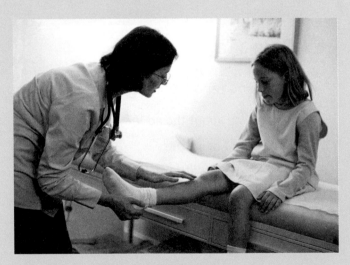

Preventive Care

Preventive Care covers services such as well-child visits and regular check-ups.

	NP	OAP
	$20.00 co-pay	No charge

THINGS TO DO

❶ Warm Up

Discuss these questions with your classmates.

1. What are some different ways to find a job? How did you or someone you know find a job?

2. Read the job ads on page 93. Which job would you prefer? Why?

❷ Listen and Take Notes 🎧 050

Listen to conversations about some of the job ads on page 93. Write two questions each applicant asks. Then write the answers.

Job	Questions	Answers
1. Biomedical Equipment Technician		
2. Home Health Aide		
3. Community Health Worker		

❸ Role-Play 🎧 051

Listen. Then work with a partner. Role-play the telephone conversation between a receptionist and a person looking for a job. Replace the highlighted words with the ideas below or your own ideas.

A: Hi. I'm calling about the ad for an orderly .

B: Yes. How can I help you?

A: Can you tell me a little about the job?

B: Sure. We're looking for someone with at least two years' experience.

A: I have a lot of experience.

B: Do you have a high-school diploma ?

A: Yes, I do.

B: And are you able to work part-time ?

A: Yes. What should I do if I'm interested?

B: Apply in person at our Human Resources Office.

> **Target Grammar**
>
> **Be able to**   *page 184*

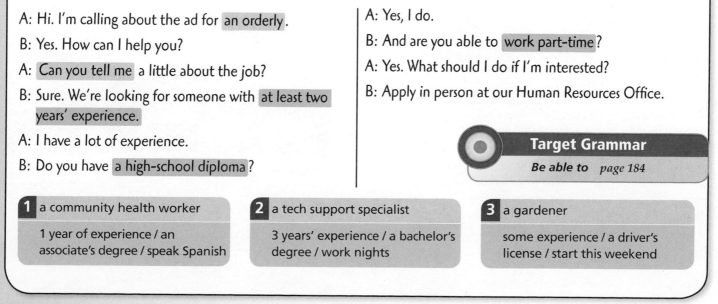

1 a community health worker

1 year of experience / an associate's degree / speak Spanish

2 a tech support specialist

3 years' experience / a bachelor's degree / work nights

3 a gardener

some experience / a driver's license / start this weekend

THE TIMES • CLASSIFIED ADS

Healthcare Jobs

Biomedical Equipment Technician

Clean, assemble, store, and maintain medical devices.

Must have Biomedical Equipment Technician certificate, plus 2 years' experience. Excellent communication skills.

Send **résumé** to
Belmont Community Hospital
2345 Ralston Ave.
Belmont, CA 94002

Home Health Aide

Provide personal care in the home to clients who are unable to perform these activities independently: bathing, dressing, food preparation.

Qualifications: Valid HHA certificate, 1 year of experience as a home health aide. Excellent oral communication skills. Must enjoy working with seniors!

Call 888-555-9786 or pick up application at Sunnyside Home Health Services,
456 Guerrero Street
San Jose, CA 95101

Orderly

Lift patients onto and from beds, transport patients, set up equipment, and deliver meals.

Two years' experience and high-school diploma required. Part-time; $10.50/hour.

Apply in person at the Human Resources Office,
Room 78B
San Mateo County Hospital
345 Grand Street
San Mateo, CA 94401

Community Health Worker

The County of San Mateo is seeking an experienced Community Health Worker to provide nutrition education, supplemental foods, and referrals to other community services.

The candidate must have 2 years' experience, an Associate's degree, a Community Health Worker Certificate, and excellent communication skills. Bilingual Spanish-English a plus.

To apply, send résumé and **cover letter** to County Health Dept.
234 B Street, San Mateo, CA 94401

Medical Records Specialist

Huntington Medical Center is hiring a Medical Records Specialist to organize and maintain patient records.

6 months' to 1 year's experience in a medical office + high-school diploma or GED required. Excellent communication and organizational skills.

Send résumé and cover letter to:
Huntington Medical Center
555 Bay Street
San Francisco, CA 94983

COMMUNICATION STRATEGY

Asking Polite Questions

Asking questions directly can sometimes be impolite. Words such as *could, can,* and *would* make questions sound more polite.

Could you tell me . . . ?

Can you tell me . . .?

Would you mind telling me . . . ?

❶ Warm Up

Discuss these questions with a partner.

1. What is the purpose of a résumé? What kind of information does it usually have?

2. Have you ever written a résumé?

❷ Read and Respond

Read the résumé. Then answer the questions.

Hana Nasser

11510 South Lake Drive
Atlanta, GA 30318
770-555-5482 • hanacooks@global.net

JOB OBJECTIVE

Work as a pastry chef with a catering company

WORK EXPERIENCE

Rosie's Bakery

Shift supervisor, 2009 present

- Head baker, 1st shift
- Supervise baking assistants
- Manage supply inventory
- Cater for large parties

Bread For It

Baker, 2007–2009

- Sole bread baker
- Developed new recipes
- Helped manager with inventory

Lebanon Café

Server, 2005–2007

- Waited tables
- Operated the cash register
- Assisted in the kitchen

---

1. What kind of job does Hana want? _____

2. How can someone contact her? _____

3. How many years has she been in the food business? _____

4. Does she have supervisory experience? _____

5. Does she have experience working with customers? _____

6. Besides cooking, what other skills does she have? _____

❸ Apply

Complete the form with information about you. Then write a résumé like Hana Nasser's.

Name: _____

Address: _____

Telephone number : _____ Email: _____

Job you are applying for:: _____

WORK EXPERIENCE (start with your most recent job)

1. Position: _____ Dates: _____ Company: _____

Duties: _____

_____

2. Position: _____ Dates: _____ Company: _____

Duties: _____

_____

WINDOW ON MATH

Understanding Payroll Deductions

A Read the information.

Gross Pay = the amount you earn per hour/week/month/year

Deductions = the amount subtracted from your gross pay before you get your paycheck
Deductions can include medical and dental insurance, retirement plans, and taxes.

Net Pay = your total pay, minus the deductions

B Look at the pay stub. Compute the total deductions and net pay for this pay period and for the year to date.

Employee name: **Eva Haslam**		Pay Period: **3/15/12 to 3/31/12**	
Earnings/Wage	Hours This Pay Period	Earnings This Pay Period	Earnings Year to Date
$16.00/hour	80	$1,280.00	$7,680.00
Federal taxes deducted		$230.40	$1,382.40
State taxes deducted		$140.80	$844.80
Medical insurance deducted		$40.00	$240.00
Dental insurance deducted		$15.00	$90.00

	Gross Pay	Total Deductions	Net Pay
1. This pay period:	$1,280	_____	_____
2. Year to date:	$7,680	_____	_____

Making Inferences

MAKING INFERENCES

When you make an inference, you draw a logical conclusion from evidence or facts.

Evidence: Maria has lived her whole life in <u>Spain</u>.
Inference: Maria speaks Spanish.

Evidence: David is a <u>computer programmer</u>.
Inference: David knows how to use a computer very well.

Evidence: For this position, you will need a valid <u>driver's license</u> and your own <u>car</u>.
Inference: You will have to drive in this job.

❶ Practice the Strategy

Read the evidence. Circle the correct inference.

1. Evidence: Lee was born in the United States.
Inference:

   A. Lee is 20 years old.
   B. Lee is an American citizen.
   C. Lee lives in New York.

2. Evidence: Vera plays soccer every day.
Inference:

   A. Vera doesn't have a broken leg.
   B. Vera likes to swim.
   C. Vera's parents like soccer.

3. Evidence: I graduated from the University of California in 1978.
Inference:

   A. I am a doctor.
   B. I finished high school.
   C. I am married.

4. Evidence: Sales associate: four years of experience needed.
Inference:

   A. To apply for this job, you need four years of work experience.
   B. To apply for this job, you need four years of sales experience.
   C. To apply for this job, you need four years of higher education.

5. Evidence: You need excellent computer skills for this position.
Inference:

   A. You will have to use a computer in the job.
   B. The supervisor likes computers.
   C. There are three computers in the office.

❷ Preview

Survey the article on page 97. What's the topic? What's the main idea?

❸ Listen and Read 🎧 052

Read the article. Then read the statements and check (✔) if they are *True* or *False*. For each statement, write a piece of evidence from the reading that supports your answer.

How to Get Your Dream Job: Never Give Up!

When she was a small child in El Salvador, Yolanda decided to become a nurse. This was her dream job. She wanted to work with doctors and take care of patients. Getting a good education can be expensive, so Yolanda knew that achieving her goal might be difficult.

Yolanda and her family came to the United States when she was a teenager. Yolanda did well in school. She learned English quickly. This was her first step to achieving her goal. But Yolanda had an obstacle . Even though her parents worked very hard, they didn't have enough money to send Yolanda to college.

This didn't stop Yolanda. She got a part-time job in a nursing home while she was in high school. This helped Yolanda in two ways. She got useful experience for her dream job. She also was able to save a little money for college.

Yolanda received a scholarship to a nursing program. Her parents were very proud, especially when Yolanda's wish finally came true . In 2010, Yolanda graduated from community college. She got her first job in a hospital emergency room in Chicago.

Emergency room work is hard. Patients arrive all the time. They often have serious problems that need attention immediately. Emergency room nursing can be stressful, but Yolanda loves the fast pace of her work. Yolanda never gave up, and today she has her dream job.

1. Yolanda didn't come from a wealthy family.   ✔ True ___ False
   Evidence: <u>Even though her parents worked hard, they didn't have money for Yolanda's education.</u>

2. Yolanda's first language was Spanish.   ___ True ___ False
   Evidence: _____

3. The work you do in a nursing home is similar to the work that a nurse does.   ___ True ___ False
   Evidence: _____

4. Yolanda's parents didn't want her to go to college.   ___ True ___ False
   Evidence: _____

5. Yolanda got good grades in high school.   ___ True ___ False
   Evidence: _____

6. Yolanda doesn't work well under pressure.   ___ True ___ False
   Evidence: _____

❹ Understand the Reading

Discuss these questions with a partner.

1. What do the highlighted words and phrases mean? Use the context to guess.

2. What was Yolanda's obstacle? What did she do to remove the obstacle?

3. What kind of a person is Yolanda? Are you like Yolanda? Why or why not?

WRITING AND REVISING A COVER LETTER

When you send someone your résumé for a job, you often include a cover letter. A cover letter introduces you and summarizes your résumé. It should make the reader want to read your résumé. A cover letter has these parts:

Parts of a Cover Letter	Location and Purpose
Top: Return address, date, inside address, and salutation	• Put your address in the upper right corner so the employer can contact you. • Put the date under this, so the employer knows when you wrote the letter. • On the left side below the return address, include the name and address of the person you are writing to. • Follow this by the salutation: title, or Mr., Ms., Mrs. and last name.
Middle: Body	• In the first paragraph below the salutation, explain why you are writing, what position you want, and how you heard about it. • In the next paragraph, explain your strengths and achievements. Refer to your résumé here. • In the final paragraph, restate your interest in the position. Say you look forward to hearing from the person and express your appreciation.
Bottom: Closing and signature	• After your last paragraph, close the letter with *Sincerely*, a comma, and your handwritten signature. • Type or print your name below your signature.

Revising is an important part of writing a cover letter. When you revise your cover letter, you change the content to make the writing stronger. Ask yourself these questions before you send a cover letter:

1. Have I clearly explained why I am writing?

2. Will the reader easily understand my strengths and see why I am a good match for the position?

3. Does my letter refer to my résumé?

4. Does it make the reader want to read my résumé?

❶ Practice the Skill

Read the cover letter on page 99 and label the parts. Then answer these revision questions:

1. Has Hana clearly explained why she is writing?

_____

2. Will the reader easily understand Hana's strengths and see why she is a good match for the job?

_____

3. Does the letter refer to Hana's résumé?

_____

4. Does the letter make the reader want to read her résumé?

_____

11510 South Lake Drive
Atlanta, GA 30318 – – – – – – *Return*
June 16, 2012   *address*

Howard Smith
President
A Formal Affair Catering   } – – – – – – – – – – – – – – – – – – –
43 East Monroe Street
Chicago, IL 60603

Dear Mr. Smith,   –

    I am writing in response to your ad on Foodservice.com for a pastry chef. I would enjoy the opportunity to meet you and speak to you about this position.

    As you will see in the enclosed résumé, I worked for many years in the food   – – – service industry. For the past three years, I have specialized in baking and pastry making. I am very well organized, have excellent communication skills, and I am able to work well under pressure.

    I am truly interested in the position of pastry chef at A Formal Affair Catering and would appreciate the opportunity to discuss my qualifications in person. I can be reached at your convenience at the email address or telephone number at the top of my résumé.

Sincerely, –

Hana Nasser –

❷ Plan Your Writing

Work with a partner. Talk about your dream job or one of the jobs in the classified ads on page 93. Explain why you want the job and why you are a good match for the job. As you talk, complete the form below:

Job Title / Name of Position: _____

My Strengths and Achievements: _____

_____

_____

_____

❸ Write

Write a cover letter to accompany your résumé. Write to May Lee, Manager, ABC Company, 55 East Monroe Street, Chicago, ILL 60603. Use your notes from Activity 2. Follow the model cover letter above. Answer the revision questions about your letter.

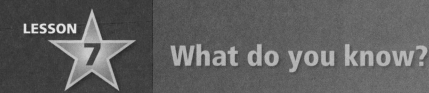
① Listening Review  053

Part 1

Listen to what is said. When you hear the question, *Which is correct?*, listen and choose the correct answer: *A, B,* or *C*. Use the Answer Sheet.

Part 2 054

You will hear the first part of a conversation. To finish the conversation, listen and choose the correct answer: *A, B,* or *C*. Use the Answer Sheet.

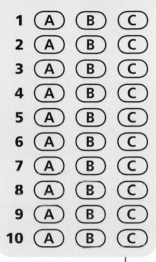

Answer Sheet

1	Ⓐ	Ⓑ	Ⓒ
2	Ⓐ	Ⓑ	Ⓒ
3	Ⓐ	Ⓑ	Ⓒ
4	Ⓐ	Ⓑ	Ⓒ
5	Ⓐ	Ⓑ	Ⓒ
6	Ⓐ	Ⓑ	Ⓒ
7	Ⓐ	Ⓑ	Ⓒ
8	Ⓐ	Ⓑ	Ⓒ
9	Ⓐ	Ⓑ	Ⓒ
10	Ⓐ	Ⓑ	Ⓒ

② Grammar Review

Circle the correct answer: A, B, or C.

1. I want _____ a physician assistant.
   A. to be
   B. be
   C. been

2. Jenny likes _____ outdoors.
   A. works
   B. work
   C. working

3. Salim hates _____ alone.
   A. study
   B. studying
   C. studies

4. She _____ work on a team than alone.
   A. prefer
   B. would prefer
   C. would rather

5. Ron would rather _____ a doctor.
   A. to be
   B. being
   C. be

6. Ivan would prefer _____ indoors.
   A. works
   B. to work
   C. work

Work-Out CD-ROM

Unit 7: Plug in and practice!

❷ Grammar Review (continued)

7. Are you able _____ 50 pounds?
A. lifting
B. lift
C. to lift

8. He _____ able to buy a car soon.
A. will be
B. be
C. being

9. The applicant must be able _____ a truck.
A. drive
B. to drive
C. driving

10. A: Will you be able to come in tomorrow?
B: _____
A. Yes, I am.
B. Yes, I will.
C. Yes, I was.

LEARNING LOG

I know these words:

NOUNS AND NOUN PHRASES
- admittance clerk
- benefits
- biomedical equipment technician
- community health worker
- co-pay
- cover letter
- deductible
- deductions
- dependents
- domestic partner
- gross pay
- home health aide

- lab technician
- medical records specialist
- net pay
- network
- objective
- obstacle
- orderly
- physician assistant
- premium
- preventive care
- résumé
- tech support specialist
- working conditions

VERBS
- give up
- revise

OTHER
- come true
- need attention
- open access
- out-of-pocket

I practiced these skills, strategies, and grammar points:

- identifying qualities of a job or workplace
- understanding workplace medical benefits
- calling about a job
- asking polite questions
- giving reasons for a preference

- taking notes
- reading for specific information
- listening for specific information
- reading and writing a résumé
- understanding payroll deductions
- making inferences
- writing and revising a cover letter

- using verbs followed by gerund or infinitive
- using *prefer, would prefer, would rather* for preferences
- using *be able to*

THINGS TO DO

❶ Warm Up

Discuss these questions with your classmates.

1. What forms of communication did you use yesterday?
- talked to someone in person
- sent an email
- sent someone a text message
- left a message on someone's voicemail
- wrote a letter

2. What are some other ways people communicate?

3. What types of communication can you find in the picture?

> **Body language** is using the body to communicate instead of using words. It includes facial expressions, gestures, and other body movements.

❷ Identify

Which of these examples of body language can you find in the picture? Check (✔) them.

- ○ waving to someone
- ○ pointing at something
- ○ rubbing a chin
- ○ smiling
- ○ frowning
- ○ pointing at oneself
- ○ holding up a finger
- ○ shaking hands
- ○ shaking a fist
- ○ holding out both hands

❸ Decide

Look at the picture. Who is probably saying these things? Write each person's name.

1. "Put it over there, please." _____Jon_____

2. "Nice to meet you." _____

3. "That looks great!" _____

4. "Wait just a minute." _____

5. "Are you talking to me?" _____

6. "I don't know." _____

7. "Come here." _____

8. "I'm thinking about it." _____

Now, discuss your answers with a partner.

Examples: *Jon could be saying, "Put it over there, please." I think Leo is saying, "I don't know" because he's holding out both hands.*

Andy

Beth

HAN

KATE

Target Grammar

Indefinite pronouns *page 186*

Improving Communication Skills

THINGS TO DO

❶ Talk about It

Discuss these questions with your classmates.

1. Look at the pictures on page 105. In which situations are the speakers friends or family members? In which situations are they probably strangers?

2. Is there a difference in the way you speak to people you know well and people you don't know well? Explain the difference and find examples in the pictures.

❷ Match

Read the comments in the boxes on page 105. Match each comment with a response below. Then say the comments and responses with a partner.

a. ___2___ Thanks.

b. _____ It looks good, but I think the neckline could be higher.

c. _____ You're welcome.

d. _____ I'm sorry. I have to work tomorrow.

e. _____ Sure. Go ahead.

f. _____ Sure. I'd be glad to. That looks heavy.

g. _____ You look great!

h. _____ Yes. I'd like to fill this prescription.

i. _____ That's a good idea.

❸ Listen and Write 🎧 055

Listen to the conversations. Write the number of the conversation next to the kind of communication.

a. _____ make a suggestion

b. _____ interrupt

c. _____ make a request

d. _____ express appreciation

e. _____ ask for an opinion

f. _____ offer help

❹ Use the Vocabulary

Write the missing word forms. Complete the questions below. Then ask and answer the questions with a partner.

Noun	Verb
interruption	_____interrupt_____
expression	_____
_____	appreciate
_____	suggest

a. Did anything _____interrupt_____ your sleep last night?

b. How do people _____ sadness?

c. When someone gives you a gift, how do you show your _____?

d. Do you have a _____ for improving this letter?

Target Grammar

Will and *would* for formal requests   *page 188*

THINGS TO DO

❶ Warm Up

Who do you think the people are in pictures 1, 2, and 3? Write the number of each picture next to a pair of people below.

_____ a husband and wife   _____ a doctor and a patient

_____ a supervisor and an employee   _____ two friends

_____ two coworkers   _____ a teacher and a student

❷ Listen and Write 🎧 056

Listen to the conversations. Write *M* (man) or *W* (woman) next to the kind of communication.

Conversation #1			
1. offers help	_____	**3.** compliments	_____
2. asks for feedback	_____	**4.** makes a suggestion	_____

Conversation #2			
1. interrupts	_____	**3.** asks for feedback	_____
2. makes a request	_____	**4.** expresses appreciation	_____

Conversation #3			
1. makes a request	_____	**3.** makes a suggestion	_____
2. offers help	_____	**4.** compliments	_____

❸ Role-Play 🎧 057

Listen. Then work with a partner. Role-play the conversation between two students. Replace the highlighted words with the ideas below or your own ideas. Use the communication strategy.

A: I think you might be able to help me. Can you come here for a minute?

B: Sure. What is it?

A: Can you show me how to save a picture from a website?

B: Okay. That's not hard. All you have to do is click the mouse here and drag the picture to your desktop. Did you get that?

A: Yes. Thanks a lot. You must be a genius.

B: Not really.

send a text message

get to the nearest bank from school

COMMUNICATION STRATEGY

Checking for Understanding

When you give someone help or feedback, it's a good idea to check for understanding. Notice the formal and informal ways to check for understanding:

Is there anything that you didn't understand? (formal)

Is that clear? (formal)

Did you get that? (informal)

Got it? (informal)

Understand? (informal)

○ **Target Grammar**

May and *might* for possibility;
must for conclusion   *page 189*

Becoming a Better Listener

❶ Warm Up

Before you read the article, look at the statements about listening and speaking skills. Check (✔) *True* or *False*.

	True	False
1. A good listener thinks about the speaker's supporting ideas while he or she is speaking.	○	○
2. A good listener restates a speaker's ideas out loud, while he or she is speaking.	○	○
3. A good speaker doesn't look the listener in the eyes while he or she is speaking.	○	○
4. A good speaker asks questions such as: "Did you get that?" or: "Do you have any questions?"	○	○

❷ Read and Respond

Read the article. Check your answers in Activity 1. Then answer the vocabulary questions below.

How to Be a Better Listener and Speaker

Listening is one of the most important skills in communication. Everyone appreciates a good listener, and good listening can make you more successful in all areas of your life, including at work and school. So, how can you become a better listener? Here are a few tips to improve your listening skills:

- When someone is speaking, **anticipate** what you think he or she will say next. This helps you remember what the speaker said.
- Pay attention to the speaker's supporting ideas as you listen. This helps you to understand and remember the ideas.
- Make mental summaries as you listen. In your mind restate what you think the person is saying.
- If possible, take notes as you listen.

What if you have to speak to a poor listener? Here are some things you can do to deliver your message **effectively** :

- Pay attention to your body language. The way you hold your body and make eye contact can tell the listener that you are saying something important. Tone of voice—the way you stress words and use intonation—also helps the listener.
- Be specific and **get to the point.** Don't speak about things that are off your main topic.
- Check for understanding. It's probably the best way to be sure that the listener has heard you.

It's not always easy to be a good listener, but clear communication can improve all parts of your life!

Vocabulary Questions

1. What word means *well*? _____

2. What word means *think ahead*? _____

3. What words mean *stay on the topic*? _____

❸ Listen and Apply 🎧 058

Listen to a short presentation. Practice your listening skills while you take notes. Then answer the questions. Compare your answers with a partner.

While you listened . . .	Yes	No
1. did you anticipate what the speaker might say?	○	○
2. did you pay attention to the way the speaker supported the main ideas?	○	○
3. did you make mental summaries as you listened?	○	○
4. did you take notes?	○	○

How much do you remember?

1. What was the topic of the presentation? _____

2. What was the speaker's main idea? _____

_____

3. How did the speaker support her main idea? Write one example. _____

_____

_____

_____

WINDOW ON PRONUNCIATION

Using Stress for Emphasis 🎧 059

One way to help listeners pay attention is to stress important words. To do this, the speaker gives the most stress to the words in a sentence that he or she thinks convey the most important idea.

A Listen to the sentences. Then listen and repeat.

<u>Anticipate</u> what you <u>think</u> the person will say <u>next</u>.

Make <u>eye</u> <u>contact</u>.

B Listen to the sentences. Underline the stressed words in each sentence.

1. Set aside some time to talk.

2. Ask your children's opinions.

3. Don't interrupt your children when they are speaking.

Now, discuss this question with a partner: Why did the speaker stress those words?

C Talk with a partner. Summarize the presentation in Activity 3. Pay special attention to words and phrases that need stress.

Fact or Opinion?

DISTINGUISHING FACT FROM OPINION

Fact	Opinion
Facts are statements that we can prove. **Examples:** • *Most people speak at about 125 words a minute.* • *He apologized for being late.*	Opinions express a person's feelings or beliefs. **Examples:** • *My best friend is very beautiful in my opinion.* • *I think that it's hard to be a good listener.*

❶ Practice the Strategy

Read the statements. Write *fact* or *opinion*. If it's an opinion, underline the words that help you know it's an opinion.

1. <u>In my opinion</u>, it's rude to criticize someone older than yourself.
_____opinion_____

2. Paris is the capital of France. _____

3. I believe that there are aliens. _____

4. Nevada is between California and Utah. _____

5. I feel strongly that we need to save more money. _____

6. Switzerland has four official languages: German, French, Romansh, and Italian. _____

7. The telephone was the most important invention of the 20th century. _____

8. I think that there are too many people in the world. _____

9. There are more computers in the world today than there were 50 years ago. _____

10. There are more than five billion people in the world today. _____

Now think of one more fact and one more opinion. Write them below.

Fact: I know that _____.

Opinion: I think that _____.

❷ Preview

Survey the article on page 111. What is the topic?

_____

_____

❸ Listen and Read 🎧 060

Read the article below. Underline three facts in the article. Find at least one opinion and circle the words that help you know it's an opinion.

Do Men and Women Speak the Same Language?

By Jake Kline

"Mike, my boss, is so rude!" my friend Jane complained. I asked why. She said, "Every time he wants me to do something, he says, 'Jane, get me the Smith report.' Or: 'Jane, come into my office for a minute.'"

Now, I'm a man, so what Mike said sounded fine to me. I asked Jane why she thought her boss was so rude. Jane explained. "I would say: 'Jane, would you *please* get me the Smith report?' Or: 'Jane, would you *mind* coming into my office for a minute?'"

Now, Jane's version didn't sound strange to me, but neither did Mike's. I wondered what the problem really was, so I decided to do a little research. According to some of the experts, there actually is a difference in the way that men and women communicate. They've even done studies to prove it.

Here's what one expert found: Most North American men learn to be competitive as young children. They play competitive games with each other. They participate in team sports. Because of these activities, they learn to give and take orders. On the other hand, girls in North American cultures learn to play "pretend" games with each other and with dolls. They participate in relationship games, such as playing house. Therefore, girls learn to cooperate with each other. This has an effect on both boys' and girls' communication styles as they grow up. As a result, North American men often give orders and use fewer words to get a message across. North American women make polite requests and include a lot of detail in their speech.

So it's actually pretty easy to see why Jane might think that her boss is rude. Her boss might think that Jane is too polite and too talkative! In my opinion, the best thing to do is to understand why men and women speak differently. I believe that we should try to understand what the other person is really trying to say, and not worry about how they're saying it.

❹ Understand the Reading

Discuss these questions with a partner.

1. Did anything in the article surprise you? What was it?

2. Do you agree with the writer when he says, "we should try to understand what the other person is really trying to say, and not worry about how they're saying it?" Why or why not?

3. Do you think that there are similar differences in the way men and women speak in your native language? Give examples.

Supporting Your Ideas

> ## SUPPORTING YOUR IDEAS
>
> In a piece of **persuasive** writing, the writer expresses an opinion. The writer provides facts, examples, and personal stories to convince the reader that this opinion is correct. We call these facts, examples, and stories **supporting ideas** . The writer uses these supporting ideas to persuade the reader.

❶ Practice the Skill

Read each paragraph on page 113 and identify the writer's opinion. Then list the ideas the writer gives to support this opinion.

The Writer's Opinion or Main Idea	The Supporting Ideas
1. Limit the time children communicate online.	
2.	• Many people die in car accidents caused by drivers on their cell phones. •
3.	

❷ Plan Your Writing

Choose a topic you have a strong opinion about. Then brainstorm a list of facts, examples, or personal stories to support your opinion. Record your ideas in the chart below.

Topic: _____

My opinion: _____

_____

Supporting ideas:_____

_____

_____

_____

❸ Write

Write a persuasive paragraph about your ideas. Use the information from your chart in Activity 2. Read your paragraph to the class and try to convince your classmates that your opinion is correct.

1

Texting and Teens

If parents want their children to get better grades, they should limit the amount of time they let them communicate online. Texting and emailing give teens bad writing habits because they use informal writing styles. I have been a high school teacher for many years, and I think student writing is much worse today than it was only five years ago. In one study I have read, 50 percent of teens said they use informal writing styles instead of proper capitalization and punctuation in their school assignments. I think teens should spend more time doing real writing, and less time texting and emailing.

2

Stop Talking or Stop Driving

Driving while talking on a cell phone is a very bad habit. Every year many people die in car accidents caused by drivers who are using cell phones while they drive. It is especially bad to talk on a cell phone when you are driving on the highway. At highway speeds, you need to focus on the road and not on your friend on the phone. I hope every state makes it illegal to drive while you are talking on a cell phone.

3

Social Networking Sites

College students and job seekers should be careful about using social networking websites. Many people write personal details and post silly pictures of themselves on these sites. They think that the messages and photos are private, and that only their friends will see them. Unfortunately, anyone can find them, and worse, the information often stays on the site for a long time. Employers check social networking sites regularly when they are interviewing job seekers. So if you hope to have a good job someday, be careful when you post messages on networking sites. Better yet, my advice is to stay away from these sites altogether.

❶ Listening Review 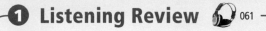 061

Part 1

First you will hear a question. Next, listen carefully to what is said. You will hear the question again. Then choose the correct answer: *A*, *B*, or *C*. Use the Answer Sheet.

Part 2 🎧 062

You will hear the first part of a conversation. To finish the conversation, listen and choose the correct answer: *A*, *B*, or *C*. Use the Answer Sheet.

Answer Sheet

1	Ⓐ	Ⓑ	Ⓒ
2	Ⓐ	Ⓑ	Ⓒ
3	Ⓐ	Ⓑ	Ⓒ
4	Ⓐ	Ⓑ	Ⓒ
5	Ⓐ	Ⓑ	Ⓒ
6	Ⓐ	Ⓑ	Ⓒ
7	Ⓐ	Ⓑ	Ⓒ
8	Ⓐ	Ⓑ	Ⓒ
9	Ⓐ	Ⓑ	Ⓒ
10	Ⓐ	Ⓑ	Ⓒ

❷ Grammar Review

Circle the correct answer: *A*, *B*, or *C*.

1. It _____ rain today, but I'm not sure.

   A. must
   B. might
   C. will

2. That man is rubbing his chin. He may _____ thinking about something.

   A. be
   B. being
   C. to be

3. The boss is yelling and shaking his fist, so he _____ be angry.

   A. might
   B. must
   C. will

4. _____ you take this, please?

   A. Might
   B. Must
   C. Will

5. Would you _____ me a hand?

   A. give
   B. gives
   C. to give

6. Will you _____ a window, please?

   A. opening
   B. to open
   C. open

Work-Out CD-ROM

Unit 8: Plug in and practice!

❷ Grammar Review (continued)

7. Can you help me with _____?

    A. anyone

    B. something

    C. nothing

8. A: Is _____ there? B: No, _____ is home.

    A. someone / anyone

    B. no one / anyone

    C. anyone / no one

9. We didn't understand _____ .

    A. anything

    B. nothing

    C. nobody

10. Someone _____ you on the phone.

    A. want

    B. wants

    C. wanting

LEARNING LOG ✓

I know these words:

NOUNS AND NOUN PHRASES

- ○ appreciation
- ○ body language
- ○ communication style
- ○ expression
- ○ feedback
- ○ interruption
- ○ request
- ○ research
- ○ suggestion
- ○ supporting ideas

VERBS

- ○ anticipate
- ○ appreciate
- ○ compliment
- ○ express
- ○ give orders
- ○ interrupt
- ○ offer
- ○ suggest
- ○ take orders

ADJECTIVES

- ○ competitive
- ○ persuasive
- ○ rude

ADVERB

- ○ effectively

IDIOMS

- ○ get to the point
- ○ make a request
- ○ make a suggestion

I practiced these skills, strategies and grammar points:

- ○ identifying ways people communicate
- ○ interpreting body language
- ○ communicating in social situations
- ○ listening for specific information
- ○ checking for understanding
- ○ analyzing good communication skills

- ○ using context to guess the meaning of a word
- ○ using listening skills effectively
- ○ summarizing a presentation
- ○ taking notes
- ○ expressing an opinion
- ○ distinguishing fact from opinion

- ○ supporting your ideas
- ○ using indefinite pronouns
- ○ using *may* and *might* for possibility and *must* for conclusion
- ○ using *will* and *would* for formal requests
- ○ writing a persuasive paragraph

THINGS TO DO

1 Warm Up

Discuss these questions with your classmates.

1. Where are the people in the pictures? What are they doing?
2. What differences do you see between the two pictures?

2 Identify

Complete the paragraph with words from the picture. Then compare your paragraph with a partner.

The United States Congress

The United States ___Congress___ is responsible for making national laws, such as laws that have to do with taxes. Members of Congress discuss and vote on _____. These are suggestions for new laws. The U.S. Congress is divided into two groups, the _____ and the _____. There are 100 _____ and 435 _____ in the U.S. Congress. The leader of the Senate is the Vice President of the United States and he or she is called the _____. The leader of the House of Representatives is the _____. In the House of Representatives, _____ sit on the left side of the Speaker of the House. In the Senate, _____ sit on the right side of the President of the Senate. Visitors can watch the Senate and House at work. The _____ also watches and reports on Senate and House activities.

President of the Senate
(Vice President)

3 Talk about It

Read the list of suggestions for U.S. laws. Check (✔) the laws that you think would be a good idea. Then discuss your ideas with the class.

Provide free healthcare for all citizens.	○
Make guns illegal.	○
Provide low-cost or free college education for all citizens.	○
Require "English Only"—everyone must speak only English all the time.	○
Let people born outside the U.S. **run for** President.	○

Example: *I think guns should be illegal. Too many people are killed because it's easy to get guns in the United States.*

🎯 **Target Grammar**

Phrasal verbs *page 191*

United States Congress

Senate

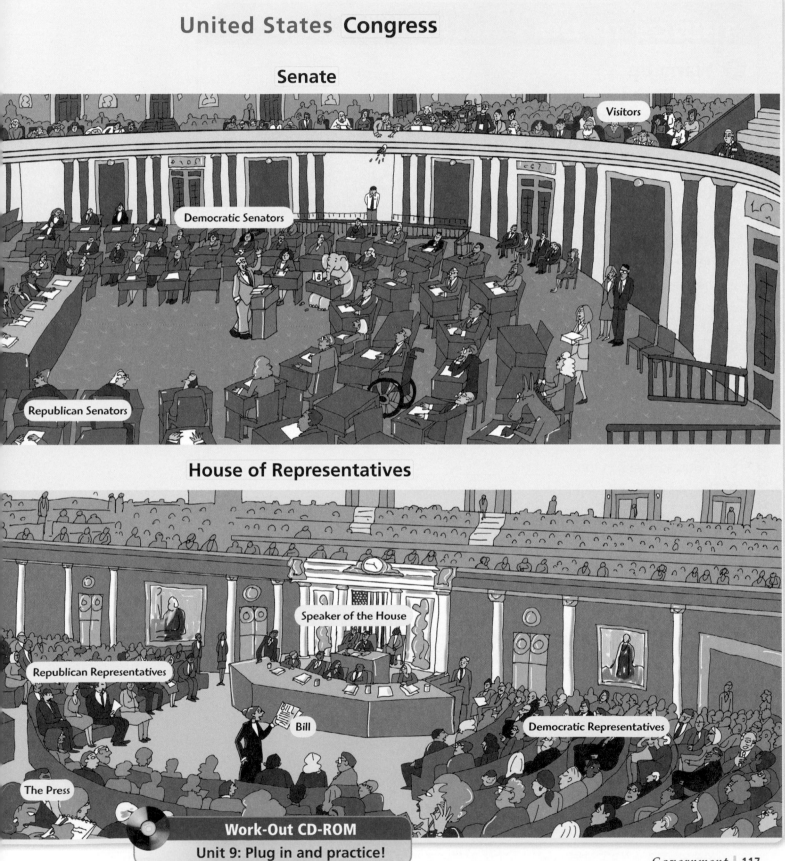

Visitors

Democratic Senators

Republican Senators

House of Representatives

Speaker of the House

Republican Representatives

Bill

Democratic Representatives

The Press

Work-Out CD-ROM

Unit 9: Plug in and practice!

THINGS TO DO

❶ Warm Up

Discuss these questions with your classmates.

1. How is the government organized in your home country?
2. Compare the government of your home country with the picture. What are the similarities? What are the differences?

❷ Use the Vocabulary

Use the words in the diagram on page 119 to complete the sentences.

1. The Supreme Court is part of the _____ branch of the government.
2. The President can _____ a bill.
3. Congress _____ bills for new laws. Then they discuss them and vote.
4. When Congress accepts a bill, they _____ it.
5. If a law is **constitutional**, that means it doesn't break the rules of the _____.
6. The _____ must decide if a law is constitutional.
7. The President is part of the _____ branch of the government.
8. Congress meets in the _____ building.
9. The President and the Vice President work in the _____.
10. The Senate is part of the _____ branch of the government.

❸ Listen and Write 🎧 063

Listen to the news report about what the three branches of government are doing. Write each activity in the correct place in the chart.

Legislative Activities	Executive Activities	Judicial Activities

Target Grammar

Must, have to and *have got to*
for necessity and prohibition   *page 193*

THE THREE BRANCHES OF GOVERNMENT

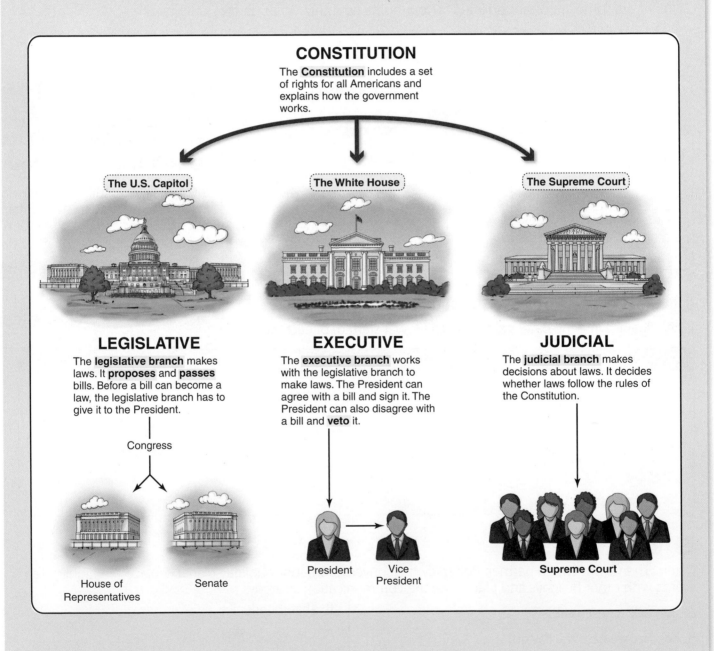

CONSTITUTION

The **Constitution** includes a set of rights for all Americans and explains how the government works.

The U.S. Capitol

The White House

The Supreme Court

LEGISLATIVE

The **legislative branch** makes laws. It **proposes** and **passes** bills. Before a bill can become a law, the legislative branch has to give it to the President.

Congress

House of Representatives

Senate

EXECUTIVE

The **executive branch** works with the legislative branch to make laws. The President can agree with a bill and sign it. The President can also disagree with a bill and **veto** it.

President

Vice President

JUDICIAL

The **judicial branch** makes decisions about laws. It decides whether laws follow the rules of the Constitution.

Supreme Court

Major National Holidays

THINGS TO DO

❶ Warm Up

Discuss these questions with your classmates.

1. Look at the holidays on page 121. When are they? What do people usually do on these days?

2. What are some important holidays in your home country? What do they celebrate?

❷ Listen for General Information 🎧 064

Listen to the information about holidays. Write the name of the holiday and check (✔) if the holiday celebrates an event or a person.

Holiday	Event	Person
1. _____	○	○
2. _____	○	○
3. _____	○	○
4. _____	○	○
5. _____	○	○

❸ Listen for Specific Information 🎧 065

Listen again. Write the date and the origin (how it started) of each holiday.

	Date	Origin
1.		
2.		
3.		
4.		
5.		

COMMUNICATION STRATEGY

Declining an Invitation

If you don't want to accept an invitation, it's polite to show interest but explain why you can't accept. Try these phrases:

I'm sorry. I have other plans that day.

Oh, I'd love to, but …

That sounds nice. Unfortunately, …

❹ Role-Play 🎧 066

Listen. Then work with a partner. Role-play the conversation about holiday plans. Replace the highlighted words with other holidays and plans. Use the communication strategy.

A: July 4th is next week.

B: Yes, and we have the day off.

A: I know. We're having a big picnic in the park on that day .

B: That sounds nice.

A: Can you join us?

B: I'm sorry. I have other plans that day.

NATIONAL HOLIDAYS

Martin Luther King , Jr. Day

Presidents' Day

Memorial Day

Independence Day

Labor Day

❶ Warm Up

Discuss these questions with a partner.

1. Have you ever voted?

2. What are the laws about voting in your home country?

3. Why should people vote?

❷ Read and Respond

Read the voting website information. Rules about voter registration vary from state to state. Check the state where you live.

Secretary of State   ⊟ ⊞ ⊠

Secretary of State

Home | Contact Us | Site Map | FAQ

Search ⬤ **GO**

Elections & Voter Information

Election Dates

Register to Vote

Voter Information

Political Parties

Resources

Voter Registration

Registering to Vote

You may register to vote if:

- you are a United States citizen;
- you are a resident of this state;
- you are at least 18 years of age (or will be by the next election);
- you are not in prison.

How You Can Register to Vote in This State

1. Fill out a voter registration form. Click here to complete a <u>voter registration form</u> online.
2. Receive a voter registration form in the mail. Click here to fill out a request for a <u>voter registration form</u> for you to complete and return to your county elections office.
3. Pick up a voter registration form. You can pick up a voter registration form at your county elections office, public library, or post office.

Voter Registration Deadlines

The deadline to register to vote is 15 days before each election. You ought to register early!

Additional Assistance

For more help with voter registration, please contact the Secretary of State's office at the following numbers:

English:	(800) 555-VOTE
Cantonese:	(800) 555-2857
Mandarin:	(800) 555-2857
Japanese:	(800) 555-2865
Korean:	(800) 555-1558
Spanish:	(800) 555-VOTA
Tagalog:	(800) 555-2957
Vietnamese:	(800) 555-8163

⬤ **Target Grammar**

Should and *why don't* for advice   *page 195*

Read the statements below. Circle *True* or *False*.

1. You must be 18 years old to vote.	True	False
2. You can vote if you are in prison.	True	False
3. You can get a voter registration form at a post office.	True	False
4. You cannot vote on November 2 if you registered on October 10.	True	False
5. If you speak Cantonese, call (800) 555-VOTE for information in your language.	True	False

❸ Listen and Write 🎧 067

Listen to the conversations about voting. Match the conversation with the topic.

Conversation	Topic
1. _____	**a.** vote for a new **mayor**
2. _____	**b.** **Proposition** 3: more money for public schools
3. _____	**c.** vote for state senator
4. _____	**d.** Proposition B: a high-speed train

❹ Read and Apply

Read the situations. Discuss your opinions with your classmates.

1. Rafael is a citizen of Mexico. He is studying at a university in this state. Can he register to vote?

2. Rachel is 17. She will be 18 on November 1st. She wants to vote in an election on November 2. Can she register?

3. Steve is a U.S. citizen. He just got out of prison. Can he register to vote?

4. Natalia does not speak English. Can she register to vote?

WINDOW ON PRONUNCIATION

Intonation in Clauses 🎧 068

When a sentence has two clauses, each clause has its own intonation pattern. Each clause sounds like a sentence, usually with rising-falling intonation.

A Listen to the sentences. Then listen and repeat.

1. You may register to vote if you are a United States citizen.

2. You may register to vote if you are 18 years of age or older.

3. If you speak Cantonese, you should call the special telephone number.

B Listen to the sentences. Listen again and mark the intonation patterns of each sentence. Then practice the sentences with a partner.

1. For more help with voter registration, please contact the Secretary of State's office.

2. If you are a resident of this state, you may register to vote.

3. Click here if you want to complete a voter registration form online.

Using the Dictionary

> ## USING THE DICTIONARY
>
> Sometimes you can guess the meaning of a new word when you are reading. If you can't guess, look it up in the dictionary. The dictionary can tell you many things about a word. For example, it can tell you:
>
> - how to pronounce a word
> - the part(s) of speech of a word
> - the meaning(s) of a word
>
> **par•ty** /pahr' tee/ n **1** a gathering of people for a pleasurable event: *a birthday party.* **2** a group of people with similar political opinions: *the Democratic or Republican party;* **3** a group of people who work together
>
> If a word has more than one meaning, the first one is usually the most common. Use a dictionary with sample phrases or sentences; they help you understand the different meanings of a word.

❶ Practice the Strategy

Read this dictionary entry and answer the questions with a partner.

> **serve** /surv/ v **1** to work for a country: *She served in the U.S. Senate.* **2** to give food or drinks: *We served dinner at 6 P.M.* **3** to provide something necessary or useful: *The community center serves newcomers to the city.*

1. What word is this dictionary entry for? _____

2. How do you pronounce the word? Say it for your partner.

3. What part of speech is the word? _____

4. How many meanings are given? _____

5. Which is the correct meaning for the way the word is used in this sentence?
Wu is the first Chinese-American to <u>serve</u> in the U.S. House of Representatives.

_____

6. Which is the correct meaning for the way the word is used in this sentence?
Wu's firm <u>served</u> the high technology industry.

_____

❷ Preview

Survey the reading passage on page 125. What's the topic?

_____

❸ Listen and Read 🎧 069

Read the passage below. Look up the highlighted words in a dictionary. For each word, write the part of speech, the number of definitions given for the word, and the correct dictionary definition for the way the word is used in the paragraph.

Profile: Congressman David Wu

Congressman David Wu is the first and only Chinese-American to serve in the U.S. House of Representatives. Wu is a Democrat from Oregon. He represents Oregon's First Congressional District, which **stretches** from Portland to the Oregon Coast.

Congressman Wu has lived the American dream. In October of 1961, at six years of age, he moved with his family to the United States after President John F. Kennedy signed an executive order **updating** unfair immigration **quotas**. He attended public schools and **earned** a Bachelor of Science degree from Stanford University. In 1982, he received a law degree from Yale University.

Before he was elected to the House of Representatives, Wu had a **distinguished** career as a lawyer. In 1988, he co-founded the law firm of Cohen & Wu. For a decade, the firm served the high technology industry and many small businesses in Northwest Oregon.

Congressman Wu's **priorities** include improving our nation's public education system and making college less expensive. He is also interested in improving our nation's healthcare system and protecting our natural environment.

Word	Part of Speech	Number of Definitions	Definition as Used Here
1.			
2.			
3.			
4.			
5.			
6.			

❹ Understand the Reading

Discuss these questions with a partner.

1. What kind of background and experience does Wu have? Do you think this helps him to be a good representative?
2. What qualities make a good representative?
3. Would you like to be a politician? Why or why not?

STATING YOUR POSITION IN A LETTER

People often write letters to a member of Congress to explain their **position** on—or opinion of—an issue that Congress is discussing. The writer wants to try to influence the way the senator or representative will vote. To do this, it's important to:

- identify the issue you are concerned about at the beginning of the letter;
- clearly state your position on the issue;
- include reasons, or supporting ideas, for your position;
- tell the representative what you want him or her to do;
- use strong expressions of persuasion such as, "I urge you to . . ." "You must . . ."
- use a formal style in the letter;
- proofread and revise your letter, if necessary.

❶ Practice the Skill

Read the letter. Then work with a partner to answer the questions on page 127.

The Honorable David Wu
House Office Building
United States House of Representatives
Washington, DC 20515

Dear Representative Wu:

Last year, Congress passed a bill to give **universal** health insurance to children in low-income families, and the President vetoed it. Next year, Congress will vote on this bill again. I believe that the government must provide free healthcare to all children, but especially to the children of hard-working, poor people.

 Health care is very expensive in the United States. Many parents work at jobs that do not provide health insurance. And even though they work hard, they do not make enough money to pay for insurance on their own. Therefore, when a child gets sick, low-income working parents have no place to go. With government-supported health insurance, no child will have to suffer. In addition, it will provide preventive care programs for children so that they stay well and grow up to be healthy, productive citizens.

 I urge you to support universal heath insurance for children when this bill comes up for discussion again next year.

Sincerely,

Lina Taylor

Lina Taylor
5532 SE 30th Street
Apartment 223
Portland, OR 97231

Questions

1. Who is Lina writing to? _____

2. What issue is she concerned about? _____

3. What is Lina's position on the issue? _____

_____

4. What are Lina's supporting ideas? Where does she explain these ideas? _____

_____

_____

_____

5. Where does Lina tell the representative to do something? Underline the expression of persuasion that

she uses. _____

6. Did Lina make any mistakes in her letter? _____

❷ Plan Your Writing

Choose one of the possible laws on page 116 or any issue that interests you. Complete the chart. State your position on the issue. Write three supporting ideas for your position.

Issue: _____

My position: _____

_____

Supporting ideas: _____

_____

_____

_____

_____

❸ Write

Now, write a letter to Representative Wu or your own local representative. Use the ideas in your chart in Activity 2 and the letter on page 126 as an example.

What Do You Know?

❶ Listening Review 🎧 070

Part 1

Listen to what is said. When you hear the question *Which is correct?*, listen and choose the correct answer: *A*, *B*, or *C*. Use the Answer Sheet.

Part 2 🎧 071

First you will hear a question. Next, listen carefully to what is said. You will hear the question again. Then choose the correct answer: *A*, *B*, or *C*. Use the Answer Sheet.

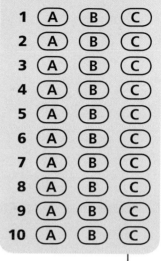

Answer Sheet

1	Ⓐ	Ⓑ	Ⓒ
2	Ⓐ	Ⓑ	Ⓒ
3	Ⓐ	Ⓑ	Ⓒ
4	Ⓐ	Ⓑ	Ⓒ
5	Ⓐ	Ⓑ	Ⓒ
6	Ⓐ	Ⓑ	Ⓒ
7	Ⓐ	Ⓑ	Ⓒ
8	Ⓐ	Ⓑ	Ⓒ
9	Ⓐ	Ⓑ	Ⓒ
10	Ⓐ	Ⓑ	Ⓒ

❷ Grammar Review

Circle the correct answer: *A*, *B*, or *C*.

1. How many senators _____ for the vote?

   A. showed on
   B. showed up
   C. called on

2. He can't run _____ president because he wasn't born here.

   A. in
   B. for
   C. to

3. The president is _____ our support to pass the new health care bill.

   A. counting on
   B. finding out
   C. showing up

4. The Speaker of the House called _____ the representative.

   A. with
   B. by
   C. on

5. Congress must _____ the bill to the President.

   A. to send
   B. sending
   C. send

6. The President _____ sign the bill by midnight.

   A. has to
   B. has
   C. have to

❷ Grammar Review (continued)

7. The Supreme Court _____ decide if a law follows the Constitution.

  A. has to
  B. have to
  C. have

8. You really _____ register to vote.

  A. had
  B. should
  C. have

9. We should _____ "Yes" on Proposition 9.

  A. voting
  B. to vote
  C. vote

10. _____ to the meeting with us?

  A. Why you not come
  B. Why you not coming
  C. Why don't you come

LEARNING LOG

I know these words:

NOUNS AND NOUN PHRASES

- bill
- branch
- Congress
- Democrat
- the press
- House of Representatives
- Independence Day
- Labor Day
- Martin Luther King, Jr. Day
- mayor
- Memorial Day
- origin
- party
- position
- president
- Presidents' Day

- priority
- proposition
- quota
- registration
- representative
- Republican
- Senate
- senator
- Speaker of the House
- Supreme Court
- the Constitution
- vice president

VERBS

- earn
- pass a bill
- propose a bill
- run for

- serve
- stretch
- update
- veto
- vote for
- vote on

ADJECTIVES

- constitutional
- democratic / Democratic
- distinguished
- executive
- judicial
- legislative
- republican / Republican
- universal

I practiced these skills, strategies and grammar points:

- identifying the functions of government
- understanding the branches of government
- understanding major national holidays
- identifying the purpose of holidays
- declining an invitation

- learning rules about voting
- taking notes
- listening for general information
- listening for specific information
- understanding a website
- using a dictionary
- stating a position on an issue

- writing a formal letter
- using phrasal verbs
- using modals of necessity and prohibition
- using *should* and *why don't* for advice

Work-Out CD-ROM

Unit 9: Plug in and practice!

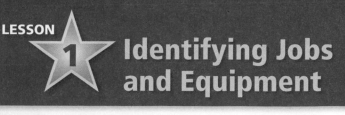
THINGS TO DO

❶ Warm Up

Discuss these questions with your classmates.

1. Where are the people in the picture? What are they doing?

2. What tools and equipment are they using?

3. Which job would you like to have?

❷ Identify

Study the picture and read the sentences. Write the person's name next to the job.

1. A **ticket agent** makes reservations and prints **boarding passes** . _____Tonya_____

2. An **airport security screener** checks passengers' luggage and uses a **metal detector** . _____

3. A **gate agent** keeps track of passengers who are boarding the plane. _____

4. An **air traffic controller** helps pilots take off and land. _____

5. A **baggage handler** loads baggage onto a plane. _____

6. Planes can't back up by themselves, so an **aircraft maintenance technician** tows them to the runway. _____

7. A **ground service equipment mechanic** fuels the plane. _____

❸ Match

Match the equipment with the person who uses it.

____ **1. X-ray scanner**
____ **2. ticket reader**
____ **3. conveyor belt**
____ **4. tow tractor**
____ **5.** computer
____ **6.** headset

a. gate agent
b. baggage handler
c. airport security screener
d. air traffic controller
e. aircraft maintenance technician
f. ticket agent

❹ Talk about It

Discuss these questions with a partner.

Do you think the airport is a safe place to work? A stressful place to work? A happy place to work? Give reasons for your answers.

Tonya

Target Grammar

Possessive and reflexive pronouns *page 197*

THINGS TO DO

❶ Talk about It

Discuss these questions with your classmates.

1. For what reasons might a person take off work?
2. Look at the leave schedule. Who is taking the most time off? For what reason? Who is taking a short time off? For what reason?
3. Have you ever taken the types of **leave** in this schedule?

❷ Match

Match the type of leave with the meaning.

> **To take (time) off (from) work**
> means not to go to work.

Type of Leave	Means Time Off . . .
1. _____ bereavement leave	**a.** to take a trip, rest, or spend time with others.
2. _____ childcare emergency leave	**b.** to have a baby and/or take care of a new baby.
3. _____ jury duty	**c.** to take care of children when there's no one to help.
4. _____ leave of absence	**d.** because someone died.
5. _____ maternity/paternity leave	**e.** to do something other than work, for example, go to school.
6. _____ medical leave	**f.** for a serious medical reason, such as surgery.
7. _____ military leave	**g.** to serve in the military, such as the Army or the Marines.
8. _____ vacation	**h.** to serve on a jury; to help make a decision in a court of law.

❸ Listen and Take Notes 🎧 072

Listen to the employees ask for time off. Write the type of leave.

Conversation	Type of Leave
1	
2	
3	
4	

> **Target Grammar**
>
> *Because* and *since*
> *for reasons* page 199

Sunday	Monday
	Marta: **maternity leave** to 4/1
7	Mark: **vacation** to 3/19
14	Ron: **medical leave** to 3/31
21	Amir: **childcare emergency leave** to 3/26
28	

SPEEDY DELIVERY • LEAVE SCHEDULE • MARCH

Tuesday	Wednesday	Thursday	Friday	Saturday
1	Sandy: **jury duty** to 3/5 **3**	**4**	**5**	**6**
8	**9**	Nigel: **bereavement leave** to 3/15 **11**	**12**	**13**
	10			
15	**16**	Jake: **paternity leave** to 3/31 **18**	**19**	**20**
	17			
22	Rosa: **military leave** to 12/31 **24**	Lin: **leave of absence** to 6/1 **25**	**26**	**27**
	23			
29	**30**	**31**		

Leaving Phone Messages

THINGS TO DO

❶ Warm Up

Discuss these questions with your classmates.

1. What are the people in the pictures doing?

2. What do you say when you leave a message for someone you don't know? for a friend?

❷ Listen and Take Notes 🎧 073

Listen to the phone calls. Write the information in the chart.

	Who Called?	Phone Number	Message
1	Dan	[didn't leave a phone number]	
2			
3			

Now match the phone calls to the pictures.

❸ Role-Play 🎧 074

Listen. Then work with a partner. Role-play two conversations. Replace the highlighted words with your own ideas.

A: Mr. Green's office.

B: Hello. This is Jane Grant . May I please speak to Mr. Green ?

A: Mr. Green isn't in right now. May I take a message ?

B: Yes. Would you please tell him that I will be about 10 minutes late?

A: Certainly.

B: Thank you.

A: Hello.

B: Hi. This is Linda . Is Rafael there?

A: He can't come to the phone right now. Can I take a message?

B: Sure. Tell him I've been waiting at the theater since 6 P.M.

A: Sorry, Linda . I'll tell him.

B: Thanks. Bye.

COMMUNICATION STRATEGY

Asking for a Message

There are many ways to say that someone isn't available to speak on the phone. Notice the difference between the formal and informal phrases.

... isn't in. (formal)

... isn't here right now. (informal)

... can't come to the phone right now. (informal)

May I take a message? (formal)

Would you like to leave a message? (formal)

Can I take a message? (informal)

Do you want to leave a message? (informal)

⊙ Target Grammar

Present perfect continuous *page 201*

Understanding W-2 Forms

❶ Warm Up

Discuss these questions with a partner.

1. Have you ever received a W-2 form? What kind of information was on it?

2. When do you usually pay **income taxes**?

3. Have you ever gotten a tax **refund**?

❷ Read and Respond

Read the W-2 form and answer the questions on page 137. Then check your answers with a partner.

a Control number 12378945	22222	Void ☐	For Official Use Only ▶ OMB No. 1545-0008		
b Employer identification number XXX-XXX-XXX			1 Wages, tips, other compensation 19,500		2 Federal income tax withheld 1592.00
c Employer's name, address, and ZIP code Dino's Bakery 1492 Ponce St. Pacoima, CA 91331			3 Social security wages 19,500		4 Social security tax withheld 816.17
			5 Medicare wages and tips 19,500		6 Medicare tax withheld 283.00
			7 Social security tips		8 Allocated tips
d Employee's social security number 000-12-3456			9 Advance EIC payment		10 Dependent care benefits
e Employee's first name and initial Jennifer	Last name Smith		11 Nonqualified plans		12a See instructions for box 12
3127 South Pleasant St. Reseda, CA 91335			13 Statutory employee ☐ Retirement plan ☐ Third-party sick pay ☐		12b
			14 Other		12c
					12d
f Employee's address and ZIP code					

15 State CA	Employer's state ID number XXX-XXX-XXX	16 State wages, tips, etc. 19,500	17 State income tax 961.30	18 Local wages, tips, etc.	19 Local income tax	20 Locality name

Form **W-2** Wage and Tax Statement

2011

Department of the Treasury—Internal Revenue Service

Copy A For Social Security Administration — Send this entire page with Form W-3 to the Social Security Administration; photocopies are **not** acceptable.

For Privacy Act and Paperwork Reduction Act Notice, see back of Copy D.

Cat. No. 10134D

Do Not Cut, Fold, or Staple Forms on This Page — Do Not Cut, Fold, or Staple Forms on This Page

Questions

1. Who is the employer? _____

2. Who is the employee? _____

3. Wages are money that you   a. earn.   b. pay the government.   c. put in the bank.

4. Money that is **withheld** is money that   a. you get in your paycheck.   b. you put in the bank.
c. the company deducts for taxes.

5. How much did the employee earn this year? _____

6. Which is the largest amount withheld for this employee? _____

❸ Listen and Apply 🎧 075

Listen to the conversation and complete the chart.

	Wages	Federal Income Tax Withheld	State Income Tax Withheld
Ting (wife)			
Wei (husband)			

❹ Talk about It

Discuss these questions with a partner.

1. Who received higher wages, Ting or Wei?

2. Who had more federal and state income tax withheld?

3. For both employees, which withholding is higher, state income tax or federal income tax?

4. What might Ting and Wei do with their tax refund? What would you do with a tax refund?

WINDOW ON MATH
Percentages

A Read the information.

The amount withheld from your wages for federal and state taxes is a percentage of your income (wages). To calculate withholding amounts, you need to multiply.

B Compute the withholding amounts.

1. $25,000 x 15% (.15) = _____   **3.** $35,000 x 25% (.25) = _____

2. $30,000 x 15% (.15) = _____   **4.** $40,000 x 25% (.25) = _____

Pronoun Reference

PRONOUN REFERENCE

Good writers use pronouns so that they don't have to repeat nouns. This makes a reading passage sound better. Pronouns often **refer to** nouns in a previous sentence or another part of the same sentence. It's important to understand what a pronoun refers to. This helps you understand what you are reading.

Examples:

Mark asked his boss for vacation leave. **He's** going to visit his father next week.

Maternity leave is another type of leave. Women take **it** when they are going to have a baby.

Jack works with Sandy. He enjoys being on a team with **her**.

---

❶ Practice the Strategy

Read the pairs of sentences. Write the word or phrase that the bolded pronoun refers to.

Sentences	What the Pronoun Refers to
1. An air traffic controller uses a headset to communicate with pilots. **He** wears it on his head.	_____
2. My sister used to be a gate agent. **She** worked at O'Hare International Airport.	_____
3. I need a week off from work. I'm going to take **it** in March.	_____
4. Sylvana and Joe both have jury duty next week. **They**'ll be gone for five days.	_____
5. Computers are an important piece of equipment at an airport. Ticket agents use **them** to print tickets.	_____
6. Tow tractors help planes back up. Pilots can't get to the runway without **them**.	_____
7. Ron is taking time off work to stay home with the baby. **She** was born a few days ago.	_____
8. I'm taking a few days off. I'm taking **them** because I really need a vacation.	_____

❷ Preview

Survey the passage on page 139. What is the topic?

_____

❸ Listen and Read 🎧 076

Read the passage below. Draw arrows from the bolded pronouns to the words that they refer to. Compare your pronoun references with a partner.

Teamwork

Teamwork means working together with other people to achieve a goal. **It's** an important part of almost any job. In order for teamwork to be successful, you need to become a good team player. How do you become a team player? Here are some tips:

- Take responsibility for tasks, even though **they** aren't part of your job. If something needs to be done, do it yourself. Show people that you are willing to work hard and learn more. If something goes wrong, take the blame. Do not make your team members take responsibility.

- If you are good at a certain task, train another person to do it. The more skills that your team has, the better it is for everyone. Don't be afraid to ask other people for help, if necessary, and be open when **they** ask you for help.

- Encourage discussion and exchanging ideas. Never criticize other people's ideas. Give positive feedback, and learn how to accept feedback on your own ideas.

- Be a good communicator. Make sure that you always let your team members know what you are doing. Take the time to listen to **them**. Make eye contact—**it** lets people know that you are really paying attention.

- Build relationships at work. In many cases, you have been spending more time with your co-workers than with your own family. You're with your team members a lot, so get to know **them**. Be friendly. Find out about their families, their birthday, and other special events in their lives.

❹ Understanding the Reading

Discuss these questions with a partner.

1. What does taking responsibility for tasks tell other people?

2. Why should you teach someone else how to do something that you know how to do?

3. What's one way to show people that you are listening to them?

❺ Talk about It

Discuss these questions with your classmates.

What are the advantages of working on a team? What are the advantages of working alone? Which do you prefer? Why?

Writing Professional Emails

WRITING PROFESSIONAL EMAILS

Work emails are more formal than personal emails. They are similar to formal letters.

It's important to **make a good impression** when sending emails at work. Here are some tips for writing professional emails.

Tip	Reason
Write a clear subject in the subject line. Keep the message short, and stay on the topic.	People at work are busy. They don't have a lot of time to read emails.
Don't use ALL CAPITAL LETTERS.	According to email rules or **etiquette**, this is like shouting.
Edit your email. Make sure you correct spelling and punctuation mistakes. Always read your email one more time before you hit the "Send" button.	This is important for making a good impression. You want your readers to think that you are a careful worker.
Don't say anything that you cannot say to everyone in the company.	Work email isn't private! It belongs to the company. Anyone can see it.

❶ Practice the Skill

Read the email. Then work with a partner and answer the questions on page 141.

FROM: RLee@spd.com
SUBJECT: Request for Medical Leave
DATE: October 12, 2012
TO: SJones@spd.com

Dear Ms. Jones:

I am emailing you to request a one-week medical leave from November 1 to November 5.

I need to take a one-week medical leave to have minor surgery on my foot. The surgery is scheduled for November 1, and I am not supposed to walk for about five days afterwards.

The doctor has told me that if I stay home and do not walk for that week, it will be okay for me to return to work by November 8.

Please let me know if you have any questions, and if my medical leave is approved.

Thank yu.

Ron Lee

Questions

1. What is in the subject line of this email?

_____

2. What is the topic of the email? Does it match the subject line?

_____

3. What is the writer asking for? Is it clear?

_____

4. Where does the writer explain the reason for his request?

_____

5. Has the writer made any mistakes?

_____

❷ Plan Your Writing

Choose one of the types of leave on pages 132–133. Think of the amount of time that you would need to take off from work and a brief explanation for your request. Complete the outline.

Type of leave: _____

Time you need to take off: _____

_____

Explanation: _____

_____

_____

_____

_____

_____

❸ Write

Now write an email to Ms. Jones (SJones@spd.com). Ask for time off from work. Use your ideas from Activity 2.

❶ Listening Review  077

Part 1

First you will hear a question. Next, listen carefully to what is said. You will hear the question again. Then choose the correct answer: *A, B,* or *C.* Use the Answer Sheet.

Part 2 🎧 078

Listen to what is said. When you hear the question *Which is correct?*, listen and choose the correct answer: *A, B,* or *C.* Use the Answer Sheet.

Answer Sheet

1 Ⓐ Ⓑ Ⓒ
2 Ⓐ Ⓑ Ⓒ
3 Ⓐ Ⓑ Ⓒ
4 Ⓐ Ⓑ Ⓒ
5 Ⓐ Ⓑ Ⓒ
6 Ⓐ Ⓑ Ⓒ
7 Ⓐ Ⓑ Ⓒ
8 Ⓐ Ⓑ Ⓒ
9 Ⓐ Ⓑ Ⓒ
10 Ⓐ Ⓑ Ⓒ

❷ Grammar Review

Circle the correct answer: *A, B,* or *C.*

1. Rick fixed the computer by _____.

A. itself
B. herself
C. himself

2. The pilots _____ are responsible for many aspects of flight safety.

A. herself
B. yourselves
C. themselves

3. Joe: Please help _____ to another cup of coffee.
Ann: Thank you.

A. myself
B. yourself
C. itself

4. These aren't our bags. They must be _____.

A. their
B. they
C. theirs

5. I've got my ticket, but where's _____?

A. mine
B. your
C. yours

6. Bob asked for time off _____ a medical emergency.

A. because he has
B. because having
C. since has

❷ Grammar Review (continued)

7. Sam just started work here. He _____ very long.

A. 's been
B. hasn't been working
C. wasn't working

8. I have been _____ for over an hour.

A. wait
B. waited
C. waiting

9. Wei _____ been working here since 2010.

A. have
B. has
C. having

10. Who have you been _____?

A. talking to
B. talk to
C. talking

LEARNING LOG

I know these words:

NOUNS AND NOUN PHRASES

- ○ air traffic controller
- ○ aircraft maintenance technician
- ○ airport security screener
- ○ baggage handler
- ○ bereavement leave
- ○ boarding passes
- ○ childcare emergency leave
- ○ conveyor belt
- ○ etiquette
- ○ fuel truck
- ○ gate agent
- ○ ground service equipment mechanic

- ○ headset
- ○ income taxes
- ○ jury duty
- ○ leave (of absence)
- ○ maternity leave
- ○ medical leave
- ○ metal detector
- ○ military leave
- ○ paternity leave
- ○ refund
- ○ team player
- ○ teamwork
- ○ ticket agent

- ○ ticket reader
- ○ tow tractor
- ○ vacation
- ○ wages
- ○ X-ray scanner

ADJECTIVE

- ○ withheld

VERBS

- ○ refer to
- ○ take time off
- ○ withhold

OTHER

- ○ make a good impression

I practiced these skills, strategies and grammar points:

- ○ identifying jobs and equipment
- ○ understanding different types of leave from work
- ○ asking for time off from work
- ○ leaving, taking, and asking for phone messages

- ○ understanding W-2 forms
- ○ listening for specific information
- ○ understanding pronoun reference
- ○ writing professional emails
- ○ explaining reasons for taking leave from work
- ○ using possessive and reflexive pronouns

- ○ using *because* and *since* for reasons
- ○ using the present perfect continuous

Work-Out CD-ROM

Unit 10: Plug in and practice!

UNIT 1 SETTING GOALS

Simple Present - Statements

We use the **simple present** to talk about facts and routines.

Statements			Negative Statements		
I You	**cook**		I You	**do not** **don't**	
He She	**cooks**	dinner on Saturdays.	He She	**does not** **doesn't**	**cook** dinner on Saturdays.
We You They	**cook**		We You They	**do not** **don't**	

1 **Complete the paragraph about the Taylor family. Use the simple present.**

The Taylors _____have_____ (have) a lot of responsibilities. Amy usually _____ (buy) food on
　　　　　(1)　　　　　　　　　　　　　　　　　　　　　　　　　　　　　　(2)

Wednesdays, but she _____ (cook / not) dinner. Michael always _____ (cook)
　　　　　　　　　　　　(3)　　　　　　　　　　　　　　　　　　　　　(4)

dinner on Wednesdays and Amy sometimes _____ (help) him. Nick usually
　　　　　　　　　　　　　　　　　　　　　　　(5)

_____ (finish) his homework before dinner. Michael and Nick always _____
　　(6)　　　　　　　　　　　　　　　　　　　　　　　　　　　　　　　　　　　　(7)

(clean) the kitchen after dinner. They _____ (eat / not) dinner together on Wednesdays,
　　　　　　　　　　　　　　　　　　　　　(8)

because Ron _____ (attend) a class on Wednesday evenings. Amy _____
　　　　　　(9)　　　　　　　　　　　　　　　　　　　　　　　　　　　　　　　　(10)

(go / not) to school in the evenings. She _____ (stay) home with the children. Once a
　　　　　　　　　　　　　　　　　　　(11)

month, Amy and Ron _____ (go) to a PTA meeting.
　　　　　　　　　(12)

2 **Look at the Walters family's chore list. Write sentences about what they do and don't do on
Saturday. Use contractions.**

CHORES • SATURDAY, MARCH 18

wash the dishes - Mark　　　　buy food - Al

put the dishes away - Annie　　cook dinner - Jane

sweep the kitchen floor - Sam　wash the car - Annie and Al

1. Mark washes the dishes on Saturday. He doesn't wash the car.

2. _____

3. _____

4. _____

5. _____

6. _____

Simple Present - Questions

Yes / No Questions				Short Answers	
Do	you			Yes, I **do**.	No, I **don't**.
Does	she	**work** on weekends?		Yes, she **does**.	No, she **doesn't**.
Do	they			Yes, they **do**.	No, they **don't**.

Wh- Questions				Answers	
What	**do**	you	**do** on Saturday mornings?	I clean the house.	
When	**does**	she	**pay** bills?	She pays bills on weekends.	
Where	**do**	they	**work?**	They work at a hotel.	

❸ Talk with a partner. Look at Oscar's schedule. Ask and answer questions in the simple present.

	Monday	Tuesday	Wednesday	Thursday	Friday
MORNING	ESL class at Greenville Adult School	work at the BigBuy store	ESL class at Greenville Adult School	work at the BigBuy store	ESL class at Greenville Adult School
AFTERNOON	do homework at the library	clean the house and go grocery shopping	do homework at the library	clean the house and go grocery shopping	do homework at the library

Examples: *A: Does Oscar work on Monday mornings? B: No, he doesn't.*
            A: What does Oscar do on Monday mornings? B: He goes to ESL classes.

❹ On a separate piece of paper, make a schedule like Oscar's. Work with a partner. Ask and answer questions about your schedules.

Want, Need, and Would like pages 6–7

Want, Need, and Would like

Want, need, and *would like* are sometimes followed by an infinitive (*to* + verb)
Would like means the same as *want,* but it is more polite.

I You	want need	to start a company. to learn English.	I You He She We You They	would like 'd like	to start a company. to learn English.
He She	wants needs				
We You They	want need				

① Write sentences about people's long- and short-term goals. Use *want* or *would like* and *need*.

	Long-Term Goal	Short-Term Goal
Ray:	get better grades	study
Jack and Annie:	buy a house	save money
Jennifer:	improve math skills	get a tutor
Mark:	go to college	see an academic counselor
The Smiths:	pay off debts	reduce expenses
Sam:	start a business	take continuing education classes

1. Ray wants to get better grades. He needs to study.

2. _____

3. _____

4. _____

5. _____

6. _____

② Make a list of things you would like to do someday. Then tell your partner what you would like to do and what you need to do first.

Example: *I would like to go to college. First, I need to see an academic counselor.*

Will - Statements and Questions

We use ***will* + verb** to talk about scheduled events in the future.

Statements				Negative Statements		
I You He She We They	**will** **'ll**	**get** a high school diploma.	I You He She We They	**will not** **won't**	**get** a high school diploma.
Questions				Short Answers		
Will	you he they	**take** the GED?	Yes,	I he they	**will.**	No,	I he they	**won't.**

① **Read Raul's five-year plan. Then complete the paragraph. Use contractions.**

This year:	take the GED
Next year:	get a part-time job; don't get a loan; start community college
In two years:	get a good job
Three years from now:	save money; don't buy a car and don't travel
Four years from now:	get married and buy a house

This year, Raul _____will take_____ the GED. Next year, he _____ a part-time
⟨1⟩   ⟨2⟩
job, and he _____ community college. He _____ a loan. After college,
⟨3⟩   ⟨4⟩
he _____ a good job, and he _____ money. He _____
⟨5⟩   ⟨6⟩   ⟨7⟩
a car, and he _____ . In 4 years, he _____ married, and
⟨8⟩   ⟨9⟩
he _____ a house.
⟨10⟩

② **Talk with a partner. Ask and answer questions about Raul's plan. Use the information in Activity 1. If the answer is "No," give the correct information.**

Examples: *A: Will Raul take the GED this year? B: Yes, he will.*
A: Will Raul get married this year? B: No, he won't. He'll get married four years from now.

③ **Make a five-year plan like Raul's. Talk with a partner. Ask and answer questions about your plans.**

Simple Past - Statements

We use the **simple past** to talk about actions that happened before now.

Statements			Negative Statements		
I You He She We You They	**moved** **came***	to the U.S. last year. to the U.S. last year.	I You He She We You They	**did not** **didn't**	**move** to the U.S. last year. **come** to the U.S. last year.

*Note: For a list of irregular verbs, go to page 231.

1 **Complete the sentences. Use the simple past of the underlined verbs. Some answers will be negative.**

1. Sandy usually <u>meets </u>her tutor on Wednesday, but last week she _____<u>met</u>_____ her tutor on Thursday.

2. Maria usually <u>visits</u> Mexico every summer, but she _____ Mexico last summer because she wanted to save money.

3. George usually <u>goes</u> to the library on Tuesdays, but he _____ to the library on Monday last week.

4. I usually <u>eat</u> at restaurants on the weekends, but I _____ at a restaurant last weekend because I need to reduce my expenses.

5. The Taylors usually <u>make</u> dinner at 6:00 P.M., but last night, they _____ dinner at 7:00 P.M.

6. We usually <u>do</u> our homework before dinner, but last night we _____ our homework after dinner.

7. Maggie usually <u>arrives</u> on time, but yesterday she _____ late.

8. Jack usually <u>buys</u> a new jacket every year, but he _____ a new jacket last year because he needs to save money.

9. My father usually <u>goes</u> grocery shopping on Saturday, but last week he _____ shopping on Friday.

10. Ling usually <u>takes</u> a vacation in the summer, but last year she _____ any time off from work at all.

Simple Past - Questions

	Yes / No **Questions**			**Short Answers**				
Did	you he she we they	**come** here last year?	Yes,	I he she we they	**did.**	No,	I he she we they	**didn't.**

	Wh- **Questions**			**Answers**
What		you	**do** last night?	I **studied** for the citizenship test.
When	**did**	she	**come** to the U.S.?	She **came** to the U.S. last month.
Where		he	**learn** English?	He **learned** English in Turkey.
Who		they	**live** with?	They **lived** with their family.

2 Read the list of events in Asad's life. Write *yes/no* and *Wh-* questions about his life. Then ask and answer the questions with a partner.

2005	Came to the United States. Arrived in New York. Didn't like the weather!
2006	Moved to San Diego. Lived with my brother. Loved the weather!
2007	Started school. Took ESL classes.
2008	Got a job at the airport!
2009-2011	Saved a lot of money. Studied for the citizenship exam.
2012	Became a U.S. citizen!

1. When did Asad come to the United States?   He came to the United States in 2005.

2. _____

3. _____

4. _____

5. _____

6. _____

3 Talk with a partner. Ask and answer the questions.

1. When did you come here? _____

2. Did you come alone or with your family? _____

3. Where did you live first? Did you like it?_____

Quantifiers

We use **some, any, many, a few, several, a little,** and **much** with nouns to talk about amounts.

		Affirmative	Negative	Question
Count Nouns		There are **some flowers** in the garden.	There aren't **any flowers** in the garden.	Are there **some flowers** in the garden? Are there **any flowers**?
		There are **many trees** in the yard.	There aren't **many trees** in the yard.	Are there **many trees** in the yard?
		There are **several trees** in the yard.		
		There are **a few** trees in the yard.		
Noncount Nouns		There is **some food** in the refrigerator.	There isn't **any food** in the refrigerator.	Is there **any food** in the refrigerator?
		There is **a little food** in the refrigerator.	There isn't **much food** in the refrigerator.	Is there **much food** in the refrigerator?

1 **Read the conversation about a house. Circle the correct quantifier.**

A: Garden State Realty. Can I help you?

B: Yes. Hi. Do you have **some** / **any** houses for rent?
(1)

A: Yes, we have **a little** / **several** houses for rent in Greenville.
(2)

B: I want a house with a yard. Are there **any** / **much** houses with yards?
(3)

A: Yes. The house on State Street has a yard. It has **any** / **some** grass and **a few** / **a little** plants.
(4) (5)

B: Are there **any** / **much** trees?
(6)

A: No, there aren't **any** / **some** trees, but there are **a little** / **a few** big bushes.
(7) (8)

B: That's okay. How **many** / **much** rooms are there in the house?
(9)

A: There are three bedrooms, and there's also **some** / **a few** space in the back for an office.
(10)

B: Great. My wife and I would like to see it.

2 **Read the facts about the house. Then complete the sentences. Use the words in the box.**

2-Bedroom House for Sale • 234 Oak Street

Good light, 10 windows. Yard with 3 trees; no flowers, small area covered in grass. Needs work: cracks in walls; holes in roof.

_____

cracks	flowers	grass	holes	~~bedrooms~~	space	trees	windows

1. There aren't many _____bedrooms_____.

2. There are a few _____ in the yard.

3. There aren't any _____ in the yard.

4. There are some _____ in the roof.

5. There are a lot of _____.

6. There are many _____ in the walls.

7. There isn't much _____ in the yard.

8. There's some _____ in the yard.

3 **Complete the paragraph with the words in the box. You will use some words more than once. More than one answer may be correct.**

a few	any	much	some	several

I found a nice little house to rent today. The house has _____some_____ problems, but there

(1)

are _____ things that I like about it. It has _____ rooms and _____

(2) **(3)** **(4)**

space in the garden for plants. There are _____ trees and _____ tomato plants.

(5) **(6)**

There aren't _____ flowers or bushes, but I'm going to plant _____ flowers as soon

(7) **(8)**

as I move in. One problem is that there isn't _____ room to park my car.

(9)

4 **Talk with a partner. Ask and answer questions about your house or apartment. Use *some, any, much, many, a little,* and *a few*.**

Example: *A: Are there many rooms in your apartment? B: No, there aren't.*
         A: Is there any space in the yard? B: Yes, there is.

Gerunds after Prepositions pages 20–21

Gerunds after Prepositions

We often use a **gerund** (verb-*ing*) after a **verb + preposition**.

EXAMPLES

I **plan on buying** a house.

She **is thinking about buying** a house.

Common **verb + preposition** combinations:

plan on   think about   dream about   talk about

We also use a **gerund** after **be + adjective + preposition**.

EXAMPLES

I **am interested in renting** an apartment.

They **are excited about renting** an apartment.

Common **be + adjective + preposition** combinations:

be interested in   be excited about   be used to

be concerned about   be worried about   be afraid of

---

1 **Complete the sentences with the gerund form of the verb in parentheses.**

1. Rachel is thinking about _____putting_____ (put) her piano in the corner.

2. Jennifer dreams about _____ (get) new furniture.

3. Luis is concerned about _____ (fix) the cracks in the ceiling.

4. Ana is used to _____ (live) in an apartment.

5. Rob is excited about _____ (have) a nice kitchen.

6. Nino and Sue are talking about _____ (find) a bigger place.

7. Lara is worried about _____ (pay) the rent.

8. Mark plans on_____ (move) into the apartment on June 1st.

2 **Ask and answer these questions with a partner.**

What is something that you are

{
worried about doing?
excited about doing?
concerned about doing?
interested in doing?
thinking about doing?
planning on doing?
used to doing?
}

Example: *A: What is something that you are interested in doing?*
         B: I'm interested in going to college.

Simple Present vs. Present Continuous		
	Notes	**Examples**
Simple Present	→ for facts	He **lives** in Chicago. I **don't have** a brother.
	→ for routines	They **work** from 9:00 to 5:00 every day. **Do** you **exercise** in the morning?
Present Continuous	→ for actions that are happening right now	I'm **washing** the dishes. Ella **isn't working** now. We're **having** fun at this party!
	→ for actions that are happening in this time period, but not right at this moment.	She **is working** at a restaurant this summer. He's **taking** an ESL class this year. **Are** you **studying** Spanish this semester?

Note: Not all verbs take the present continuous. Verbs that do *not* usually take the present continuous include: *want, have, be, like, need, understand*.

1 Complete the paragraph. Use the simple present or the present continuous.

<u>I'm not going</u> (go / not) to work today because I _____ (move) into a new
　　　①　　　　　　　　　　　　　　　　　　　　　　　　②

apartment. René _____ (help) me move into the apartment. René _____ (be)
　　　　　　　　③　　　　　　　　　　　　　　　　　　　　　　　　　　④

my friend. He _____ (have) a van. We _____ (put) all my furniture in
　　　　　　⑤　　　　　　　　　　　　　　⑥

René's van, and I _____ (take) my clothes in my car. We _____ (make) only
　　　　　　　　⑦　　　　　　　　　　　　　　　　　　　　　　⑧

one trip. I really _____ (like) the apartment. It _____ (have) two bedrooms and a
　　　　　　　⑨　　　　　　　　　　　　　　　　⑩

nice kitchen.

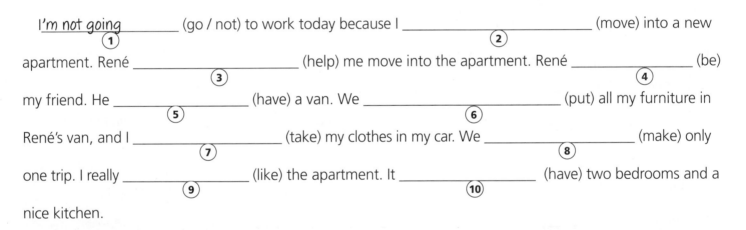

Present Continuous for Future

We sometimes use the **present continuous** for actions that will happen in the future. In these sentences, we often use a future time word or expression like *tomorrow* or *next year*.

The landlord **is coming** at 5:00 P.M. today.
We're **taking** a vacation next summer.
I'm **leaving** tomorrow.

2 **Read the email. Circle the correct verbs.**

To: rlopez@mymail.net
From: lyee@mymail.net

Hi Rafael,

I **have /** (**'m having**) a bad day today! I usually **work / am working** from 8 to 5, but today I **work / 'm working** from
8 to 3. I **go / 'm going** home early this afternoon because the landlord **comes / is coming**. She **fixes / 's fixing** my
refrigerator. Usually, the refrigerator **works / is working** fine, but today, it **doesn't work / 's not working** at all. We
have / are having an important meeting at work every Thursday at 4 P.M., but today, I **miss / 'm missing** it because
of my refrigerator!

Talk to you soon,

Lara

3 **Complete the conversation with the simple present or the present continuous. Use contractions.**

A: Hi, Carly. How _____are_____ (be) you?
    ①

B: I _____ (be) fine. What _____ (be) new?
         ②   ③

A: Not much. What _____ (you / do) right now?
                          ④

B: I _____ (clean) the apartment. My parents _____ (come) over today.
         ⑤   ⑥

A: When _____ (they / come) over?
              ⑦

B: They _____ (come) at 6:00 P.M.
              ⑧

A: Where _____ (they / live)?
               ⑨

B: They _____ (live) in Sacramento.
              ⑩

A: What _____ (you / make) for dinner?
              ⑪

B: My stove _____ (work / not), so I _____ (be / not) sure.
                  ⑫   ⑬

A: Hey, I _____ (have) an idea!
               ⑭

B: What?

A: I _____ (make) lasagna right now! _____ (you / want) me to bring it over?
        ⑮   ⑯

B: That's a great idea! Thanks so much.

Present Perfect - Statements

We use the **present perfect** to talk about an action that happened in a time period that isn't completed yet.

I **have exercised** today. (Today isn't finished.)

She **has been** sick twice this month. (This month isn't completed.)

Statements				Negative Statements			
	Have/has	Past participle			*Have/has*	Past participle	
I You	have	exercised	today.	I You	haven't	exercised	today.
He She	has	had	a check-up this year.	He She	hasn't	had	a check-up this year.
We They	have	been	sick twice this month.	We They	haven't	been	sick this month.

Note: For a list of irregular past participles, see page 231.

1 Look at Asha's schedule. It's 6:30 P.M. Complete the sentences about what Asha has and has not done today. Use the verbs in parentheses.

> **Monday, March 2**
>
> 7 A.M: Run in the park – use sunblock! (✓) done
>
> 9 A.M: Go to work. Lots of work! No smoking! (✓) done
>
> 7 P.M: Attend PTA meeting. No smoking! (✓) done
>
> 9 P.M: Watch TV and relax. No smoking!

1. Asha ___has exercised___ today. (exercise)

2. She _____ sunblock today. (put on)

3. She _____ to work today. (go)

4. She _____ today. (smoke)

5. She _____ a PTA meeting today. (attend)

6. She _____ TV today. (watch)

7. She _____ today. (relax)

Present Perfect - *Yes/No* Questions

Questions				Short Answers						
Have	you	exercised today?	Yes,	I we	**have.**	No,	I we	**haven't.**
Has	he she			he she	**has.**		he she	**hasn't.**
Have	we they			we they	**have.**		we they	**haven't.**

2 **Look at Sam's schedule. Complete the questions and answers.**

Wednesday July 8

6 AM: Go to gym   (✔) done

8 AM: Meet Sally for breakfast   (✔) done

9 AM: Go to work   (✔) done

3 PM: Go to doctor   (✔) done

6 PM: Go shopping

8 PM: Have dinner with Peter

1. ____Has____ Sam ____worked out____ (work out) today? ____Yes, he has.____

2. _____ Sam and Sally _____ (meet) today? _____

3. _____ Sam _____ (have) breakfast today? _____

4. _____ Sam _____ (go) to the store? _____

5. _____ Sam _____ (see) the doctor? _____

6. _____ Sam and Peter _____ (eat) dinner? _____

Present Perfect with *Ever, Never, Yet,* and *Already*

Notes		Examples
ever = at any time	for questions	A: Have you **ever** smoked? B: No, I haven't.
never = at no time	makes a statement negative	A: Do you smoke? B: No, I've **never** smoked.
yet = until now	for questions and negative statements	A: Have you seen the new movie **yet**? B: No, I haven't seen it **yet**.
already = before now	for affirmative statements	A: Would you like to have lunch with us? B: Thanks, but I've **already** eaten.

3 Circle the correct word in each sentence.

1. Mark has **ever** / (**never**) eaten fast food. He is very healthy.

2. We haven't taken a vacation **already** / **yet**, but we are planning to soon.

3. I don't want to go to that movie. I have **ever** / **already** seen it.

4. The pool hasn't opened **already** / **yet**. It opens next month.

4 Complete the sentences with the present perfect. Use the verbs in parentheses.

1. Marta _____has_____ already _____taken_____ (take) her vitamins.

2. Alex _____ (be / not) sick yet this year.

3. They _____ (go / not) for a check-up yet this year.

4. You _____ already _____ (eat) too much junk food today.

5 Complete the questions and answers about Luisa's medical chart.

Name: _____Luisa Rodriguez_____ Date of Birth: _____2/11//89_____ Today's Date: _____5/6/2010_____

Have you ever had the following?					
	Yes	No		Yes	No
surgery		✓	asthma		✓
infection	✓		allergies	✓	
Have you seen the following healthcare providers this year?					
dentist				✓	
dermatologist					✓

1. _____Has_____ Luisa ever _____had_____ surgery? _____No_____, she _____hasn't_____.

2. _____ Luisa ever _____ an infection? _____, she _____.

3. _____ Luisa ever _____ asthma? _____, she _____.

4. _____ Luisa _____ a dentist this year? _____, she _____.

Simple Past vs. Present Perfect   pages 34–35

Simple Past vs. Present Perfect	
Simple Past	**Present Perfect**
We use the **simple past to** talk about:	We use the **present perfect** to talk about:
1) an action that ended in the past.	1) an action that started in the past and continues now.
I **had** a toothache <u>last Tuesday</u>. (I don't have the toothache now.)	I'**ve had** a toothache <u>since last Tuesday</u>. (The toothache started last Tuesday. I still have the toothache.)
They **lived** here <u>for three years</u>. (They don't live here now.)	They'**ve lived** here <u>for three years</u>. (They started living here three years ago. They still live here.)
2) an action that happened at a specific time in the past.	2) an action that happened at a non-specific time in the past.
I **went** to the dentist <u>last week</u>. (We know when I went to the dentist.)	I'**ve been** to the dentist <u>many times</u>. (We don't know the specific times that I went to the dentist.)

① Complete the paragraph about Sara and Sam. Use the simple past or the present perfect.

Sara is an amazingly healthy person. She _____<u>has never been</u>_____ (be / never) in the hospital, and
1

she _____ (have / never) surgery. She hardly ever takes a sick day. Last year she
2

only _____ (miss) two days of work, but not because she was sick. She _____
3   4

(stay) home to take care of Sam because he _____ (be) sick. Sam is just the opposite of Sara.
5

He _____ (have) surgery twice this year, and last year he _____ (spend) a week in the
6   7

hospital. It's not that Sam is unhealthy. It's just that he is a little careless. He _____ (break)
8

his right arm twice this year. Two years ago he _____ (break) his right leg when
9

he _____ (fall) off his motorcycle.
10

② On a separate piece of paper, complete the paragraph with your own ideas. Use the simple past and the present perfect.

> Two years ago, Chen was a full-time student and had a security job at night. He never had time to exercise or get enough sleep. He always felt tired and he was sick a lot. Last year, he decided to make a change. He started exercising three times a week and he cut back his hours at work. Since then, he has not been sick at all. He _____

❸ Read Mike's plans for 2012. Then complete the paragraph with the verbs in parentheses. Use the simple past or the present perfect.

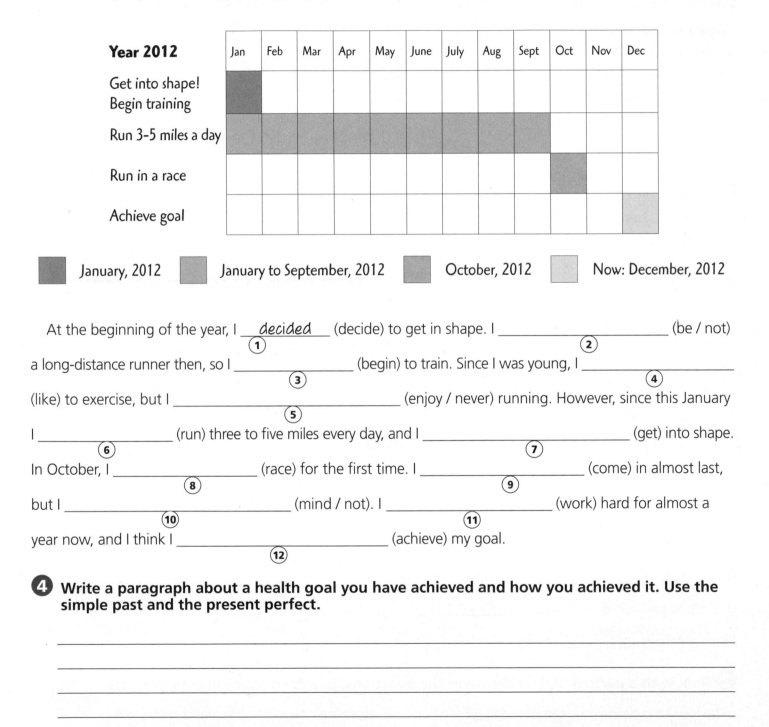

Year 2012	Jan	Feb	Mar	Apr	May	June	July	Aug	Sept	Oct	Nov	Dec
Get into shape! Begin training	■											
Run 3–5 miles a day	■	■	■	■	■	■	■	■	■			
Run in a race										■		
Achieve goal												■

■ January, 2012   ■ January to September, 2012   ■ October, 2012   ■ Now: December, 2012

At the beginning of the year, I __*decided*__ (decide) to get in shape. I _____ (be / not)
    (1)   (2)
a long-distance runner then, so I _____ (begin) to train. Since I was young, I _____
                                  (3)   (4)
(like) to exercise, but I _____ (enjoy / never) running. However, since this January
                                      (5)
I _____ (run) three to five miles every day, and I _____ (get) into shape.
   (6)   (7)
In October, I _____ (race) for the first time. I _____ (come) in almost last,
              (8)   (9)
but I _____ (mind / not). I _____ (work) hard for almost a
                  (10)   (11)
year now, and I think I _____ (achieve) my goal.
                                    (12)

❹ Write a paragraph about a health goal you have achieved and how you achieved it. Use the simple past and the present perfect.

_____

_____

_____

_____

_____

_____

Present Perfect with *For* and *Since*

We use the **present perfect** to talk about an action that started in the past and is still happening now.

We ask questions with **how long** and we answer with **for** or **since**.
- *For* tells the length of time of an action.
- *Since* tells when an action started.

I've **had** an earache for two days.

Wednesday
My earache started.

Friday (today)
I still have the earache.

Question	Answer with *for*	Answer with *since*
How long have you **had** an earache?	I've **had** an earache **for** two days.	I've **had** an earache **since** Wednesday.
	For two days.	**Since** Wednesday.

---

1 **Read the situation and complete the conversation. Use the verbs in parentheses and *for* or *since*.**

Right now, it's Monday morning, May 12. Rita has a fever. It started on Saturday night, May 10. She also has a sore throat. It started on Friday, May 9. Rita is at the doctor's office. She arrived at 9:00 A.M. and sat in the waiting room for a long time. She finally got to see the doctor at 9:45 A.M.

Doctor: Sorry I'm late. How long _____*have*_____ you _____*been*_____ (be) here?
                                                                                    ①

Rita: Oh, I _____ (be) here _____ about 45 minutes.
                                ②   ③

Doctor: So, it looks like you have a fever. How long _____ you _____ (have) it?
                                                                                            ④

Rita: _____ about two days.
              ⑤

Doctor: _____ yesterday? How long _____ your throat _____ (be) sore?
                ⑥   ⑦

Rita: Oh, _____ about three days.
                  ⑧

Doctor: So you've had a sore throat _____ Saturday as well?
                                              ⑨

Rita: No, _____ Friday.
                ⑩

2 **Talk with a partner. Ask and answer the questions. Use *for* or *since* in your answers.**

1. How long have you been here today?
2. How long have you lived here?
3. How long have you been at this school?
4. How long have you studied English?

Used to pages 42–43

Used to	
We use ***used to*** + verb to talk about something that was true in the past but is not true now.	
Statements	**Negative Statements**
I **used to eat** a lot of junk food. (Now, I don't.)	I **didn't use to have** a healthy diet. (Now, I do.)
She **used to drive** to work. (Now, she doesn't.)	She **didn't use to ride** her bike to work. (Now, she does.)
Questions	**Answers**
Did you **use to walk** to school?	Yes, I **did.**	No, I **didn't.**
Where did you **use to exercise?**	I **used to exercise** at the gym.

Note: In negative statements and questions, *use to* is spelled without the *d*.

1 Look at the information about Pat's health habits. Then complete the sentences.

Before	**Now**
eat a lot of junk food	have a healthy diet
drink a lot of soda	drink water all the time
not exercise	go to the gym three times a week
not go to the doctor	have a check-up once a year
be overweight	have a healthy weight
ride a motorcycle without a helmet	wear a helmet

1. Pat <u>used to eat a lot of junk food</u>, but now she <u>has a healthy diet</u>.
2. Pat _____, but now she _____.
3. Pat _____, but now she _____.
4. Pat _____, but now she _____.
5. Pat _____, but now she _____.
6. Pat _____, but now she _____.

2 Talk with a partner. Ask and answer questions about Pat.

Examples: *A: Did Pat use to ride a motorcycle without a helmet? B: Yes, she did.*

3 Talk with a partner. Talk about things that you used to do or didn't use to do.

Examples: *A: I used to smoke, but now I don't.*
B: I didn't use to exercise very much, but now I exercise every day.

UNIT 4 MONEY AND CONSUMERISM

LESSON 1 Gerunds as Subjects pages 46–47

Gerunds as Subjects

We sometimes use a **gerund** (verb-*ing*) as the subject of a sentence. A gerund subject always takes a singular verb.

EXAMPLES:

Shopping **is** fun.

  SUBJECT   VERB

Not paying your bills **is** a bad idea.
Paying with a credit card **saves** time.

---

1 Complete the sentences with the gerund form of a verb in the box and the correct form of the verb in parentheses. You can use the verbs in the box more than once.

buy	get	pay	use	save

1. <u>Buying</u> things on sale ___<u>saves</u>___ (save) you money.

2. _____ with a debit card _____ (help) you keep track of your bank balance.

3. _____ cash often _____ (save) time in the checkout line.

4. _____ a credit card _____ (be) a big responsibility.

5. Not _____ off debts _____ (be) a mistake if you want to buy a house.

6. _____ a pre-owned car _____ (make) sense if you don't have a lot of money.

7. Not _____ into debt _____ (be) sometimes difficult.

8. _____ online banking _____ (be) a good way to save time.

9. _____ money _____ (take) self-control.

10. _____ out of debt _____ (feel) good.

2 Talk with a partner about these money matters or your own ideas. Say whether you think the action is a good or a bad idea. Give a reason for your opinion.

- paying with a credit card
- buying something on sale
- using online banking
- paying off your debts
- memorizing your PIN
- opening a savings account
- using an ATM
- paying a service charge

Example: *Paying a service charge for your bank account is a bad idea because there are many banks that do not have service charges.*

Gerunds as Objects of Verbs pages 48–49

Gerunds as Objects of Verbs

Some verbs are followed by a **gerund** (verb-*ing*) object.

EXAMPLES:

I avoid   **using** a credit card.
    VERB   OBJECT

                She **dislikes paying** with cash.

                He **keeps spending** money.

We use gerunds after these verbs:

admit	appreciate	avoid	consider	discuss	dislike	enjoy	finish
keep	mind	miss	permit	postpone	practice	quit	suggest

❶ Read the paragraph. Circle the gerunds. Underline the verb that comes before each gerund.

My coffeemaker <u>keeps</u> (breaking). I'm considering returning it to the store. I don't enjoy taking things back to the store. There's always a big line at the returns counter, and I really dislike waiting in line. However, I do appreciate saving money. Probably the store will suggest replacing it, but I'm considering asking for a refund. I usually postpone returning things, but I'm going to do it right now!

❷ Complete the conversation with the gerund form of the verb in parentheses.

Reporter: Today, we're asking why people shop here at BigBuy. Excuse me sir. Why do you shop here?

Ivan: Actually, I dislike ___*shopping*___ (shop). I come here because I enjoy _____ (watch) people.
                         ①   ②

Reporter: I see. Miss, why do you shop here?

Sue: I enjoy _____ (get) things on sale. And I don't mind _____ (wait) in line.
                  ③   ④

Reporter: Thank you. And you, ma'am, why do you shop here?

Sylvia: I don't enjoy _____ (be) here at all. In fact, I avoid _____ (shop) here.
                     ⑤   ⑥

Reporter: Then why are you here?

Sylvia: I'm with my husband. He enjoys _____ (buy) things here because he appreciates
                                               ⑦

_____ (get) a good deal.
     ⑧

Reporter: Thanks. Ah, here's an employee. Excuse me, sir. Why do you work here at BigBuy?

Bing: Oh, I really enjoy _____ (help) people. It's a great place to work, too. I'm going to keep
                              ⑨

_____ (work) here for a long time!
     ⑩

3 Complete the sentences. Use the correct form of the words in parentheses. Use the simple present or past.

1. (enjoy / shop) Oscar _____*enjoys shopping*_____ with his wife.

2. (dislike / pay) Luisa _____ by credit.

3. (suggest / pay) The clerk _____ by cash.

4. (not / enjoy / wait) Ana _____ in line.

5. (avoid / shop) Mia _____ with her children.

6. (quit / work) Jennifer _____ at the department store.

7. (keep / get) Lara and her husband _____ new credit card applications.

4 Write answers to the questions. Then ask a partner the questions.

1. What do you enjoy doing on weekends?

_____

2. What do you dislike about shopping?

_____

3. What do you avoid doing?

_____

4. What is something you would like to quit doing?

_____

5. What do you enjoy doing with your friends or family?

_____

6. What is something that you are considering doing soon?

_____

7. What is something that you don't mind doing?

_____

8. What is something that you miss doing?

_____

9. What do you appreciate having?

_____

10. What do you sometimes postpone doing?

_____

Comparative and Superlative Adjectives;
as Adjective as pages 50–51

Comparative and Superlative Adjectives

We use **comparative adjectives** to compare **two** things.

EXAMPLE: My new car is **safer** than my old car.

We use **superlative adjectives** to compare **three or more** things.

EXAMPLE: The KMC is **the safest** car on the lot.

Adjective		Comparative	Superlative
One-syllable	fast	fast**er** (than)	**the** fast**est**
Two-syllable	modern	**more** modern (than)	**the most** modern
Ending in a single vowel and a consonant	big	big**ger** (than)	the big**gest**
Two-syllable ending in -*y*	happy	happ**ier** (than)	**the** happ**iest**
Irregular	good	**better** (than)	**the best**
	bad	**worse** (than)	**the worst**
	far	**farther** (than)	**the farthest**

1 Write the comparative and superlative forms of the adjectives below.

	Comparative Form	Superlative Form
1. affordable	more affordable	the most affordable
2. economical		
3. expensive		
4. hot		
5. important		
6. large		
7. reasonable		
8. uncomfortable		
9. heavy		
10. good		

2 Complete the article with the comparative form of the adjective in parentheses.

Two New Computers: The DataBook versus the ZBook

	DataBook	ZBook
Price	$2,000	$3,500
Weight	4.5 pounds	5 pounds
Speed	2 GHz	3 GHz

In a survey, we asked 100 people: Which laptop computer is ____better____ (good), the DataBook or the
①

ZBook? Most people prefer the DataBook. Here's why:

Most people liked the DataBook because it's _____ (cheap). With a price of
②

$3,500, the ZBook is definitely _____ (expensive). At 2 GHz, the DataBook
③

is actually _____ (slow), but because the price is _____ (low), this isn't a
④ ⑤

problem for most people. People also like the DataBook because it's _____ (light). The ZBook is
⑥

only half a pound _____ (heavy), but most people could tell the difference. Because of the price,
⑦

most people agree that the DataBook is _____ (good) than the ZBook.
⑧

3 Complete the sentences with the comparative or superlative form of the adjective in
parentheses. Use the information below.

	DataBook	ZBook	S-250
Price	$2,000	$3,500	$1,500
Weight	4.5 pounds	5 pounds	5.5 pounds
Speed	2 GHz	3 GHz	1.5 GHz

1. The S-250 is _____ (cheap) of the three computers.

2. The DataBook is _____ (light) of the three computers.

3. The ZBook is _____ (light) than the S-250.

4. The S-250 is _____ (slow) of the three.

5. The DataBook is _____ (good) buy of the three computers.

as Adjective as

Notes	Examples
We use **as adjective as** to say that two things are equal.	My new car is **as economical as** my old car.
We use **not as adjective as** to say that two things are not equal.	A sedan is **not as expensive as** a van. (The sedan is less expensive.)

4 **Rewrite each sentence. Make sentences with *as* adjective *as* or *not as* adjective *as*.**

1. Both the new car and the old car are attractive.

_____*The new car is as attractive as the old car.*_____

2. The new car is more comfortable than the old car.

_____

3. The Mini Sedan is smaller than the Sport Van.

_____

4. The Sport Van is more expensive than the Mini Sedan.

_____

5. Both the Mini Sedan and the Sport Van are economical.

_____

6. Both the old laptop and the new laptop are light.

_____

7. Both the red sweater and the blue sweater are warm.

_____

8. The red sweater is nicer than the blue sweater.

_____

5 **Tell a partner about something you purchased recently. Explain why you bought it by comparing it to other things. Use comparative and superlative adjectives and *as* adjective *as*.**

Examples: • *I bought a DataBook laptop because it's cheaper than a ZBook laptop.*
• *I bought the red wool sweater because it was the warmest.*
• *My new MP3 player is not as good as my old one.*

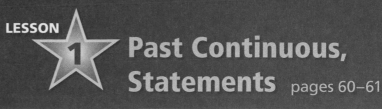

UNIT 5 ACCIDENTS AND EMERGENCIES

LESSON 1 Past Continuous, Statements pages 60–61

Past Continuous - Statements

We use the **past continuous** to talk about an action in progress at a specific time in the past.

Statements					Negative Statements			
I He She	was	working sleeping	at 9:00 last night.		I He She	wasn't	working sleeping	at 9:00 last night.
We You They	were				We You They	weren't		

1 Complete the sentences. Use the past continuous form of the verb in parentheses.

1. Juan _____was wearing_____ (wear) a helmet at work yesterday.

2. We _____ (drive) at 10:00 A.M. this morning.

3. I _____ (talk) to Jim before dinner last night.

4. The worker _____ (wear / not) safety glasses.

5. I _____ (take) a nap at 3:00 yesterday afternoon.

6. He _____ (use / not) ear plugs yesterday.

7. The machine _____ (make) a lot of noise yesterday afternoon.

8. The repairman _____ (fix) the washing machine at 8:00 A.M. this morning.

2 Look at the chart. Then complete the sentences. Use the past continuous.

	Carlos	Marta and Lou
7:00 A.M.	shop	drive to work
10:00 A.M.	do laundry	work
2:00 P.M.	pick up son	eat lunch

1. At 7:00 A.M., Carlos _____.

2. Marta and Lou _____ at 7:00 A.M.

3. At 2:00 P.M., Carlos _____.

4. Marta and Lou _____ at 10:00 A.M.

5. At 2:00 P.M., Marta _____.

Past Continuous with Time Clauses

When and *While* introduce time clauses.

While + **past continuous** shows an action in progress.

EXAMPLES:

The fire started **while** he **was cooking**.
                    ACTION IN PROGRESS

She **was listening to** music **while** she **was driving**.
     ACTION IN PROGRESS   ACTION IN PROGRESS

When + **simple past** introduces an action that interrupts an action in progress.

EXAMPLE:

We were standing in the kitchen **when** the fire **started**.
     ACTION IN PROGRESS   INTERRUPTING ACTION

The time clause can come *before* or *after* the main clause. When it comes first, we use a comma after it.

EXAMPLES:

When the fire started, we were cooking.
While she was driving, she was listening to music.

---

1 **Complete the sentences with the past continuous form of the verb in parentheses. Then underline the time clause.**

1. I _____was standing_____ (stand) on the scaffolding <u>when I saw the crash</u>.

2. The accident happened while we _____ (eat) lunch.

3. I _____ (talk) to Ali when the boss called us into his office.

4. The boss _____ (inspect) the equipment when Carl fell from the scaffolding.

5. While the men _____ (carry) the beam, one of them tripped.

6. The driver hit the pole while he _____ (talk) on his cell phone.

7. While the workers _____ (take) a break, the supervisors checked the equipment.

8. The lights went out while Trang _____ (study).

2 **Complete the sentences with information about you. Use the past continuous.**

1. When the sun came up this morning, I _____.

2. This morning while I was having breakfast, _____.

3. At 10 P.M. last night, I _____.

4. When the teacher came in to class today, I _____.

5. While the teacher was taking attendance, _____

_____.

3 Complete the paragraph with the simple past or the past continuous form of the verb in parentheses.

Hard Luck Harry's vacation _____ *didn't go* _____ (go / not) very well. On his vacation,
(1)

he _____ (have) a lot of problems. He _____ (injure)
(2)   (3)

his back while he _____ (carry) his suitcase. He _____
(4)   (5)

(get) heat exhaustion while he _____ (hike). He _____
(6)   (7)

(fall) while he _____ (walk) along the beach. He _____
(8)   (9)

(get) a bad shock while he _____ (dry) his hair with the hotel hairdryer.
(10)

There _____ (be) a big explosion in the hotel kitchen, and he _____
(11)   (12)

(have) to evacuate the hotel! Poor Hard Luck Harry _____ (spend) several weeks in the
(13)

hospital when he _____ (get) home.
(14)

Past Continuous- Questions

Yes / No Questions			Short Answers	
Were	you		Yes, I **was**.	No, I **wasn't**.
Was	she	**working** last weekend?	Yes, she **was**.	No, she **wasn't**.
Were	they		Yes, they **were**.	No, they **weren't**.

Wh- Questions				Answers
What	**were**	you	**doing** at 3:00 PM?	I **was working** at the site.
Who	**was**	she	**working** with?	She **was working** with John.
Where	**were**	they	**working?**	They **were working** at the shop.

4 Complete the questions about an accident in a kitchen.

1. What _____ *were* _____ you _____ *doing* _____ (do) in the kitchen last night?

2. What _____ you _____ (cook)?

3. What _____ you _____ (wear)?

4. Who _____ you _____ (talk) to when the accident happened?

5. _____ you _____ (pay) attention while you were cooking?

6. _____ you _____ (wear) your gloves?

LESSON

3

Simple Past vs. Past Continuous pages 64–65

Simple Past vs. Past Continuous		
	Notes	**Examples**
Simple Past	→ for an action that began and ended in the past	She **fell off** the ladder yesterday. We **finished** work at 5:00 PM.
Past Continuous	→ for an action that was in progress at a specific time in the past	We **were fixing** the roof at 8:00 AM yesterday. Last year at this time, I **was not working**. I was **going** to school.
	→ for an action that began earlier and was in progress when another action happened	She **was climbing** the ladder when she fell. While we **were fixing** the roof, it started to rain.

1 Circle the correct form of the verb to complete each conversation. Practice with a partner.

1. A: What **happened** / **was happening** to your hand?

   B: I **broke** / **was breaking** my wrist.

   A: Really? How did you do that?

   B: I **slipped** / **was slipping** while I **climbed** / **was climbing** up a ladder at home.

   A: You're lucky you didn't get hurt worse.

2. A: What's wrong with Tom?

   B: He **hurt** / **was hurting** his back.

   A: How did he do that?

   B: He **pulled** / **was pulling** a muscle while he **moved** / **was moving** some boxes.

   A: That's too bad.

3. A: Did you know that Adam **got** / **was getting** something in his eye?

   B: No, I didn't. How did he do that?

   A: He **cut** / **was cutting** some wood, but he **didn't wear** / **wasn't wearing** safety glasses.

   B: That's too bad!

4. A: What did you do to your hand?

   B: Oh, I **burned** / **was burning** it.

   A: How did you burn it?

   B: Well, I **cooked** / **was cooking** and some grease **caught** / **was catching** on fire.

5. A: Randy **had** / **was having** an accident at the construction site yesterday.

   B: Really? What **did he do** / **was he doing**?

   A: He **climbed** / **was climbing** up the scaffolding when he **tripped** / **was tripping**.

   B: How far **did he fall** / **was he falling**?

   A: About 20 feet. He **was** / **was being** lucky he **didn't hurt** / **wasn't hurting** himself more.

TARGET GRAMMAR: UNIT 5 **171**

Real Conditionals pages 66–67

Real Conditionals

Real conditional sentences tell what will happen if something else happens. They show a **cause** and **result**.

EXAMPLE:
If it **rains** this weekend, we **won't go** to the beach.

    CAUSE   RESULT

If clause = *If* + simple present	Result clause = *will / be going to /* modal + verb
If I **decide** to stay home,	I**'ll call** my supervisor.
If he **has** time,	he **might take** a first aid class.
If you **work** on scaffolding,	you **should wear** a safety harness.
If you **need** help,	you **can call** me anytime.
If we **don't finish** the work today,	we**'re going to come** back tomorrow.

Note: The *if* clause can come first or second. When it comes second, do not use a comma.

Example: I'll call my supervisor if I decide to stay home.

1 **Match the *if* clause with the result clause.**

If clause

1. __f__ If Alice wants to protect her hands,

2. _____ If John needs to protect his ears,

3. _____ If Lucy wants to protect her eyes,

4. _____ If you work on scaffolding,

5. _____ If there are sharp objects on the ground,

6. _____ If Rob wants to protect his face,

7. _____ If Rafael wants to protect his head,

8. _____ If I want to be safe on the job,

9. _____ If Sam isn't careful,

10. _____ If Lucy doesn't follow safety rules,

Result clause

a. he'll get a hard hat.

b. I'll follow all the safety rules!

c. you must wear a safety harness.

d. he should wear a face mask.

e. she should get some safety glasses.

f. she'll wear gloves.

g. you should wear boots.

h. he'll wear ear plugs.

i. she is going to get fired.

j. he might have an accident.

2 **Complete each sentence. Use *should* or *must*. Use the cues in parentheses.**

1. If you get something in your eyes, (you / cover them / with gauze)

   _____*you should cover them with gauze.*_____

2. If this isn't a serious emergency, (you / not call / 911)

   _____

3. If someone is bleeding, (you / apply direct pressure / on the wound)

   _____

4. If Mario has a minor burn on his hand, (you / submerge it / in water)

   _____

5. If Sun-mi has a sharp object in her eye, (you / not try / to remove it)

   _____

6. If you are helping someone who is bleeding, (you / put on gloves / first)

   _____

3 **Answer the questions. Use real conditionals in your answers. Then, ask a partner the questions.**

1. What should you do if someone at work has a serious accident?

   _____

   _____

2. What can you do if you want a safer workplace?

   _____

   _____

3. What should you do if you see a dangerous situation at work?

   _____

   _____

4. What can you do if you want to become healthier?

   _____

   _____

5. What should you do if you see a crime?

   _____

   _____

Verbs Followed by Infinitives

Some verbs are followed by an **infinitive** (to + verb) object.

	Verb	**Infinitive**
Dog owners	**need**	**to keep** their dogs on a leash.
We	**agreed**	**to pick up** the litter in the park.

We use infinitives after these verbs:

agree	decide	expect	learn	need	plan	refuse
promise	refuse	try	volunteer	want	would like	remember

1 **Read the paragraph. Circle the infinitives. Underline the verb that comes before each infinitive.**

This year, I plan to make my community a better place. We need to clean up our city park, so I've decided to start a cleanup organization. So far, five people have volunteered to help, but I would like to get at least 20 volunteers. We plan to meet once a month at the park with trash bags. I have volunteered to buy gloves for everyone. The mayor promised to come to our first meeting, and he agreed to make a little speech. We expect to have a lot of fun and to do good work at the same time!

2 **Complete the conversation with the infinitive of the verb in parentheses.**

Grant: All right. We've all agreed _____to discuss_____ (discuss) ways to improve our apartment complex.
①
Who wants _____ (volunteer) for the first problem?
②

Bill: I do. I would like _____ (clean) the graffiti off the walls.
③

Grant: Thanks, Bill. Jesse, what do you want _____ (do)?
④

Jesse: I volunteer _____ (start) a recycling program.
⑤

Grant: Great. What about the pet problem? Who's going to try _____ (fix) that?
⑥

Lise: I'd like _____ (put) up signs around the courtyard. People might agree
⑦
_____ (keep) their pets on a leash with just a little reminder like that.
⑧

Grant: This all sounds great! Okay, everybody! Now we need _____ (get) to work!
⑨

3 Complete the sentences with the correct form of the words in parentheses. Then complete the form for yourself.

Clean Up the Beach Day!

When: *Sunday, June 25, 9 A.M.*

Where: *Greenville Beach*

> *Join your friends and neighbors for a good time and a cleaner beach!!*
> *There's a job for everyone! Sign up today!!*

Complete the form below and return it to the community center office.

- -

Name: _____

Address: _____

Phone number: _____ Email: _____

❏ I <u>volunteer to join</u> (volunteer / join) a clean-up crew.

❏ I _____ (want / organize) a clean-up crew.

❏ I _____ (volunteer / buy) trash bags.

❏ I _____ (plan / come) to the information meeting on June 25.

❏ I can't come to Clean Up the Beach Day, but I _____ (agree / give) $ 20 for expenses.

❏ I _____ (promise / bring) food for five people.

❏ I _____ (need / get) a ride to the beach on June 25.

❏ I _____ (agree / provide) a ride for three people.

❏ I _____ (would like / have) more information.

---

4 Talk with a partner. Ask and answer the questions.

1. How do you plan to help your community this year?_____

2. What will you volunteer to do this year?_____

3. What is something that you promise to do this year?_____

4. What is something that you need to do tomorrow?_____

Be allowed, Be permitted, and Be illegal pages 76–77

Be allowed, Be permitted, and Be illegal

We use an **infinitive** (*to* + verb) after *be allowed*, *be permitted*, and *be illegal*.

EXAMPLES:

I	am (not)	allowed	to watch TV	after 9:00.
Children	are (not)		to ride	bikes without helmets.
You	are not	permitted	to fish	unless you have a license.
It	is	legal	to park	here.
		illegal	to talk	on a cell phone while you are driving.

1 Write sentences about the park. Use (*not*) *be allowed* or (*not*) *be permitted* and an infinitive.

Welcome to Blue Lake State Park

Please . . .

- No alcohol
- No motor vehicles off paved roads
- Swim only in the lake
- No loud music

- Barbecue in cooking area
- No camping
- Fish with a license
- Don't leave garbage behind

Blue Lake State Park

1. <u>You aren't permitted to drink alcohol here.</u>

2. _____

3. _____

4. _____

5. _____

6. _____

7. _____

8. _____

2 **Complete the conversation. Use the infinitive form of the verb in parentheses.**

Teacher: Okay, class, today we're going to review some California driving laws. What about texting?

Marcus: It's illegal _____to text_____ (text) while driving.
①

Teacher: Right. What about cell phones? Is it legal _____ (use) a cell phone while driving?
②

James: It's illegal _____ (use) handheld cell phones while driving.
③

Teacher: Right. What's the seatbelt law?

Jenny: It's illegal _____ (drive) without your seatbelt on.
④

Teacher: What are some other rules of the road?

Ali: It's illegal _____ (drive) through a crosswalk if someone is in it.
⑤

Teacher: Right. Can you make a right turn if the light is red?

Rob: Yes. It's legal _____ (make) a right turn on a red light if you stop first.
⑥

Teacher: Good. Can you drive in a bicycle lane?

Danny: No, it's illegal _____ (drive) in a bicycle lane.
⑦

Eva: What if you just cross a bicycle lane to park your car?

Teacher: It's actually legal _____ (cross) a bicycle lane if you are parking or turning a corner.
⑧

3 **Complete the sentences. Then talk about your answers with a partner.**

1. In our class, we are not permitted _____

2. In my community, it is illegal _____

3. In the U.S., it is illegal _____

4. I think it should be legal _____

5. We should be permitted _____

6. When I was a teenager, I was not allowed _____

7. I think teenagers should be allowed _____

8. Your idea: _____

Verbs Followed by Object + Infinitive pages 78–79

Verbs followed by Object + Infinitive

Some verbs take a noun or pronoun **object** before the **infinitive**.

	Verb	Object	Infinitive
The officer	**told**	**the man**	**to slow** down.
I	**advise**	**you**	**to watch** your speed.
They	**warned**	**us**	**not to be** late.

Verbs that take an object before the infinitive include:

advise   ask   expect   need   order   pay   require   tell   want   warn

❶ Complete the conversation. Use the infinitive form of the verb in parentheses.

Officer Lee: Hey, Jane, I heard about the teenagers in the park today.

Officer Ruiz: Yes. I had to ask them _____not to loiter_____ (loiter / not). I had to order them

_____ (leave) the park.
②

Officer Lee: What else happened?

Officer Ruiz: Oh, yeah. I had to tell a man _____ (stop) fishing. I advised him
③

_____ (get) a license right way.
④

Officer Lee: Weren't some people drinking alcohol?

Officer Ruiz: Yes, I told them _____ (drink / not) in the park. I also told
⑤

them _____ (turn down) the music.
⑥

Officer Lee: Didn't someone sneak in without paying today?

Officer Ruiz: Yes. I ordered her _____ (pay) the fee.
⑦

Officer Lee: Sounds like you had a crazy day!

Officer Ruiz: And it's not over yet! I have to go home and tell my kids _____ (do) their
⑧

homework and clean up their rooms!

2 Complete the sentences about class rules. Use the correct form of the words in parentheses.

1. The teacher _____requires us to turn_____ (require / us / turn) homework in on time.

2. The teacher _____ (want / us / be) on time.

3. The teacher _____ (expect / us / not miss) more than three classes.

4. If we are absent, the teacher _____ (expect / us / call) a classmate.

5. The teacher _____ (tell / us / turn) off our cell phones in class.

6. The teacher _____ (warn / us / not copy) other people's work.

7. The teacher _____ (require / us / raise) our hand before we speak.

8. When other students are speaking, the teacher _____ (want / us / listen) politely.

3 Talk with a partner. Ask and answer the questions.

1. Think about when you were growing up:

a) What chores did your parents expect you to do?

_____

b) What did your parents warn you not to do?

_____

c) What did your parents advise you to do?

_____

2. Think about a job you've had:

a) What tasks did your boss expect you to do?

_____

b) What did your employer pay you to do?

_____

3. Think about school: What does your school require you to do?_____

_____

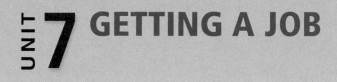

UNIT 7 GETTING A JOB

LESSON 1 — Verbs Followed by Gerund or Infinitive pages 88–89

Verbs Followed by Gerund or Infinitive: Same Meaning

A **gerund** *or* **infinitive** can follow some verbs and have the same meaning.

EXAMPLES:

I <u>love</u> **to be** outdoors all day. = I <u>love</u> **being** outdoors all day.
　　INFINITIVE　　　　　　　　　　　　GERUND

He <u>likes</u> **to work** with people. = He <u>likes</u> **working** with people.
　　INFINITIVE　　　　　　　　　　　GERUND

Gerunds and infinitives have the same meaning after these verbs:

begin	continue	hate	like	love	prefer	start

1 **Complete the conversation with the infinitive or the gerund form of the verb in parentheses. In some cases either a gerund or infinitive is possible.**

A: What kind of job would you like to have?

B: I'd like ____to be____ (be) a landscaper.
　　　　　　　①

A: I guess you don't like _____ (work) indoors.
　　　　　　　　　　　　　②

B: Right. I prefer _____ (be) outdoors all day. And I love _____ (work) around plants.
　　　　　　　　③　　　　　　　　　　　　　　　　　　　④

　I started _____ (work) with plants when I was a child.
　　　　　⑤

A: Don't you like _____ (be) with other people?
　　　　　　　　⑥

B: No. I prefer _____ (be) alone. How about you?
　　　　　　　⑦

A: I wouldn't like _____ (work) outdoors all day. I like _____ (help) people. I'd like
　　　　　　　⑧　　　　　　　　　　　　　　　　　⑨

　_____ (be) a nurse.
　　⑩

2 **Complete the sentences with information about you. Use an infinitive or a gerund.**

1. I love _____

2. I hate _____

3. I like _____

4. I prefer _____

Verbs Followed by Gerund or Infinitive: Different Meaning

Some **verbs** can be followed by a **gerund** or **infinitive**, but the meaning is different.

Verb	Example	Meaning
remember	She remembered **to buy** some flowers.	She remembered to do something, and then she did it.
	She remembered **buying** flowers.	She did something, and then she remembered it.
stop	On his way to work, he stopped **to buy** some flowers.	He interrupted what he was doing and did something else.
	He stopped **buying** flowers because it was too expensive.	He stopped a habit.
try	I tried **to walk** to work today, but it took too long.	I attempted to do something, but I was not successful.
	I tried **snowboarding** last week.	I experimented with something new.

3 Complete the sentences with a gerund or an infinitive. In some cases, either a gerund or an infinitive is possible.

It's a new year, so I have made some New Year's resolutions. This year, I am going to stop _____*eating*_____ (1)

(eat) sweets. I tried _____ (stop) last year, but I couldn't. I remember _____ (stop) (2)   (3)

for only a day. I'm going to try _____ (exercise) every day, too. I remember (4)

_____ (join) a gym last year, but I didn't really like it. This time, I'm going to try (5)

_____ (walk) every day. I'm also going to remember _____ (be) a (6)   (7)

better employee. I stopped _____ (concentrate) last year, but this year, I'm going to (8)

try _____ (do) my best. (9)

4 Write answers to these questions. Then ask and answer the questions with a partner.

1. What did you remember to do today? _____

2. What do you remember doing when you were a child? _____

_____

3. What have you stopped doing? _____

4. What did you try doing last year? _____

Prefer, Would prefer, and *Would rather* for Preferences pages 90–91

Prefer, Would prefer, and *Would rather*

We use **prefer** or **would prefer** before a noun, an infinitive, or a gerund to express preference. **Would prefer** is more polite than **prefer**. We often use the short form: **'d prefer**.

EXAMPLES:
I **prefer** the Network Plan. [+ noun]
I **would prefer** to have the Network Plan. [+ infinitive]
I**'d prefer** having the Network Plan. [+ gerund]

We also use **would rather (not)** + **verb** to express preference. We often use the short form: **'d rather.**

EXAMPLES:
I **would rather have** the Network Plan.
I**'d rather get** the Network Plan.
He**'d rather not choose** a plan now.

---

1 Read the choices. Express your preference. Use *prefer, 'd prefer, would rather,* or *'d rather (not)* and the correct form of the verb in parentheses, if there is one.

1. a fast computer / an inexpensive computer (buy) _____ *I'd rather buy an inexpensive computer.* _____

2. a full-time job / a part-time job _____

3. a trip to New York City / a trip to Mexico City (take) _____

4. a high salary / good benefits (have) _____

5. nurse / physician assistant (be) _____

6. a high deductible / a high co-pay _____

7. indoors / outdoors (work) _____

8. with machines / with people (work) _____

2 Read the information about the health plans. Complete the sentences. Use *prefer, 'd prefer,* or *'d rather (not)* and the verb in parentheses, if there is one.

	Health Plan A	Health Plan B
age of children	covers children to age 19	covers children to age 21
co-pay	$15 a visit	$20 a visit
deductible	$100	$0
premium	$25	$30
out-of-pocket cost	$1,000	$1,250
preventive care	$15	$0

1. Nabil: I _____prefer Plan A_____ because the co-pay is only $15 a visit.

2. Lin: (have / not) _____I'd rather not have Plan A_____ because the deductible is too high.

3. Nabil: (take) _____ because my children are young.

4. Lin: _____ because the deductible is $0.

5. Nabil: (get / not) _____ because the out-of-pocket is too high.

6. Lin: _____ because it covers children up to age 21.

7. Nabil: _____ because the premium is only $25.

8. Lin: (sign up for / not) _____ because there's a $15 charge for preventive care.

3 Complete the sentences about you. Use *prefer, 'd prefer,* or *'d rather (not)*.

1. I _____ (be) _____.

2. I _____ (have) _____.

3. I _____ (not go) _____.

4. I _____ (work) _____.

5. I _____ (buy) _____.

6. I _____ (not have) _____.

7. I _____ (live) _____.

8. I _____ (not be) _____.

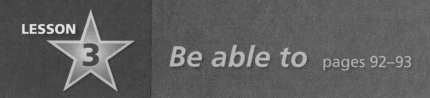
Be able to	
Be able to + **verb** has the same meaning as *can*, but it is more formal.	
Present Statements	**Negative Statements**
I **am able to lift** 50 pounds. She**'s able to drive.** They**'re able to come.**	I**'m not able to lift** 50 pounds. She**'s not able to drive.** They**'re not able to come.**
Future Statements	**Negative Statements**
I**'ll be able to come** at 10:00 A.M. He**'ll be able to help** you.	I **won't be able to come** at 10:00 A.M. He **won't be able to help** you.
Questions	**Answers**
Are you **able to lift** 50 pounds?	Yes, I **am.**　　　No, I **am not.**
Will he **be able to help** us?	Yes, he **will.**　　　No, he **won't.**

1 **Complete the conversation with the correct form of the verb in parentheses. Use present or future forms of *be able to*.**

Mr. Lee: Thank you for coming in. I have a few questions. Mrs. Gomez weighs about 130 pounds.

_____Are you able to lift_____ (lift) a 130-pound patient?
　　　　　　　　 (1)

Sara: Yes, I am, but _____ Mrs. Gomez _____ (walk) at all?
　　　　　　　　　　　　　　　　　　　　　　　　　 (2)

Mr. Lee: Yes, she _____ (walk) a little. Now, _____ you _____
　　　　　　　　　　　 (3)　　　　　　　　　　　　　　　　　　　　　　　　　 **(4)**

(speak) Spanish?

Sara: Yes, I am. _____ Mrs. Gomez _____ (communicate) in English?
　　　　　　　　　　　　　　　　　　　　　　　　　 (5)

Mr. Lee: Yes, but she's only _____ (speak) a little. _____ you
　　　　　　　　　　　　　　　　　 (6)

_____ (drive)?
　　　　 (7)

Sara: Yes, I am.

Mr. Lee: If you get this job, _____ (you) _____ (work) 40 hours a week?
　　　　　　　　　　　　　　　　　　　　　　　　　　　 (8)

Sara: Yes, I _____.
　　　　　　　　 (9)

Mr. Lee: _____ you _____ (come) on weekends?
　　　　　　　　　　　　　　　　　　　　　 (10)

Sara: No, I _____. I'm sorry.
　　　　　 (11)

2 Ana is going to school so she can get a better job. When she finishes, she will have more skills. Complete the sentences about her abilities when she finishes school next year. Use the words in parentheses.

Class Schedule • Fall Semester	Class Schedule • Spring Semester
Spanish 110: Intermediate Conversation	Spanish 210: Advanced Conversation
Business English 101: Writing Memos	Business English 212: Writing Reports
Computer Technology 100: Computer Repair	Management 211: Managing Projects

1. Ana <u>will be able to speak Spanish.</u> _____ (speak Spanish)

2. Ana _____ (write memos)

3. Ana _____ (repair computers)

4. Ana _____ (manage projects)

5. Ana _____ (write Spanish)

6. Ana _____ (write reports)

7. Ana _____ (write computer programs)

3 Talk with a partner. Look at the list of abilities or use your own ideas. Ask and answer questions. Use *be able to*.

- lift patients onto beds
- transport patients
- use a computer
- repair a computer

- work on weekends
- work 40 hours a week
- speak Spanish
- drive a truck

Examples: *A: Are you able to speak Spanish? B: Yes, I am.*
A: Are you able to drive a truck? B: No, I'm not.

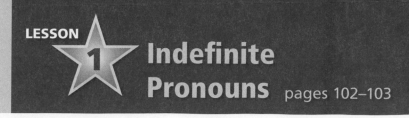
Indefinite Pronouns

An **indefinite pronoun** refers to one or more persons or things. The persons or things are not specific. Indefinite pronouns are always singular. We use a singular verb with them.

	someone somebody	**Somebody** called.
For people	anyone anybody	I didn't talk to **anyone**. Does **anybody** want coffee?
	no one nobody	**No one** called.
	everyone everybody	**Everyone** is here. Is **everyone** here?
For things	something	**Something** is missing.
	anything	There isn't **anything** in the refrigerator. Is there **anything** on TV?
	nothing	There is **nothing** in the refrigerator.
	everything	**Everything** was good. Was **everything** Okay?

① **A teacher is talking to her class. Complete the sentences with the correct form of the verb in parentheses.**

Well, it looks like everyone _____is_____ (be) here today. No one _____ (seem) to be absent. So
①   ②

let's get started. _____ anyone _____ (know) the answer to question number 1? Well, I see
③

someone in the back _____ (be) raising her hand. I'm glad that someone
④

_____ (know) the answer! _____ anyone else _____ (know) the answer? Great! I
⑤   ⑥

guess everyone _____ (have) done the homework for today. Uh-oh! I hear a cell phone.
⑦

_____ someone _____ (have) a cell phone on? Remember, no one _____ (be)
⑧   ⑨

allowed to use a cell phone in class. Please turn it off.

2 Complete the conversation. Use one of the indefinite pronouns in the box. You can use a pronoun more than once.

| anyone | anything | everyone | no one | nothing | someone | something |

Luisa: Did you do _____anything_____ this weekend?
(1)

Amy: Yes, I went to Sam's party.

Luisa: Did you meet _____ new?
(2)

Amy: No, I didn't meet _____ new, but I saw a lot of old friends.
(3)

Luisa: Was _____ from work there?
(4)

Amy: Yes, there was _____ from work there, but I can't remember her name.
(5)

Luisa: Did you have _____ interesting to eat?
(6)

Amy: No, _____ was very interesting. I did eat _____ that tasted very good,
(7)   (8)
though. Did you do _____ this weekend?
(9)

Luisa: I went over to my neighbor's house. I knocked on the door, but _____ answered.
(10)

Amy: Was there _____ on TV?
(11)

Luisa: No, there was _____ good on TV. I did see _____ at the Rialto Movie Theatre.
(12)   (13)

Amy: Oh, the new Clint Eastwood movie? Did you go with_____?
(14)

Luisa: No, _____ wanted to go. _____ has seen that movie already.
(15)   (16)

3 Write answers to the questions. Then ask and answer the questions with a partner.

1. Are you afraid of anything? If so, what are you afraid of?

_____

2. Does anything bother you? If so, what is it?

_____

3. Have you met anyone new recently? If so, who is it?

_____

LESSON 2

Will and *Would* for Requests pages 104–105

Will and Would for Requests	
We use **will** and **would** + verb to ask someone to do something. Both **will** and **would** are formal, but **would** is a little more polite than **will**. Adding *please* makes the request more polite.	
REQUESTS	ANSWERS
Will you **give** me a hand?	I'd be happy to.
Would you please **give** me some feedback?	Of course.
Would you **open** the door, please?	Sure.

1 **Complete the sentences with *will* or *would* and the correct form of the verb in parentheses.**

1. (please / move) <u>Would you please move</u> _____ your car?

2. (please / give) _____ me your opinion of this?

3. (take) _____ a look at this?

4. (please / move) _____ over a little?

5. (please / answer) _____ the phone for me?

2 **Make a request for each situation. Use *will* or *would*. Add *please* for politeness.**

1. You want someone to close the door.

    <u>Would you close the door, please?   /   Would you please close the door?</u>

2. You need some help with a project.

_____?

3. You need to look up a word.

_____?

4. It's cold in here with the window open.

_____?

5. You're thirsty.

_____?

6. You are looking for a post office and you are lost.

_____?

7. You don't get your paycheck until Friday and you don't have any money.

_____?

8. You are trying to study in the library and some people are talking.

_____?

9. Your friend is driving and you think he is going too fast.

_____?

188 **TARGET GRAMMAR: UNIT 8**

May and *Might* for Possibility; *Must* for Conclusion pages 106–107

May and *Might* for Possibility

We use **may** and **might** + **verb** to talk about present or future possibility.

EXAMPLES:
I **might go** to the movies. = It's possible I will go.
Bob **might be** at the library. = Maybe Bob is at the library.

Statements				Questions		Answers
I You He/She We They	**may** **might (not)**	come.	Will	you he	come?	I **may come.** He **might.**

1 **Read the situation. Then re-write each statement using *may (not)* or *might (not)*.**

Tariq and Sushila are paying bills. Tariq looks very upset, but Sushila doesn't seem worried at all. She goes online to see how much money they have in their savings account.

1. Maybe Tariq is worried.

  _____Tariq might be worried._____

2. It's possible that Tariq is worried about paying bills.

  _____

3. Perhaps Tariq and Sushila are married.

  _____

4. It's possible that they don't have very much money.

  _____

5. Perhaps Sushila has an idea.

  _____

6. Maybe they have some money that they forgot about.

  _____

7. It's possible that there's enough money in the account to pay all the bills.

  _____

2 **Talk with a partner. Ask and answer the questions. Use *may* or *might*.**

1. What is something you might do this weekend?

2. What are two things you may do next summer?

3. What are five things you might do some time in the future?

Must for Conclusion

We use *must* + verb when we are making a guess, and we are almost sure we our guess is right.

EXAMPLES:

Situation: Jane is frowning.

Conclusion: She **must be** unhappy.

Situation: Sara is not coming to the picnic.

Conclusion: She **must not feel** well.

❸ **Match the situation and the conclusion.**

___f___ **1.** Sue is waving to Raul.

_____ **2.** Yolanda is rubbing her chin.

_____ **3.** Raul is smiling.

_____ **4.** Sara is frowning.

_____ **5.** Ana is holding up both hands.

_____ **6.** Jane is pointing at herself.

_____ **7.** John and Maria are shaking hands.

_____ **8.** Rob is shaking his fist.

a. They must be saying *hello* or *goodbye*.

b. He must be angry.

c. She must be unhappy.

d. She must be saying, "Are you talking to me?"

e. She must be thinking about something.

f. She must be saying, "Hello, Raul!"

g. He must be happy.

h. She must be saying, "I don't know."

❹ **Write a conclusion for each situation.**

1. John won a million dollars in the lottery.

_____ *He must be excited.* _____

2. Van and Lee are absent today.

_____

3. Everyone is wearing a coat.

_____

4. Jack is coughing.

_____

5. Luisa is yawning.

_____

6. Ali is studying very hard tonight.

_____

7. Reggie can't go to the restaurant with his friends.

_____

Phrasal Verbs

There are many **phrasal verbs** (verbs with two or three words) in English. Phrasal verbs have a verb and a particle (for example: *on, in, up, for, to, out, at*). The particle changes the meaning of the verb.

Here are some phrasal verbs and their meanings.

Phrasal Verb	Meaning	Example
call on	ask someone to speak	The teacher **called on** me, but I didn't know the answer.
count on	expect someone to be supportive	Can I **count on** you to vote for me?
figure out	understand	She **figured out** the answer to the puzzle.
fill out	complete (a form)	Could you please **fill out** this form?
find out	discover	I **found out** that I passed the test.
get on	enter public transportation	He **got on** the train at 7:00 A.M.
get off	exit public transportation	I **got off** the bus near my house.
get up	stand, or rise from bed in the morning	Ellen **got up** very early this morning.
look forward to	anticipate with good feelings	We're **looking forward to** our vacation.
pass out	give to others; distribute	The teacher **passed out** the tests.
run into	meet unexpectedly	I **ran into** an old friend at the grocery store yesterday.
run for	campaign as a candidate for election	People born outside the U.S. cannot **run for** president.
show up	appear	Ryan **showed up** at the party two hours late.

1 **Rewrite the sentences. Replace the underlined words with a phrasal verb from the list above. Use the correct form.**

1. The vice president <u>stood</u> and spoke to the representatives.
   <u>The vice president got up and spoke to the representatives.</u>

2. The Speaker of the House <u>asked</u> the representative to answer the question.

3. The candidate <u>gave</u> flyers to the audience.

4. The problem was hard to <u>understand</u>.

5. Because of the storm, no one <u>appeared</u> at the rally.

6. Senator Smith is <u>expecting</u> us to vote for her in the next election.

_____

7. We are <u>anticipating</u> visiting Washington next summer.

_____

8. The senator from Texas is <u>campaigning for</u> president.

_____

9. We <u>unexpectedly met</u> the new senator at the supermarket.

_____

2 **Complete the paragraph with the correct words from the box.**

forward	on	out	up	to

I was in Washington D.C. last week, and I found _____out_____ that you can visit Congress in session.
                                                    (1)

I showed _____ at the House gallery, and I saw my representative get _____ and pass
              (2)   (3)

something _____ to the rest of the representatives. I figured _____ that it was a report
              (4)   (5)

of some kind. She called _____ the other representatives to read the report carefully. Then
                              (6)

she said that she was looking _____ _____ the vote. She said she hoped she
                                     (7)   (8)

could count _____ everyone to vote "Yes" on the bill.
                   (9)

3 **Answer the questions about you. Then ask and answer the questions with a partner.**

1. What are you looking forward to?

_____

2. Who do you count on? What do you count on this person for?

_____

3. Does anyone count on you? Who? What for?

_____

4. Who have you run into recently? Where did you run into him or her?

_____

5. What have you figured out recently?

_____

Must, Have to, and Have got to for Necessity and Prohibition pages 118–119

Must, Have to, and Have got to for Necessity

We use **must, have to,** and **have got to** + verb to talk about things that are necessary or required.

Statements			Negative Statements		
I We They	**have to** **have got to** **must**	**vote** on the bill today.	I You	**don't have to**	**work** today.
The court Congress	**has to** **has got to** **must**	**decide** on the law. **send** bills to the president.	He She	**doesn't have to**	**agree** with the bill.
			We They	**don't have to**	**work** today.

Notes:
- *Don't / doesn't have to* means that it is *not* necessary to do something.
- We don't use *have got to* in the negative.

Must not for Prohibition

We use **must not** + verb to talk about something that is prohibited or not allowed.

I You He / She We They	**must not** **mustn't**	**break** the laws of the Constitution. **smoke** in this building.

❶ Complete the sentences with the correct form of the words in parentheses.

According to the Constitution and the Bill of Rights:

1. There _____*must be*_____ (must / be) three branches of government.

2. The legislative branch _____ (have to / write) the laws for the country.

3. The executive branch _____ (have to / work) with the legislative branch to establish laws.

4. The judicial branch _____ (have got to / decide) if laws are constitutional.

5. The government _____ (must / not / let) soldiers stay in private citizens' homes.

6. The government _____ (must / not / search) a private citizen's home without a warrant.

7. A citizen _____ (not / have to / say) anything in a court of law that might make her look guilty.

8. The government _____ (must / not / take) private property and use it for public purposes without paying for it.

2 **Rewrite the rules. Complete the sentences with *must, must not, have to,* or *don't have to.* More than one answer may be possible.**

1. Don't cross here. You _____*must not*_____ cross here.

2. Clean up when you walk your dog. You _____ clean up when you walk your dog.

3. It's illegal to throw trash on the ground. People _____ throw trash on the ground.

4. Stop for pedestrians. You _____ stop for pedestrians.

5. Dogs can run free in this park. You _____ put your dog on a leash.

6. No smoking. You _____ smoke here.

7. You can't turn left here. You _____ go another way.

8. You can park here for free. You _____ pay to park here.

3 **Answer the questions. Use *must, must not, have/has to, don't/doesn't have to.* Then discuss your answers with a partner.**

1. What aren't you allowed to do in your home country?

_____

_____

2. What are you allowed and not allowed to do in the place where you live now?

_____

_____

3. What aren't you allowed to do in your school?

_____

_____

4. What aren't you allowed to do in your classroom?

_____

_____

5. What must you do this week?

_____

_____

6. What don't you have to do this week?

_____

_____

Should and *Why don't* for Advice   pages 122–123

Should for Advice

We use *should* + **verb** to ask for and give advice.

Questions					Statements	
What	should	I you he she we they	do?	I You He She We They	should shouldn't	register to vote.

1 **Complete the sentences with *should* or *shouldn't*.**

1. The election is next month. Raul _____should_____ register soon.

2. You _____ vote "Yes" on Proposition A. It will give more money to the schools.

3. Ana only speaks Spanish. She _____ call 555-VOTA for voter information in Spanish.

4. Wei is only 17, so he _____ register to vote until next year.

5. You _____ vote unless you understand the issues.

6. They _____ become citizens so they can vote.

7. If you don't have time to register at your county elections office, you _____ register online.

8. The mayor is doing a terrible job. We _____ reelect him.

9. Everyone says the new show is excellent. We _____ miss it.

Why don't for Suggestions

We use *Why don't* and *Why doesn't* to give suggestions or advice. It is less formal than *should*.

Suggestions				Answers
Why	don't	you we they	register online?	Good idea. Maybe I'll do that.
	doesn't	he she		He doesn't have a computer.

2 Complete the conversation with *Why don't you* or *Why don't we* and one of the verbs in the box.

take	go	~~make~~	watch	read

Ana: I'm bored.

Rick: _____ Why don't you make _____ some cookies?

Ana: It's too hot to bake.

Rick: _____ a book?

Ana: I don't have any good books.

Rick: _____ some TV?

Ana: I don't want to stay inside.

Rick: _____ a walk in the park?

Ana: Good idea. _____ together?

Rick: No thanks, I'm reading a good book.

3 Read the situations. Write advice using *should, why don't, or why doesn't.*

1. Pete doesn't like the government. He complains about everything, but he never votes.

   _____

   _____

2. Marta's town has a bad traffic problem, and she has to drive a lot. In the next election, she has the chance to vote on a proposition to build a new road in her town.

   _____

   _____

3. Alan's town has financial problems. There's never enough money for important services. Two people are running for mayor. One, Sue Green, is a successful businessperson. The other, Robert Smith, is a schoolteacher.

   _____

   _____

4. In the next election, people can vote on Proposition 2. Proposition 2 will raise taxes to pay for new schools. Ping doesn't have children and she doesn't want to pay more taxes.

   _____

   _____

5. Our senator spends all his time playing golf with rich businesspeople. He never votes in the Senate, and he doesn't listen to the people who elected him.

   _____

   _____

Possessive Pronouns

We use a **possessive pronoun** in place of a possessive adjective and noun.

Possessive Adjective	Possessive Pronouns
This is **my** ticket.	It's **mine**.
That's **your** boarding pass.	It's **yours**.
He's got **his** passport.*	He's got **his**.
Is that **her** baggage?	No, **hers** is blue.
This is not **our** car.	**Ours** is over there.
That's not **their** car.	**Theirs** is a sedan.

*He**'s got** his passport means the same as He **has** his passport.

1 **Circle the correct word.**

1. Here are **your** / **yours** boarding passes.

2. I can't find my headset. Can I borrow **your** / **yours**?

3. The agent gave me your boarding pass by mistake. Did she give you **my** / **mine**?

4. Jane's car is in the shop. We can't take **her** / **hers**. Let's take **my** / **mine**.

5. Is that **our** / **ours** suitcase or is it **their** / **theirs**?

6. I've got **my** / **mine** sunglasses. Did your bring **your** / **yours**?

2 **Complete the conversations with the correct possessive adjective or possessive pronoun.**

1. A: Excuse me, sir. Is that _____your_____ backpack?

   B: No, it's not _____ . Did you ask that woman over there? It might be _____.

   A: OK, I'll check.

2. A: Hold on, I can't find _____ boarding pass. Do you have it?

   B: Let me look. No, I have _____ boarding pass, but not _____.

3. A: Let's find _____ gate. Is that it?

   B: No, _____ is Gate 24. It's down there.

4. A: Is this Martha's sweater?

   B: No. _____ is the red one over there.

Reflexive Pronouns

We use a **reflexive pronoun** when the subject and object of the verb are the same.

EXAMPLES:

The machine turns **itself** off after an hour. = The machine turns the machine off.
Mary made **herself** lunch. = Mary made lunch for Mary.

We also use a **reflexive pronoun** to mean *alone* or *without help*. We often use *by* with the reflexive pronoun.

EXAMPLES:

Airplanes can't back up **by themselves**. = Airplanes need help to back up.
The agent checked in all of the passengers **by himself**. = The agent checked in the passengers alone. No one helped him.

Subject Pronoun	Reflexive Pronoun	Subject Pronoun	Reflexive Pronoun
I	myself	it	itself
you	yourself	we	ourselves
he	himself	you	yourselves
she	herself	they	themselves

3 **Complete the sentences with the correct reflexive pronoun.**

1. Captain Lucia Rodriguez flew the plane by _____herself_____.

2. The flight attendants did the safety checks by _____.

3. Ali ran the X-ray scanner by _____.

4. The children flew to Grandma's house by _____.

5. The plane can fly by _____ on auto pilot.

6. We fixed the computer _____.

7. The baggage handlers loaded the luggage _____.

8. The conveyor belt does not shut _____ off.

9. The air traffic controllers gave _____ a break.

10. I sent _____ an email to see if the Internet was working.

11. Did you finish the work _____?

12. Sally never travels by _____.

Because and *Since* for Reasons pages 132–133

> ## *Because* and *Since* for Reasons
>
> We use *because* and *since* to give **reasons**.
>
> EXAMPLES:
>
> I need to take some time off **because** <u>I'm going to a funeral</u>.
>   REASON
>
> Jack asked for three days off **since** <u>he has to fly to New York</u>.
>   REASON
>
> When the reason clause comes first, we use a comma after it.
>
> EXAMPLES:
>
> **Because** I'm going to a funeral, I need to take some time off.
> **Since** he has to fly to New York, Jack asked for three days off.

1 **Combine the two sentences. Use the words in parentheses. Use correct punctuation.**

1. She needs to take time off. She has a dentist appointment. (because)

   _____*Because she has a dentist appointment, she needs to take time off.*_____

2. He is going ask for some time off. He has jury duty. (since)

   _____

3. The boss needs to put it on the schedule. You have to ask for time off at least a month in advance. (because)

   _____

4. His wife is going to have a baby. He asked for a one-week paternity leave. (Since)

   _____

5. He went to the hospital. He fell at work. (because)

   _____

6. She wasn't allowed to take time off for a vacation. She asked too late. (because)

   _____

7. He couldn't take time off from work. He missed his grandmother's funeral. (because)

   _____

8. The babysitter quit. Mark is going to ask for emergency childcare leave. (since)

   _____

9. You shouldn't miss class next week. We're going to have a test. (since)

   _____

10. Salim asked for a day off. He wants to visits his sister. (because)

   _____

2 Look at the schedule. Match the event with the type of leave. Then with a partner, tell what kind of leave you need and why. Use *because* or *since* and the dates in the schedule.

June

3 Monday_____

_____ **a.** (wife) have a baby _____

4 Tuesday_____

_____ **b.** have jury duty _____

5 Wednesday_____

_____ **c.** need a break from work _____

6 Thursday_____

_____ **d.** need to have surgery _____

7 Friday_____

_____ **e.** go to a funeral _____

June

10 Monday_____

_____ **f.** no childcare _____

11 Tuesday_____

_____ **g.** attend a training program

12 Wednesday_____

_____ **h.** join the Army _____

13 Thursday_____

_____

14 Friday_____

_____

Types of Leave

___e___ **1.** bereavement leave

_____ **2.** childcare emergency leave

_____ **3.** jury duty leave

_____ **4.** a leave of absence

_____ **5.** maternity / paternity leave

_____ **6.** a medical leave

_____ **7.** military leave

_____ **8.** a vacation

Example: *I need to take bereavement leave on Friday June 7 because I'm going to a funeral.*

3 Answer the questions with a complete sentence. Then ask and answer the questions with a partner.

1. Why do people sometimes need to take time off from work?

_____

2. Why are people sometimes afraid to ask for time off from work?

_____

3. Why do students sometimes miss class?

_____

4. Why should you ask for time off in advance?

_____

Present Perfect Continuous   pages 134–135

Present Perfect Continuous

We use the **present perfect continuous** to talk about actions that started in the past and are still happening now.

Statements				Negative Statements			
I You	**have**	**been waiting**	since 6:00. for an hour. all day.	I You	**have not haven't**	**been waiting**	long.
He She	**has**			He She	**has not hasn't**		
We They	**have**			We They	**haven't**		

Yes/No Questions	Short Answers	*Wh*-Questions	Answers
Have you been waiting long?	Yes, I have. No, I haven't.	How long have you been waiting?	For an hour. Since 8:00 AM.
Has he been working all day?	Yes, he has. No, he hasn't.	How long has he been working?	Since this morning.

Contractions: I have been waiting = I'**ve** been waiting   We have been waiting = We'**ve** been waiting
He has been waiting = He'**s** been waiting   They have been waiting = They'**ve** been waiting

1 Complete the sentences with the present perfect continuous. Use the words in parentheses. Use contractions or full forms.

1. I _____ have been talking _____ to Jan for five hours! (talk)

2. Tony _____ since 6:00 this morning. (drive)

3. Mark and I _____ to work every day this week. (walk)

4. Aisha _____to take a leave of absence since last month. (plan)

5. Al and Ruby _____ at this company for very long. (work / not)

6. Sue _____ soccer this summer. (play / not)

7. Ali _____ at the theater since 7:00. (wait)

8. My cell phone _____ for the past few days. (work / not)

9. How long _____ they _____ in that house? (live)

10. Angela _____ for a promotion for a year. (wait)

2 Complete the phone conversation with the present perfect continuous. Use the words in parentheses. Use contractions or full forms.

Receptionist: Sorry! __Have__ you _been waiting_ (wait) to speak to Ms. Green?
　　　　　　　　　　　　　　　(1)

Dan: Yes! I _____ (wait) for 15 minutes!
　　　　　　　　　　　　(2)

Receptionist: I'm sorry, she _____ (work) in another building today.
　　　　　　　　　　　　　　　　　　　(3)

I _____ (try) to find her all morning! Would you like to leave a message?
　　(4)

Dan: Yes. Please tell her that we _____ (read) résumés all week.
　　　　　　　　　　　　　　　　　　(5)

We _____ (have) a hard time finding the right applicant for the job.
　　　(6)

I _____ (look) for someone who already works here, someone like Robert.
　(7)

He _____ (work) in IT here this summer.
　　(8)

Receptionist: Okay . . . you _____ (read) resumes all week . . . And
　　　　　　　　　　　　　　　(9)

who _____ I _____ (speak) to?
　　　　　　　　　　　　　　　(10)

Dan: This is Dan.

Receptionist: I'll give Ms. Green the message.

3 Look at the schedule. It's Friday afternoon. Talk with a partner. Ask and answer questions about the people.

Monday_____
_____Jan: start work on the_____
construction job_____
Tuesday_____
_____Nadya: visit customers_____
Wednesday_____
_____Dan: plan the leave schedule_____

Thursday_____
_____Wei: fix the computers_____
Friday_____
_____Lucia: 8:00 a.m. to 5:00 p.m.:_____
speak to job applicants_____

Examples: *A: Has Jan been working on the construction job this week? B: Yes, she has.*
A: How long has Jan been working on the construction job? B: She's been working on the construction job since Monday.

Note: This audio script offers support for many of the activities in the Student Book. When the words on the Student Book page are identical to those on the audio program, the script is not provided here.

UNIT ONE

Lesson 1, Activity 2: Listen and Match (page 4)
Listen to the conversations. Match the conversation to the responsibility. Listen again and check your answers.

Conversation 1:

Laura: Oh, great Ed, you had time to go to the supermarket today!

Ed: Sure. I got some good deals, too.

Conversation 2:

Ed: It looks like dinner's started.

Laura: Yeah, we're having spaghetti. It'll be done about 6:30.

Conversation 3:

Ed: Smells delicious! Hey, did you get to those bills today?

Laura: Not yet. I'm going to do them right now, hon.

Conversation 4:

Julio: Mom, how do you spell "reduce?"

Laura: What are you working on?

Julio: A report.

Laura: Oh, I bet Marta knows . . .

Marta: Yeah, that's easy: r-e-d-u-c-e.

Conversation 5:

Robbie: Daddy, what are we doing tonight?

Ed: Well, after we all clean up the kitchen--

All kids: Us, too?

Ed: Yep. After we *all* clean up the kitchen, we're going to watch a movie.

All kids: A movie?!? Yay!

Conversation 6:

Laura: But don't we have a PTA meeting tonight?

Ed: No, that's next Thursday.

Laura: Oh, right.

Lesson 3, Activity 2: Listen and Take Notes (page 8)
Listen to the conversations and write the person's long-term goal. Listen again and write the suggested short-term goal.

1.

Client: I think I need some advice about my program.

Counselor: Sure. That's what academic counselors are here for. What do you need?

Client: Well, I want to become a medical technician.

Counselor: To get into a med tech program, you need a high school diploma or a GED…

Client: Really?

Counselor: …..and you'll need to take a placement test in math and English.

Client: I really have trouble with math. I just don't understand fractions.

Counselor: Maybe you need a tutor to help you with math before you do anything else.

Client: Hmm.

Counselor: You can go to the Academic Learning Center for help.

Client: What's the *Academic Learning Center*?

Counselor: It's a place where you can find tutors.

2.

Counselor: Hi, there. What can I do for you?

Client: Uh, hi. Uhm, yes. . . . uhm, I want to attend college here in the fall, but I don't have any money.

Counselor: Well, you could apply for a grant.

Client: Oh. A grant . . .

Counselor: Yes. You could apply for a grant . . .

Client: Uhm, can you tell me what a *grant* is?

Counselor: Sure. A grant is money for school that you don't have to pay back.

Client: It's money I *don't* have to pay back?

Counselor: That's right.

Client: Wow, that sounds great! How do I start?

Counselor: Well, there are many types of grants. Uhm, let's see. . . . First, you'll need to get some documents together. Then we'll decide on the best grant for you.

Client: Okay!

3.

Bank officer: Hello. How can I help you?

Customer: Hello. Uh, I want to send my children to college, but first, I'll need to save a lot of money.

Bank officer: An excellent idea. We have many different ways to save for college here.

Customer: Great.

Bank officer: What kind of account do you want to open?

Customer: What kinds of accounts do you have?

Bank officer: Well, we have savings accounts and CD accounts. . . .

Customer: CD accounts? What's a *CD*?

Bank officer: A CD is a certificate of deposit.

Customer: A *certificate of deposit?*

Bank officer: Yes. With this type of account, you leave the money in the account for a certain amount of time, and it can really grow.

Customer: How long?

Bank Officer: Well, for example, how old are your children?

Customer: Oh, one is two and the other is three.

Bank officer: Well, you have many years. Let me show how much you will have in fifteen years if you open a CD today . . .

4.

Parent:	Uhm, excuse me. I'm looking for Mr. Green.
Teacher:	That's me. What can I do for you?
Parent:	My name is Hugo Vasquez.
Teacher:	Oh yes, Mr. Vasquez. It's nice to meet you. Daniela is a great kid.
Parent:	Thank you. I, uh, I want to talk to you. I want to become more involved in Daniela's education. You know, I'd like to help her with her homework, for example . . .
Teacher:	That's wonderful.
Parent:	But the problem is . . . uhm, my English isn't very good.
Teacher:	I see . . .
Parent:	I really need to improve my English. What can I do?
Teacher:	Well, I have a great idea for you: We have an English for Parents class here.
Parent:	*English for Parents*? What's that?
Teacher:	Classes that are only for parents of children in this school. You'll meet some of the other parents and learn a lot of English, too!
Parent:	Great idea. Thanks!

Lesson 4, Activity 4 Listen and Circle (page 11)
Listen to a conversation about citizenship. Then circle True or False.

Ms: Smith:	Okay, class . . . Are there any questions about becoming a U.S. citizen? Yes, Luis?
Luis:	Uhm, yes, Ms. Smith. . . Do you need to know about U.S. history to become a citizen?
Ms. Smith:	Yes, you do. You need to know basic information about United States history. Anyone else? Yes, Ana?
Ana:	But, uhm, do you need to memorize the U.S. Constitution?
Ms. Smith:	Oh, no. Not at all. You don't need to memorize the constitution. But you do need to follow U.S. laws.
Ana:	Okay. . .
Ms. Smith:	Lin? Did you have a question?
Lin:	Yes, uhm, I would like to know . . . uhm . . . Do you need to have a lot of money in the bank to become a citizen?
Ms. Smith:	A lot of money in the bank? No. Absolutely not. Money is not a requirement. You *do* need to pay an application fee, though. Yes, Wei?
Wei:	I was wondering . . . Do I need to marry an American if I want to become a citizen?
Ms. Smith:	No, Wei, you do not need to be married to an American. You can become a citizen if you are unmarried. Although, if you marry an American, you can become a citizen sooner.
Amina:	Oh, Ms. Smith. That reminds me.
Ms. Smith:	Yes, Amina?
Amina:	I have a friend. She's married to an American and she has been here for two years. Can she become a citizen yet?

Ms. Smith:	Uhm, no, two years isn't long enough. You need to live here for three years if you are married to an American citizen.
Amina:	And if you *aren't* married?
Ms. Smith:	If you *aren't* married, you can apply for naturalization after five years.
Amina:	After five years. . . Oh, I see.

Lesson 7, Activity 1: Listening Review (page 16)

Part 1
First, you will hear a question. Next, listen carefully to what is said. You will hear the question again. Then choose the correct answer: A, B, or C. Use the Answer Sheet.

1.
Where are the speakers?
  A: Hi. Can I help you?
  B: Yes. I want to take classes here.
  A: You want to enroll here at the community college?
  B: Yes.
  A: Okay. The first thing you need to do is fill out an application.

Where are the speakers?
  A. At a bank.
  B. At a company.
  C. At a college.

2.
How can the woman prepare for the citizenship test?
  A: Hi, Mary. What's new?
  B: Oh, I'm studying to become a citizen.
  A: Wow, that's great. What do you have to do to become a citizen?
  B: I have to take a test.
  A: Gee, how do you prepare for that?
  B: Well, first I have to get a tutor. I have to learn some basic information about American history and government.

How can the woman prepare for the citizenship test?
  A. Learn about American government.
  B. Take a business course.
  C. Get a loan.

3.
What does Rafael need?
  A: So, Rafael, do you have your homework today?
  B: Uh, no, Ms. Green. I didn't finish it.
  A: Rafael, this is the second time this term.
  B: Well, I'm actually having trouble understanding the assignments.
  A: Then you should go to the tutoring center and get some help.

What does Rafael need?
  A. He needs financial aid.
  B. He needs continuing education.
  C. He needs a tutor.

4.

What does the woman suggest?
A: I'd like to attend college some day.
B: Do you have your GED?
B: No. I have a high school diploma.
A: Great.
B: My problem is that I don't have enough money.
A: Oh. You should get a grant.
B: That's a great idea!

What does the woman suggest?
A. Get a GED.
B. Get a grant.
C. Get a high school diploma.

5.

What does the man want to do?
A: Hi. Can I help you?
B: Yes. I'm Lucia's dad.
A: Oh, Lucia's in my class. So nice to meet you! Is this your first time at a PTA meeting?
B: Yes. I need to get more involved in Lucia's education. I just need to make the time for it.
A: Well, this is a good place to start!

What does the man want to do?
A. Take a class.
B. Become involved in his child's education.
C. Prioritize.

Part 2
Listen to what is said. When you hear the question,
Which is correct?, *listen and choose the correct answer:*
A, B, or C. Use the Answer Sheet.

6.
A: Hey, did you get to those bills today?
B: Not yet. I'm going to pay them this evening.
A: Did you go to the supermarket today?
B: Sure. I got some good things for dinner, too.

Which is correct?
A. The man paid the bills.
B. The man bought food.
C. The man made dinner.

7.
A: Do you have to do homework tonight?
B: Yes, I do.
A: But we have to go to a PTA meeting tonight.
B: I'm going to stay home. I have too much work.

Which is correct?
A. The woman has to go to work tonight.
B. The woman has to clean the house tonight.
C. The woman has to do homework tonight.

8.
A: I want to start my own painting company, but my English isn't too good.
B: You should take some continuing education classes.

A: Do they teach English?
B: Yes. And business classes, too.

Which is correct?
A. The woman wants to take painting classes.
B. The woman wants to teach English.
C. The woman wants to start a business.

9.
A: I want to go to college, but I don't have enough money.
B: You could apply for a PELL grant.
A: Is that the same as a loan?
B: No. It's a grant. You don't have to pay it back.

Which is correct?
A. The man's goal is to go to college.
B. The man's goal is to get a grant.
C. The man's goal is to pay back his loan.

10.
A: Do you have a high school diploma?
B: No, but I have a GED certificate.
A: What's a GED certificate?
B: It's like a high school diploma.

Which is correct?
A. The man has a high school diploma.
B. The man doesn't have a GED certificate.
C. A GED certificate is like a high school diploma.

UNIT 2

Lesson 1, Activity 3: Listen and Check (page 18)
Look at the picture and listen to the conversation. Check
True *or* **False.**

Ida:	So, this is the house I was telling you about. I think it's just what you want. There are three bedrooms, two bathrooms . . .
Woman:	Yes, we did want three bedrooms and two bathrooms. . . .
Ida:	There's a nice yard for the kids, some trees . . .
Man:	Uh, what's wrong with the roof?
Ida:	The roof?
Man:	Uh, yeah, what's wrong with the roof?
Woman:	Yeah, what are the roofers doing?
Ida:	Well, there is a hole in the roof, but . . .
Woman:	A hole in the roof?!?
Ida:	Yes, but the roofers are repairing it.
Man:	And what about the plumbers. Why are they here?
Ida:	Well, there is a tiny problem with the plumbing . . .
Man:	What's wrong with the plumbing?
Ida:	Well, I, uh, . . .
Woman:	Hey, there's a crack in the wall.
Ida:	Oh, that's nothing. It'll be as good as new in no time. So, what do you think?
Man:	Honey, what do you think?
Woman:	Well, there is a nice yard. . . . .
Man:	And there are a lot of windows. I like the windows.
Woman:	Yes, a lot of windows and a nice deck. . .

Man:	On the other hand, there are a lot of problems. . .
Woman:	Yes, there are problems with the plumbing, the roof. . .
Man:	Okay. Ida, we're going to think about this and call you later.

Lesson 2, Activity 3: Listen and Match (page 20)
Listen to the conversation. Match the conversation with the ad. Write the letter.

1.
 A: Hi, I'm calling about the apartment for rent on North Street.
 B: Sure. Which one are you interested in?
 A: The two-bedroom apartment.
 B: The one that's $800 a month?
 A: No, the other one.
 B: Oh, okay.
 A: Oh, and, uhm, I'm planning on getting a cat. . .
 B: Cats are okay.
 A: Great!
 B: So, when would you like to see the place?
 A: How about Saturday morning?

2.
 Ken: Oh, hi, Julie. What are you doing in my neighborhood?
 Julie: Oh, hi, Ken. I was just looking at a house for rent down the street. James and I are thinking about renting it.
 Ken: Is it the yellow house?
 Julie: Yeah, that's the one.
 Ken: That's a beautiful house. It has a really nice front yard.
 Julie: Yeah, and it gets a lot of light because there are a lot of windows.
 Ken: Yeah, and there's room for both of your cars, too.

3.
 A: Hey, this apartment sounds good: three bedrooms, one and a half bathrooms . . .
 B: "One and half"? What does that mean?
 A: It probably means there's a small guest bathroom.
 B: Oh, O.K. Is it in a safe neighborhood?
 A: Yes. Belmont Street. That's a great neighborhood.
 B: Can we bring Spot?
 A: Yes. It's says "Pets OK."
 B: That sounds good. What about parking?
 A: It says there's a garage.
 B: Sounds perfect. One thing: we were thinking about getting a place with a laundry room this time. . .
 A: Uh, yeah, unfortunately, it doesn't say anything about a laundry room.

4.
 A: Yes, can I help you?
 B: Yes. We just moved here. We're planning on renting a house for a while.
 A: A house, huh? How many bedrooms are you looking for?
 B: Three would be nice.
 A: Three . . . yes, here it is. I have something on Lake Avenue. Three bedrooms, one bath . . .

B: That sounds good. What about pets? We have a dog . . .
A: Pets are okay. Would you like to see it?
B: Yes, that would be great.

Lesson 3, Activity 2: Listen and Take Notes (page 22)
Listen to the telephone conversations. For each conversation, write the tenant's problem. Then listen again and write the landlord's response. Match each conversation to the correct picture.

1.

Mr. Webster:	Hello.
Sun-Mi:	Is this Mr. Webster?
Mr. Webster:	Yes it is.
Sun-Mi:	Hi, it's Sun-Mi Park, your tenant in apartment 23.
Mr. Webster:	Yes, hi, Ms. Park. What can I do for you?
Sun-Mi:	Well, I'm calling about the air conditioner in our apartment. It's not working.
Mr. Webster:	The air conditioner isn't working? What seems to be the problem?
Sun-Mi:	I'm not sure. It just stopped working sometime during the night.
Mr. Webster:	It was working when you went to bed?
Sun-Mi:	Yes, that's right.
Mr. Webster:	Is the fan running?
Sun-Mi:	No, nothing is working.
Mr. Webster:	Okay. I'll send someone over.
Sun-Mi:	Will that be today?
Mr. Webster:	Yes, it will. I'll send someone before 5.
Sun-Mi:	Before 5? Great. Thanks.
Mr. Webster:	You're welcome. Bye.
Sun-Mi:	Bye.

2.

Mrs. Wright:	Hello?
Mrs. Adams:	Can I speak to Mrs. Wright, please?
Mrs. Wright:	This is Mrs. Wright.
Mrs. Adams:	Mrs. Wright, it's Mrs. Adams, your tenant in apartment 8G.
Mrs. Wright:	Yes, uh, hi, Mrs. Adams.
Mrs. Adams:	My husband and I just got home and there are bugs everywhere!
Mrs. Wright:	There are bugs everywhere?
Mrs. Adams:	Yes, that's right. Bugs are crawling all over the place. Especially in the kitchen.
Mrs. Wright:	Hmm. Bugs in the kitchen. Well, no one has ever called me about that problem before.
Mrs. Adams:	Well, it's really awful. My husband is afraid to go into the kitchen.
Mrs. Wright:	Hmm. I don't think I can do anything about this.
Mrs. Adams:	What do you mean?
Mrs. Wright:	This isn't my responsibility.
Mrs. Adams:	Are you saying that you aren't going to do anything?
Mrs. Wright:	Listen, all you have to do is go to the store and buy some insecticide. . .
Mrs. Adams:	But . . .
Mrs. Wright:	Oh, sorry, that's my other line. I have to get that.

3.

Mr. Jones:	Hello?
Dan:	Hello. Can I speak with Mr. Jones?
Mr. Jones:	This is Mr. Jones.
Dan:	Oh, hi. This is Dan Wright. I'm one of your tenants on Lake Avenue.
Mr. Jones:	Oh, yeah, sure. What can I do for you?
Dan:	Well, I'm calling because there seems to be something wrong with the clothes dryer in the basement.
Mr. Jones:	The clothes dryer? What's the matter with it?
Dan:	It isn't working. When I put my money in, nothing happens. And it won't return my money either.
Mr. Jones:	It won't return your money?
Dan:	No, and I put money in twice, too.
Mr. Jones:	Okay. I'll get over there tomorrow.
Dan:	Great. Can you give me a rough time?
Mr. Jones:	Yeah. It'll probably be in the afternoon between 3:00 and 4:00.
Dan:	Good, and can I get my money back?
Mr. Jones:	Yes, of course. What apartment are you in?
Dan:	It's number 35.
Mr. Jones:	Okay. I'll stop by tomorrow.
Dan:	Thanks.
Mr. Jones:	Sure. See you tomorrow.

4.

Jack:	Hi, Ms. Lopez?
Ms. Lopez:	Yes, this is Ms. Lopez.
Jack:	This is Jack in apartment 302.
Ms. Lopez:	Hi, Jack. What's going on?
Jack:	I'm having a problem with my freezer. I think it's broken.
Ms. Lopez:	Your freezer? Oh no! What happened?
Jack:	Well, all my ice cream is melted and everything else is thawed.
Ms. Lopez:	How about the refrigerator? Is the food in there warm, too?
Jack:	Let me check. No, the refrigerator isn't working either. Nothing is cold.
Ms. Lopez:	OK. Well, that is a pretty old refrigerator. I'll send the maintenance man up to take a look at it.
Jack:	How soon can he get here?
Ms. Lopez:	I'll send him up within the next hour.
Jack:	Great. And what if he can't fix it?
Ms. Lopez:	If he can't fix it, I'll get you a new refrigerator.
Jack:	Thanks, Ms. Lopez!

Lesson 7, Activity 1: Listening Review (page 30)

Part 1

Listen to what is said. When you hear the question, Which is correct?, listen and choose the correct answer: A, B, or C. Use the Answer Sheet.

1.

Male:	What utilities are included?
Female:	All utilities are included in the rent except for the electricity.

Which is correct?
 A. Electricity is included in the rent.
 B. Only electricity is included in the rent.
 C. Electricity is not included in the rent.

2.

Female:	Hello. How can I help you?
Male:	I'm calling about the apartment for rent.
Female:	The three-bedroom for $850 on Belmont Street?
Male:	No, the two-bedroom for $700 on State Street.

Which is correct?
 A. The man is interested in the two-bedroom apartment on Belmont Street.
 B. The man is interested in the two-bedroom apartment on State Street.
 C. The man is interested in the three-bedroom apartment on State Street.

3.

Male:	Good morning. Can I help you?
Female:	Yes. I'm calling about the house for rent on Lake Avenue.
Male:	Yes. Would you like to see it?
Female:	Well, first--uhm, are pets okay?
Male:	Cats are okay, but not dogs.

Which is correct?
 A. Pets aren't okay.
 B. Cats are okay, but not dogs.
 C. Dogs are okay, but not cats.

4.

Female:	Hello?
Male:	Hi, this is Mr. Chen in Apartment 306.
Female:	Hi, Mr. Chen. What can I do for you?
Male:	I'm calling about the refrigerator. It's leaking.
Female:	Is it working?
Male:	Yes, it's working, but it's leaking water all over the floor.
Female:	Okay. I'll send someone over by the end of the day.

Which is correct?
 A. The refrigerator is leaking.
 B. The refrigerator isn't working.
 C. The refrigerator isn't leaking.

5.

Male:	I'm sorry about your air conditioner. I'll be over as soon as I can.
Female:	Do you know when that might be?
Male:	I can probably be there sometime tomorrow between noon and 3.
Female:	Gee, that's a long time to wait. Can you come today?
Male:	Sorry. I can't get there until tomorrow after noon.

Which is correct?
  A. The man is coming today after noon.
  B. The man is coming tomorrow after noon.
  C. The man is coming tomorrow after 3.

Part 2
You will hear the first part of a conversation. To finish the conversation, listen and choose the correct answer: A, B, or C. Use the Answer Sheet.

6.
  A: Hello?
  B: Hi. I'm calling about the apartment on Lake Street.

  A. I can probably get there this afternoon.
  B. Which one are you interested in renting?
  C. I'm sorry, pets aren't okay.

7.
  A: I'm interested in renting the 2-bedroom apartment on Belmont Street.
  B: Okay.
  A: Are pets allowed?

  A. Cats are okay, but not dogs.
  B. Yes, there is.
  C. When would you like to see it?

8.
  A: Hi. I'm calling about the house for rent.
  B: Sure.
  A: I was wondering . . . Is heat included in the rent?

  A. There's a laundry room in the basement.
  B. I'm afraid there's only street parking.
  C. All utilities are included.

9.
  A: Yes. What can I do for you?
  B: Well, the refrigerator isn't working.

  A. Do you know what time?
  B. Oh, I'm sorry about that.
  C. Can someone fix it?

10.
  A: Uhm, Mr. Chen, my kitchen faucet is leaking.
  B: Oh, I'm sorry about that. I'll be over as soon as I can.
  A: Do you know when that might be?

  A. I'm sorry about that.
  B. I can be there between 9 and noon.
  C. Okay. I can come later.

UNIT 3

Lesson 2, Activity 3: Listen and Write (page 34)
Listen to a conversation between Gisela and a healthcare provider. Complete Gisela's health questionnaire with the missing information.

  A: Hmm, I see from your questionnaire that you have nasal allergies.

B: Yes. I sneeze a lot and I have a runny nose.
A: So how long have you had nasal allergies?
B: Oh, I've had nasal allergies for the past six years.
A: So they started in about 2006.
B: That's right. 2006.
A: Okay. I see you take supplements.
B: Yes. I take Vitamin C.
A: Vitamin C. Very good. And how long have you taken the calcium?
B: I just started that in 2011.
A: Okay. In 2011. Now, do you smoke?
B: No. Not at all. I've never smoked.
A: Excellent. What about alcohol?
B: Alcohol?
A: Yes, do you drink alcohol?
B: Nope. Not at all.
A: Great. Now, how would you describe your diet?
B: My diet?
A: Yes. What do you eat, in general. Do you follow any type of diet?
B: I'd say I follow a low-fat diet.
A: Okay. . . do you get annual check-ups?
B: Annual?
A: Yes. You come here about once a year, don't you?
B: Yes. I do. I get a check-up each year.
A: Okay. And finally, what kind of diseases are in your family?
B: Nothing really. Oh, wait . . . my brother has asthma.
A: Asthma?
B: Yes. He sometimes has trouble breathing. He has to use an inhaler.
A: Okay. Well, that's about it. It looks like you have some pretty good health habits. Keep up the good work.

Lesson 3, Activity 2: Listen and Take Notes (page 36)
Listen to conversation #1 and write the person's reason for visiting the doctor and when the problem started. Listen a second time and write the doctor's advice. Repeat with conversation #2.

1.
Doctor: Well, everything looks fine. Do you have any questions?
Woman: I was just wondering . . uhm, I'm having trouble sleeping.
Doctor: Trouble sleeping, yes, that's very common these days. When did this start?
Woman: Uhm, it started about a week ago.
Doctor: Do you sleep on your back or on your side?
Woman: I sleep on my back.
Doctor: Well, why don't you try sleeping on your side?
Woman: Okay.
Doctor: And what about caffeine? Have you cut down on coffee?
Woman: No, I haven't cut down yet.
Doctor: Oh, really?
Woman: I still have about two cups a day.

Doctor: Okay, you'd really better cut down on the coffee.
Woman: Do I have to stop altogether?
Doctor: No, not necessarily. First, try drinking less. I'm sure that will help.
Woman: Okay . . .
Doctor: And let me know how things are going in a few days.
Woman: Yes, I will.

2.
Doctor: Hi. I'm Doctor Lopez.
Patient: Hi, Doctor Lopez. Nice to meet you. I'm John Wong.
Doctor: Nice to meet you. It says here that you're having trouble with your ear.
Patient: Yes. It's my right ear.
Doctor: Your right ear. So what's the problem? Does it hurt?
Patient: Yes, it hurts a lot.
Doctor: Let me take a look. Hmmm, how long have you had this?
Patient: I've had this since yesterday. It's been hurting for about 24 hours.
Doctor: Hmm, 24 hours.
Patient: Yes, I couldn't sleep last night the pain was so bad.
Doctor: Well, it looks like you have an ear infection. And I see that you have a slight fever.
Patient: Yeah, that's what the nurse said.
Doctor: Okay, I suggest that you take some prescription medication.
Patient: A prescription?
Doctor: Yes. Are you allergic to any drugs?
Patient: No.
Doctor: Okay, then. This will get rid of the infection. Take three a day until the pills are all gone.
Patient: Okay. And what about going to work?
Doctor: You'd really better stay home until the fever is down.
Patient: Until the fever is down? Okay, thanks Doctor Lopez.
Doctor: You're welcome. I hope you feel better soon.
Patient: Thanks.

Lesson 4, Activity 3: Listen and Write (page 39)
Listen to phone conversations between callers and community volunteers. Write the reason for each call.
1.
   A: Parental Stress Line. How can I help you?
   B: Oh, I just don't know what to do!
   A: Now, just relax. Tell me what the problem is.
   B: My baby has been crying for hours!
   A: I see.
   B: She won't stop. It's driving me crazy!!!!
   A: Okay. That's what we're here for. Now, take a deep breath. . .
   B: [breathing]
   A: That's good. Now, I need you to listen carefully. . .

2.
   A: Community Clinic. May I help you?
   B: Yes. My daughter is sick. I think she needs to see a doctor.
   A: Okay. Tell me a little about the problem, and then we'll make an appointment.
   B: Okay, but first, uhm, I don't have any health insurance.
   A: That's not a problem. We take patients without insurance here.
   B: Really? That's great.

3.
   A: Supplemental Nutrition and Assistance Program.
   B: Oh, uhm, I'm calling about food stamps . . .
   A: Yes, you have the right number. How can I help you?
   B: Well, my husband has just lost his job. I'm worried about getting enough food for the children.
   A: Okay. If you need help buying food, just come into one of our offices . . .
   B: Okay . . .
   A: fill out some forms,
   B: Okay . . .
   A: and you'll get a special card that you can use at the super-market.
   B: Oh, thank you!

4.
   A: Alcohol and Drug Treatment Referral.
   B: Hi. Umm, I'm calling about my daughter. . .
   A; Yes. . .
   B: I think she has a drug problem.
   A: I understand.
   B: She needs help, but I'm not sure what to do. . .
   A: Well, tell me a little bit about your daughter . . .
   B: Okay . . .
   A: and then we can try to find the right treatment program for her. . .
   B: Thank you.

Lesson 7, Activity 1: Listening Review (page 44)

Part 1
You will hear the first part of a conversation. To finish the conversation, listen and choose the correct answer: A, B, or C. Use the Answer Sheet.
1.
   A: What can I do for you today, Mr. Wong?
   B: My right ear hurts. I think I have an ear infection.
   A: How long have you had it?

   A. Thank you, doctor.
   B. Since yesterday.
   C. It's my right ear.

2.
   A: Achoo!
   B: Do you have allergies?
   A: Yes, I do.

A. Dogs.
B. Since he was a child.
C. What are you allergic to?

3.
A: Do you smoke?
B: No, I don't.
A: That's good. Any history of asthma in your family?

A. No. No one has asthma.
B. For five years.
C. Yes. My mother has had skin cancer.

4.
A: How can I help you?
B: I feel hot. I think I have a fever.
A: Yes, your temperature is high.
B: What should I do?

A. I suggest that you take a fever reducer.
B. I guess I could try that.
C. For two days.

5.
A: Hello. Can I help you?
B: Yes. I'm having trouble sleeping.
A: Oh, when did this start?

A. You should stop drinking coffee.
B. A few weeks ago.
C. That sounds like a good idea.

Part 2
First you will hear a question. Next, listen carefully to what is said. You will hear the question again. Then choose the correct answer: A, B, or C.

6.
What is the man allergic to?
A: Do you have any allergies?
B: Yes, I do.
A: Are you allergic to cats?
B: No, I'm not. I'm allergic to dust.

What is the man allergic to?
A. dogs
B. cats
C. dust

7.
When did the woman go to the doctor?
A: Why did you go to the doctor yesterday?
B: I had an ear infection.
A: Oh, that's too bad. When did it start?
B: Three days ago.

When did the woman go to the doctor?
A. yesterday
B. today
C. three days ago

8.
How long has the woman taken vitamin C?
A: Do you take any supplements?
B: Yes. I take calcium and vitamin C.
A: How long have you taken them?
B: I've taken vitamin C for a long time. Uhm, since I was a child. I've taken the calcium for about a year.

How long has the woman taken vitamin C?
A. since last year
B. for a year
C. for a long time

9.
What should the patient try to do?
A: Hi, I'm Dr. Green. What can I do for you today?
B: Oh, uhm, I'm having trouble sleeping.
A: Have you cut down on coffee?
B: No, I have about 4 cups a day.
A: Okay, try cutting that in half. Have 2 cups a day and see if you sleep better.

What should the patient try to do?
A. drink 4 cups of coffee a day
B. drink 2 cups of coffee a day
C. drink no coffee

10.
What is the doctor's advice?
A: It looks like you have an ear infection.
B: What should I do, doctor? Can I go to work?
A: You should stay home from work and put some drops in your ear.
B: Do I need a prescription for that?
A: Yes. Here's a prescription to take to the drugstore.

What is the doctor's advice?
A. go to work and take an over-the counter medication
B. stay home from work and take an over-the counter medication
C. stay home from work and take a prescription medication

UNIT 4

Lesson 1, Activity 3: Listen and Circle (page 46)
Listen to the conversations. Circle True or False.

1.
A: How are you today?
B: Fine. Gee, these lines are long today.
A: Yes, we've been very busy. Okay, is that it?
B: Yes, thanks.
A: Are you paying by cash or credit?
B: Actually, I'm going to write a check. Here you go.
A: May I see your ID, please?
B: Oh, yes, here's my driver's license.
A: Thanks.

2.

B: What is all that?
A: Oh, Daddy, they're having a great sale!
B: Where's the coffee maker?
A: Look at these pants! They're 30 percent off! Aren't they great?
B: Claire, where's the coffee maker?
A: Daddy, you always said: "Buying things on sale is the best way to shop!"
B: Yes, but where's the coffeemaker? I'm almost at the end of the line here.
A: Uh, it's here. Somewhere. Uh, oh. I forgot.
B: You forgot!?!
A: I'll go get it right now.
B: And while you're at it, put all those pants back!

3.

A: Oh dear, this doesn't seem to be working . . .
B: Let me see your card. . . .
A: My card? Oh, here.
B: I'm sorry. This card has expired.
A: What do you mean?
B: Your credit card isn't valid. You can't use it.
A: I can't use it?
B: No. See the date? It expired a month ago.
A: Oh, dear. . .
B: You need a new card. Call your bank.
A: I'm so sorry. Gee, this is the credit line. Can I pay with cash?
B: All right. I guess so.

4.

A: Honey, do we really need all this stuff?
B: Need it—no. Want it—yes!
A: Well, how are we going to pay?
B: With the credit card.
A: The credit card? Paying by credit's not a good idea.
B: Why not?
A: We'll just have to pay the bill next month, and what if we don't have the money then?
B: Yeah, I guess you're right. Paying by credit doesn't seem like a good idea.
A: No. Paying with cash makes more sense. . .
B: How much do we have in our checking account right now?
A: A few hundred dollars.
B: Well, let's use the debit card then. Paying with a debit card is like using cash.
A: Good idea.

Lesson 3, Activity 2: Listen and Take Notes (page 50)
Listen to two conversations. Write the missing information in the chart below.

1.

A: Good morning. How can I help you today?
B: Well, I'm interested in looking at some of your pre-owned cars.

A: We have great deals on quite a few of our pre-owned cars right now.
B: Uh-huh . . .
A: Were you looking for a specific make or model?
B: Make and model . . . not really. I'm looking for a car that gets good gas mileage.
A: Sure. We have many that get good gas mileage.
B: Great. What kind of makes and models are they?
A: Well, over here, for example, we have a KMC Via.
B: A KMC Via?
A: Yes. It's in great shape. It's been well maintained.
B: How much is it?
A: It's only $8,998.
B: $8,998, huh? I'm afraid that's too expensive.
A: Well. . .
B: How many miles are on it?
A: Just 48,000.
B: 48,000? What year is it?
A: Uhm, let me see . . . It's a 2010.
B: 48,000 seems like a lot of miles for a 2010.
A: It's a great little car . . .
B: Do you have anything in that price range that has fewer miles on it?
A: Not at the moment.
B: Okay. What about the gas mileage? How many miles does it get per gallon?
A: Well, it gets 25 miles to the gallon.
B: Is that in the city?
A: Yes, 25 in the city. But it gets better mileage on the highway.
B: What does it get on the highway?
A: It gets 30 miles per gallon.
B: 30 miles to the gallon on the highway. . .?
A: Yes. In fact, it's really one of the best deals we have on the lot right now.
B: Uh-huh. . . .
A: It has some great features, too. You won't find a better deal anywhere.
B: Okay, but I'm concerned about the number of miles it has.
A: Well, maybe we can knock a couple of hundred off the price.

2.

B: What else can you show me? What other makes get good gas mileage?
A: Well, over here, we have a Tanaka.
B: A Tanaka? What's the model?
A: It's a Cargo.
B: And it's pre-owned, too?
A: Yes.
B: Hmm . . . What kind of mileage does this one get?
A: This one gets the same miles per gallon in the city as the KMC.
B: 25?
A: That's right. 25 in the city.
B: So it's as inexpensive to run as the KMC?
A: Basically, yes. But it does get slightly fewer miles per gallon on the highway than the KMC, I think.

B: It does, huh?

A: Yes, uhm, let me see. . . Yes, this one gets 28 on the highway.

B: 28 on the highway . . . Okay. . . .

A: But the price is lower. This one is only $7,998.

B: $7,998? So it costs a bit less than the KMC. . .

A: Right.

B: How many miles are on it?

A: It has 33,000.

B: What's the year?

A: It's a 2009.

B: 33,000 miles and it's a 2009, huh?

A: Yes, that's really a great deal.

B: What kind of condition is it in?

A: It just came in yesterday, so I'll have to check. But it comes with a great service warranty.

B: Well, this sounds a bit better than the KMC. Can I take a test drive?

A: Sure. Here are the keys.

Lesson 4, Activity 3: Listen and Check (page 52)
Listen to a conversation between a banker and a customer. Check the services the customer gets.

A: Can I help you?

B: Yes. I'd like to open an account.

A: Is this a new account?

B: Yes.

A: What kind of account are you interested in opening?

B: I'd like to open a checking account.

A: A checking account. . . Okay. This will just take a few minutes.

B: Okay. . .

A: Now, do you want a check card for this account?

B: Uhm . . . Let me see . . .

A: You may want to access your account from one of our many ATMs.

B: Sure.

A: Okay, then, I'll set you up with a check card.

B: Great.

A: So, you'll need a PIN.

B: A PIN?

A: Yes. A personal identification number.

B: Okay.

A: It's very important that you keep this number private. . .

B: Sure.

A: . . . so I'm going to ask you to think of 4 to 6 numbers. . .

B: Okay . . .uhm, 9, 1, . . .

A: No, don't tell me. Just key your PIN into this keypad here . . .

A: Great. Your PIN is all set up. Remember to keep it secret.

B: Sure.

A: The card will arrive in the mail in about two weeks. So will your checks.

B: Is the check card the same as a debit card?

A: Yes, it is.

B: How does that work, exactly?

A: You can use your check card to access your account at an ATM . . .

B: Uh-huh.

A: . . . and you can also use it instead of a check or cash at a store.

B: Okay. Thank you very much for your help.

A: Thank you for banking with us. And have a good day.

Lesson 7, Activity 1: Listening Review (page 58)
Part 1: First, you will hear a question. Next, listen carefully to what is said. You will hear the question again. Then choose the correct answer: A, B, or C. Use the Answer Sheet.

1.
How does the woman pay?
   A: Will that be cash or credit?
   B: Uh, I'm going to pay by check.

How does the woman pay?
   A. by cash
   B. by check
   C. by credit

2.
What does the woman think is the best way to pay?
   A: Let's use the debit card.
   B: I agree. It's better than paying by credit. Paying with a debit card is like paying with cash.

What does the woman think is the best way to pay?
   A. by cash
   B. by credit card
   C. by debit card

3.
Why is she returning the coffeemaker?
   A: I'd like to return this coffeemaker.
   B: What's the problem?
   A: It started making a funny noise and then it stopped working.
   B: I'll get you another one. Same color?
   A: Yes, please.

Why is she returning the coffeemaker?
   A. It's the wrong color.
   B. It doesn't work.
   C. It's too noisy.

4.
What does the man do?
   A: I'm afraid the warranty on this DVD player isn't valid.
   B: I can't exchange it?
   A: No, but we can repair it for you.
   B: Okay. I'll leave it with you.

What does the man do?
   A. He gets a new DVD player.
   B. He gets a refund.
   C. He gets the DVD player repaired.

5.
Which car has the fewest miles on it?
   A: What's the mileage on these two models?
   B: The KMC has fewer miles on it than the Tanaka.

A: What about that one over there, the America?

B: The America actually has more miles than the Tanaka.

Which car has the fewest miles on it?
   A. the KMC
   B. the America
   C. the Tanaka

Part 2:
Listen to what is said. When you hear the question,
Which is correct?, *listen and choose the correct answer:*
A, B, or C. Use the Answer Sheet.

6.
   A; How much is this phone?
   B: It's 40 dollars.
   A: Wow. That's expensive.
   B: It's our cheapest model.
   A: Oh, okay. I'll take it.

Which is correct?
   A. The phone costs 20 dollars.
   B. It's the most expensive phone.
   C. It's the cheapest phone.

7.
   A: Will that be cash or credit?
   B: Can I use a debit card?
   A: Of course.
   B: Uhm, I don't have much money in my account. . . I think I'll use my credit card.

Which is correct?
   A. The woman pays by cash.
   B. The woman pays with a debit card.
   C. The woman pays with a credit card.

8.
   A: This laptop computer stopped working.
   B: It looks like your warranty is still valid.
   A: Can I have a replacement?
   B: Yes.

Which is correct?
   A. The man's warranty is void.
   B. The man's warranty isn't valid.
   C. The man's warranty is valid.

9.
   A: I'd like to return this DVD.
   B: I'm sorry, you can't.
   A: Why not?
   B: It looks like you opened the package.

Which is correct?
   A. The DVD is worn.
   B. The DVD is opened.
   C. The DVD is unused.

10.
   A: I'm interested in the Tanaka and the KMC. Which one is better?
   B: Well, the KMC Via has only 30,000 miles on it.

A: How much does the Tanaka have?

B: It has 55,000 miles on it.

A: Which one gets better gas mileage?

B: They get the same gas mileage.

Which is correct?
   A. The KMC has fewer miles on it than the Tanaka.
   B. The Tanaka has fewer miles on it than the KMC.
   C. The cars have the same number of miles on them.

UNIT 5

Lesson 1, Activity 3: Listen and Check (page 60)
Listen to the conversations. Check **True** *or* **False.**

1.
   A: What happened here?
   B: Uh, Jake here was working on the second floor when he tripped.
   A: He tripped?
   B: Yes. While he was carrying a beam, he tripped on something on the floor.
   A: Okay. So he tripped and fell. . .
   B: Yeah. It looks like he fell about 10 feet.
   A: Whew! Don't worry, we'll take good care of him.

2.
   A: Hey, look at that car!
   B: Yeah! What happened?
   A: That woman was driving too fast.
   C: No, she wasn't driving too fast.
   A: What do you mean?
   C: I saw the whole thing!
   A: What did you see?
   C: While she was driving, she was talking on her cell phone.
   B: So she didn't see the "road closed" sign and just drove into the ditch!
   C: Yes, I'm pretty sure that's what happened.

3.
   A: Whoa! Sorry.
   B: What happened, Meg?
   A: I dunno . . .
   B: Why did you drop the beam?
   A: It looks like there's something stuck in the ground here. . .
   B: Yeah, look where you're going—there are hazards all over this place . . .
   A: Hey, it's my safety glasses!
   B: Your safety glasses?
   A: Yes, I've been looking all over for them!

4.
   A: Ow!
   B: Whoa, what just happened?
   A: Oh, my head!
   B: Hey, Bob, do you need help?
   A: I don't think so.
   B: Are you sure?
   A: Yeah, I'll be okay.
   B: What happened?

A: I was using the drill and that hook swung back and hit my head!

B: Wow! And you had your hard hat on, too!

A: Yeah. I'm glad I did. . . .

5.

A: Wait a minute . . . I can't hear anything!

B: I said be careful of that truck. It's unloading dirt and gravel.

A: Oh, thanks. I see it. And it's making a lot of noise, too.

B: So are you....with that drill.

A: That's why I wear my ear plugs!

Lesson 2, Activity 3: Listen and Write (page 62)
Listen to the conversations. Write what actions to take.

1.

A: What's going on?

B: I think Jack has heat exhaustion.

A: Heat exhaustion?

B: Yeah.

A: What should we do?

B: We should get him out of the heat right away.

A: Okay. Let's take him inside.

B: Yes. And we should give him some water, too.

A: Good idea.

2.

A: Oh, no! What happened?

B: I don't know. He was fine a minute ago.

A: It looks like he's lost consciousness.

B: Does anyone know CPR? I guess not.

A: I've already called 9-1-1.

B: 9-1-1? You did the right thing.

A: I told them what happened and gave this address.

B: Thanks.

3.

A: My goodness, what happened to you?

B: Oh, we spent the entire weekend moving.

A: And. . .?

B: And I injured my back while I was carrying a heavy box.

A: Oh, I'm sorry to hear that.

B: Thanks.

A: So what did you do?

B: I called my health clinic.

A: What did they advise?

B: They said to take a pain medication, like ibuprofen.

A: Oh?

B: Yes. It makes the pain go away and it also helps to heal muscle problems.

A: Yeah, I've heard that, too.

B: They also said to put hot and cold packs on my back.

4.

A: Hey, everyone! Out of the warehouse!

B: What? What did he say?

A: Now! Immediately!

C: What happened?

A: There's been a toxic material spill in the warehouse!

B: Oh, no! What should we do?

A: When there's a spill, we have to evacuate.

C: Okay, let's go!

A: But stay calm. I called a city agency and they'll be right over.

Lesson 3, Activity 2: Listen and Take Notes (page 64)
Listen to each conversation and identify the person's injury. Then listen again for the cause of the injury.

1.

Employer:	So, Sylvia, how are you?
Sylvia:	Much better, thank you.
Employer:	I have to fill out this accident report. Can you tell me what got in your eye?
Sylvia:	I got some paint in my eye.
Employer:	What exactly were you doing?
Sylvia:	Well, while I was painting, I got some paint on my hand.
Employer:	Uh-huh . . .
Sylvia:	And then I rubbed my eye.
Employer:	Okay. So you got paint on your hand and you rubbed your eye.
Sylvia:	Uh-huh.
Employer:	Were you wearing your safety glasses?
Sylvia:	My safety glasses . . . uhm, no, I wasn't.
Employer:	Sylvia, you know that's a rule around here. You must always wear your safety glasses.
Sylvia:	Yes, I'm sorry. It won't happen again.

2.

Employer:	I just heard that you got hurt this morning, Sandra.
Sandra:	Yes.
Employer:	It looks like you hurt your hand.
Sandra:	Yes.
Employer:	What happened?
Sandra:	I burned it.
Employer:	You burned your hand, huh? What were you doing?
Sandra:	Well, I was working in the kitchen and I slipped on something on the floor.
Employer:	You slipped?
Sandra:	Yes. And then I grabbed the stove as I fell, and my hand hit the hot grill.
Employer:	You burned you hand on the grill?
Sandra:	Yes.
Employer:	Ouch.
Sandra:	Yeah.
Employer:	Are you planning on coming back to work tomorrow?
Sandra:	Uh, I'm not sure.

3.

Boss: Is anything broken?

Joe: No. Nothing is broken.

Boss: That's good. So what happened?
Joe: The doctor said I tore a muscle in my shoulder.
Boss: A muscle in your shoulder, huh?
Joe: Yes.
Boss: I heard you fell.
Joe: Yes. I fell about five feet.
Boss: What were you doing?
Joe: I was working on that scaffolding over there . . .
Boss: Uh-huh.
Joe: . . when I slipped and fell.
Boss: Were you wearing a safety harness?
Joe: No, I wasn't.
Boss: Well, you know you're supposed to use a harness when you're on scaffolding.
Joe: Yes, I know. Believe me. I'll be more careful in the future.

Lesson 7, Activity 1: Listening Review (page 72)
Part 1:
Listen to what is said. When you hear the question, Which is correct?, listen and choose the correct answer: A, B, or C. Use the Answer Sheet.

1.
   A: Ana, did you see that?
   B: Yes. I was working on the second floor when I saw the accident.
   A: What happened?
   B: Jack was carrying a heavy box when he tripped and fell.

Which is correct?
   A. Jack was working on the second floor when he tripped and fell.
   B. Ana saw the accident while she was working on the second floor.
   C. Ana tripped and fell when she was carrying a heavy box.

2.
   A: What are hazards at this job site?
   B: Noise and dangerous machinery.
   A: Do I need to get a hard hat?
   A: No. You need safety glasses and ear plugs.

Which is correct?
   A. The man needs a safety vest.
   B. The man needs a hard hat.
   C. The man needs ear plugs.

3.
   A: Hey, Rob, have you ever gotten a bad shock?
   B: No, I haven't, but once I lost consciousness.
   A: Did it happen at home?
   B: No. I was working at a construction site when I hit my head.

Which is correct?
   A. Rob got a bad shock while he was working at a construction site.
   B. Rob hit his head while he was working at a construction site.
   C. Rob lost consciousness while he was working at home.

4.
   A: What happened to your arm?
   B: I slipped in the kitchen while I was carrying a heavy pot in my hands.
   B: Did you burn it on the stove?
   A: No, I fractured it when I hit the floor.

Which is correct?
   A. The woman fractured her arm.
   B. The woman burned her arm.
   C. The woman burned her hand.

5.
   A: What happened to Jeff?
   B: He had an accident.
   A: Did you see or hear anything?
   B: No. I had my ear plugs in and my face mask on.

Which is correct?
   A. The woman saw the accident.
   B. Jeff was wearing ear plugs and a face mask.
   C. The woman was wearing ear plugs and a face mask.

Part 2:
You will hear the first part of a conversation. To finish the conversation, listen and choose the correct answer: A, B, or C. Use the Answer Sheet.

6.
   A: Mark had an accident!
   B: Oh, my! What happened?

   A. He was using safety equipment.
   B. No, he wasn't.
   C. He was carrying a beam when he tripped over something.

7.
   A: Have you ever gotten a bad shock?
   B: Yes, I have.
   A: When did it happen?

   A. In the bathroom.
   B. Last year.
   C. I was drying my hair.

8.
   A: There was a toxic spill at the factory today.
   B: Oh, no. What did you do?

   A. We had to evacuate.
   B. We submerged it in water.
   C. We turned off the electricity.

9.
   A: What happened?
   B: I burned my hand.
   A: Were you wearing your gloves?

   A. I'm sorry.
   B. No, I wasn't.
   C. I was in the kitchen.

10.

A: What happened?
B: I was working on that scaffolding over there when I fell.
A: Were you wearing safety equipment?
B: No, I wasn't.
A: You know that's a rule around here.

A. I was on the second floor.
B. Yes, I was.
C. Yes. I'm sorry it won't happen again.

UNIT 6

Lesson 1, Activity 3: Listen and Write (page 74)
Listen to the conversation. What do the speakers say you
should *do? Which should you* **not** *do? Write S for* **should**
and SN for **should not.**

Committee Chairwoman:	Hello, everyone.
Group:	Hello.
Committee Chairwoman:	Welcome to our community meeting. Today, we're going to talk about ways we can improve life here in our little community of Greenville.
Group:	[murmuring of approval]
Committee Chairwoman:	So, the question is: What makes a community a good place to live? And: What makes our community a safe place to live? Yes, you, Ms. Smith.
Ms. Smith:	I think people should remember to pick up trash because it keeps the community clean and attractive.
Group:	[murmuring of approval]
Committee Chairwoman:	Yes. Picking up trash. I think we all agree. Uhm, Mr. Chen?
Mr. Chen:	So obviously, people shouldn't litter.
Group:	[murmuring of approval]
Committee Chairwoman:	Right. People shouldn't litter here in Greenville. Uhm, Ms. Ruiz?
Ms. Ruiz:	Well, I, uh, I think pet owners should have more rights.
Committee Chairwoman:	Rights for pet owners? What exactly do you mean, Ms. Ruiz?
Ms. Ruiz:	I don't think we should have to keep pets on a leash all the time.
Group:	[murmuring of disapproval]
Committee Chairwoman:	Why not?
Ms. Ruiz:	They need to be able to run around freely sometimes.
Group:	[rumbling]
Ms. Ruiz:	It's better for the animals!
Group:	[rumbling]
Committee Chairwoman:	Well, uhm, thank you, Ms. Ruiz. Yes. Mr. Brown?
Mr. Brown:	We have a problem with graffiti. It makes our community look unattractive …
Group:	[murmuring of agreement]
Committee Chairwoman:	I think we all want to keep Greenville attractive.
Mr. Brown:	So people shouldn't draw graffiti on buildings.
Group:	[murmuring of approval
Committee Chairwoman:	Absolutely not. What about some of our traffic issues? Uhm, yes, Ms. Lee?
Ms. Lee:	Yes, there are way too many car accidents. People should remember to wear seatbelts.
Committee Chairwoman:	Yes, we should all be wearing our seatbelts . . . it's the law, anyway, isn't it?
Group:	[murmuring of agreement]
Mr. Chen:	Uhm, excuse me. . .
Committee Chairwoman:	Yes, Mr. Chen again.
Mr. Chen:	Yes, on the same topic of traffic . . . I think more people should ride motorcycles.
Group:	[murmuring of mixed comments]
Committee Chairwoman:	Really?
Mr. Chen:	Yes. Motorcycles use less gas than cars.
Committee Chairwoman:	Well, that may be true. . .
Mr. Chen:	Motorcycles use less gas, and we need to pay attention to our resources.
Committee Chairwoman:	Yes, well, saving resources is important. . .
Group:	[murmuring of agreement]
Committee Chairwoman:	Well, I don't know if everyone agrees, but anyway . . . Ms. Jones?
Ms. Jones:	Uhm, yes, I have some concerns about cell phones.
Committee Chairwoman:	Cell phones?
Ms. Jones:	Yes. I think we should be able to use cell phones in restaurants.
Committee Chairwoman:	Yes, well, right now, there's a law against using cell phones in restaurants because they bother people.
Group:	[murmuring of agreement]
Ms. Jones:	Yes, but some of us need to use our cell phones, even in restaurants.
Group:	[murmuring of mixed comments]
Ms. Jones:	Some of us have very important jobs and we need to answer our phones all the time, even in restaurants!
Committee Chairwoman:	Well, I don't know if everyone agrees with you on that, Ms. Jones.
Group:	[murmuring of agreement]
Committee Chairwoman:	Well, it looks as though our time is up. I want to thank all of you for coming and for sharing your ideas here tonight.
Group:	[applause]

Lesson 3, Activity 2: Listen and Take Notes (page 78)
Listen to each conversation and identify the problems.
Complete the chart.

1.
Officer: Good afternoon. Did you know that you were exceeding the speed limit, sir?
Driver: Exceeding the speed limit? Oh, no. I'm sorry, officer.
Officer: You were doing 55 in a 35-mile-per-hour zone. Let me see your license and registration please.
Driver: Of course. Here they are. I'm really sorry.
Officer: I'm going to have to give you a ticket.
Driver: A speeding ticket?
Officer: That's right.
Driver: Will I have to go to court?
Officer: Not if you pay the ticket within two weeks.
Driver: Oh, okay. I'll take care of it right away.
Officer: And I advise you to watch your speed from now on.
Driver: I will. It won't happen again.

2.
Woman: Yes, officer, what can I do for you?
Officer; Ma'am, there's been a complaint about your party.
Woman: Oh, I'm sorry. What's the complaint?
Officer: Your music is too loud.
Woman: I'm sorry. What did you say?
Officer: I said your music is too loud.
Woman: Oh, we'll turn it down right now.
Officer: Thank you. Also, your guests are parked on the lawn.
Woman: Oh, is it illegal to park on the lawn?
Officer: Yes, ma'am. It's against a city ordinance.
Woman: Oh, I apologize. I didn't know that. We'll have our guests move their cars.
Officer: Thank you. And please remind them not to block any of your neighbors' driveways.
Woman: Of course. Thank you. Again, we're sorry if we caused a problem.

3.
Park officer: Excuse me, do you have a fishing license?
Man: A fishing license? No, I'm sorry, I don't. Do I need one?
Park officer: Yes. You need a license to fish in any state park.
Man: Oh, I'm sorry. I didn't know that. Where can I get one?
Park officer: You can apply online or go to the Department of Fish and Game.
Man: Okay. I'll get one right away.
Park officer: There's another problem.
Man: Yes?
Park officer: You're not allowed to drink alcoholic beverages in the park.
Man: You're not allowed to drink alcoholic beverages?
Park officer: No.
Man: But I'm not driving. . . My friend is.
Park officer: That doesn't matter. You can't have alcoholic beverages in the park. It's a park rule.
Man: Oh, okay. I'm sorry.

Lesson 4, Activity 3: Listen and Apply (page 81)
Listen to the conversations about witnessing a crime.
Write the crime. Then check either Report Online or
Call 9-1-1.

1.
A: Oh, my! Stop!
B: What happened?
A: Oh, no!
B: Are you okay?
A: No, not really. . .
C: What just happened here?
A: Some guy just grabbed my car keys!
C: Gee, I'm so sorry!
A: Then he jumped into my car and drove it away!
C: He stole your car . . . . Oh, that's terrible!
A: What am I going to do?

2.
A: What is that all over our building?!?
B: Yeah, isn't that terrible?
A: It looks awful!
B: I'm sick and tired of these kids damaging our property.
A: Yeah, graffiti is ruining our entire block.
B: This has to stop!
A: [sighs] Well, what are we going to do?

3.
A: Oh gosh, Jim, Nick!
B: What is it?
A: Look in here!
B: Oh, no!
C: Where's the TV?
A: I think someone stole it!
C: I think some other things are missing, too!
B: Yeah, it looks like someone broke into the apartment . . .
A: Well, what should we do?

4.
A: What are they doing up there?!?
B: What is it?
A: I don't know!
B: It's those darned college kids. . .
A: Yes! Every night, it's the same thing! Loud music, stomping. . .
B: It sounds like a party that never ends!
A: Well, it's driving me crazy.
B: Me, too. I'll never get to sleep with all this noise!
A: What should we do?

Window on Pronunciation • Reductions with *to*
(page 81)
B Listen to the sentences. Write the missing words. Use
the full form.

1. I have to renew my driver's license this month.
2. Sam has to pay a parking ticket.
3. We ought to do something about all this graffiti!

4. You have to slow down. You're going to get a ticket!
5. This community used to be so nice. I want to move now.

Lesson 7, Activity 1: Listening Review (page 86)
Part 1: You will hear the first part of a conversation. To finish the conversation, listen and choose the correct answer: A, B, or C. Use the Answer Sheet.

1.
A: Hey, did you see that?
B: Yes. He just dropped his trash right there on the grass.
A: That's terrible.

A. Yes. People shouldn't litter.
B. Yes. People should remember to keep pets on a leash.
C. Yes. People shouldn't draw graffiti.

2.
A: Excuse me. Sir, you can't fish there.
B: I'm sorry, what did you say?
A: See that sign over there?

A. Oh, yeah. It says no weapons or firearms.
B. Oh yeah. It says you're not allowed to swim here.
C. Oh, yeah. It says fishing isn't permitted here.

3.
A: Hey, look what those kids are doing!
B: Yes. They shouldn't be over there. It's private property.
A: I'll go talk to them.

A. Thanks. Tell them trespassing isn't permitted.
B. Thanks. Fishing without a license isn't permitted here
C. Thanks. They're not allowed to exceed the speed limit.

4.
A: Yes, officer. What can I do for you?
B: Did you know that you were exceeding the speed limit?

A. Sorry. I'll take care of it tomorrow.
B. Sorry. I'll turn it down.
C. No. I'm sorry.

5.
A: Excuse me. Do you have a fishing license?
B: A fishing license? No, sorry. Do I need one?
A: You're not allowed to fish here without a license.

A. Okay. I'll get one right away.
B. But I'm not driving.
C. I will. It won't happen again.

Part 2:
First you will hear a question. Next, listen carefully to what is said. You will hear the question again. Then choose the correct answer: A, B, or C.

6. What does the woman think makes a community good?
A: I think people need to keep their community clean.
B: What about all the noise and traffic problems we have?
A: I think that having an attractive community is more important.

What does the woman think makes a community good?
A. The woman thinks that wearing seatbelts makes a community good.
B. The woman thinks that a good community is where people don't litter.
C. The woman thinks that not riding motorcycles makes a community good.

7. What aren't you permitted to do in the park?
A: Gee, Mom, this is a great park!
B: Yes. I think we're all going to have a great time today.
A: Hey! A lake! Can we go swimming?
B: Look, Robbie. What does that sign say?
A: It says swimming is prohibited. But can we go skateboarding?
B: Yes, but you're not allowed to skateboard without your safety equipment.

What aren't you permitted to do in the park?
A. You're not permitted to swim.
B. You're not permitted to skateboard.
C. You're not permitted to skateboard with safety equipment.

8. What can't the people do today?
A: Got everything?
B: Yes. Here's Skippy's leash. We'll need that.
A: What about the kids' bicycle helmets?
B: Got 'em.
A: And the swimming suits?
B: They're right here. Oh, no! I forgot to get a fishing license!

What can't the people do today?
A. They can't go bicycling.
B. They can't walk the dog.
C. They can't go fishing.

9. What's the problem?
A: Yes, officer?
B: I have a complaint from your neighbors.
A: Oh, is the music too loud?
B: No, but your guests are parked on the lawn.

What's the problem?
A. People are walking on the grass.
B. Cars are on the grass.
C. The music is too loud.

10. What's the problem?
A: Good afternoon. May I see your license, please?
B: Oh, sorry officer. Did I exceed the speed limit?
A: No, but you drove through that last red light.
B: Oh, sorry, officer.

What's the problem?
A. The man was driving too fast.
B. The man didn't stop at a red light.
C. The man was driving without a license.

UNIT 7

Lesson 1, Activity 3: Listen and Write (page 88)
Listen to the people talking about jobs and working conditions. Write the name of the job. Then match the condition with the job.

1.
A: So, José, what kind of job would you like?
B: Well, I want to work in healthcare.
A: Healthcare? Like a doctor?
B: No. I think I'd like to be a nurse.
A: A nurse, huh? That sounds hard.
B: It's very hard work.
A: So what do you think you'd like about it?
B: The teamwork.
A: Teamwork?
B: Yes. I love to work on a team with other people. Nurses, doctors, and technicians all work together as a team to help patients.

2.
A: That sounds nice, but I wouldn't want to be indoors all day.
B: So, what's your dream job?
A: Well, first of all, I want to be outdoors all day.
B: Outdoors? So what kind of job would that be?
A: I want to be a landscape designer.
B: A landscape designer?
A: Yeah. Someone who designs gardens.
B: A gardener?
A: No. I might do gardening work too, but I really want to *design* gardens.
B: Oh, I see.
A: Yes, I'd love to work outside and be close to nature all day long!

3.
A: Lara, you like to be outdoors. What's your dream job?
B: I like to *play* outdoors, but I don't want to *work* outdoors.
A: So, what do you want to do?
B: Well, I'd like to work in a hospital, like José . . .
A: You want to be a nurse?
B: No. I think I want to be a medical records specialist.
A: A medical records specialist? That sounds very *indoors*-- you'll be in an office all day!
B: Sounds great to me!

4.
A: I wonder what kind of job Rob wants to have. Rob, what do you want to do?
B: Me? Hmm . . . I want to do something with technology.
A: Technology? Do you want to program computers?
B: No. I think I want to be a biomedical equipment technician.
A: A biomedical equipment technician?
B: Yes. They repair medical equipment.
A: So you want to work with machines?
B: Well, I like to work alone.
A: That sounds kind of lonely.
B: No. I just like to concentrate on my work.
A: Oh, I get it.

Lesson 2, Activity 3: Listen and Write (page 90)
Listen to a conversation about medical benefits. Write the information in the correct column.

A: Wonderful Foods benefits office.
B: Uhm, yes. My name is Ron Grant. I'm a new employee.
A: Hi, Ron. How may I help you?
B: I have some questions about the medical benefits plan.
A: Sure.
B: Uhm, first of all . . . can I see a dermatologist if I choose the Network Plan?
A: Yes, you can. But if you want to see a specialist like a dermatologist, he or she needs to be in the network.
B: Hmm, Dr. Jones . . .wonder if she's in the network.
A: I can check for you right now. What's her first name?
B: Susan.
A: Susan Jones . . . No, sorry, she isn't in the network.
B: So if I want to see the dermatologist I have now, I should choose the Open Access Plan?
A: That's right. If you choose the Open Access Plan, you can see any doctor you want. With the Network Plan, you can only see network doctors.
B: Okay. I have another question.
A: Sure.
B: I'm not married. I have a partner.
A: A domestic partner?
B: Right. How much will I have to pay every month if I choose the Open Access Plan?
A: With a spouse or domestic partner, you'll pay a premium of $55 a month if you go with the Open Access Plan.
B: 55 . . Okay, what's the premium with the Network Plan?
A: It's $40 a month.
B: $40 a month . . And what's the deductible if we go with the Network Plan?
A: If you choose the Network Plan, your deductible is $250.
B: $250. That sounds like a lot. And if we go with the Open Access Plan?
A: There is no deductible if you go with the Open Access Plan.
B: Nothing? And if we choose the Open Access Plan, how much will we have to pay for office visits?
A: The co-pay is $20.
B: Okay . . . $20. And if we take the Network Plan?
A: If you choose the Network Plan, the co-pay is $10.
B: Only 10, huh? What about preventive care?
A: Preventive care?
B: Yes. Is that included in either plan?
A: Absolutely. Both plans include preventive care. The Network Plan charges a $10 co-pay for preventive care.
B: A $10 co-pay? How much is it in the Open Access Plan?
A: With the Open Access Plan, there's no charge for preventive care.
B: No charge, huh?
A: That's right. No charge at all.
B: Gee, this is hard. I can't decide.
A: I know.
B: What should I do?
A: I'm sorry, I can't advise you. You have to decide yourself.

B: Well, we don't get sick very much, and I'd like to save some money this year. . .

A: Hmm . . .

B: I'll think about this and get back to you.

A: That's fine.

B: Thanks for your help.

Lesson 3, Activity 2: Listen and Take Notes (page 92)
Listen to conversations about some of the job ads on page 93. Write two questions each applicant asks. Then write the answers.

1.
A: Hello. I'm calling about the biomedical equipment technician position you've advertised.

B: Yes. How can I help you?

A: Would you mind telling me if you provide medical benefits?

B: Medical benefits—yes, we have a medical benefits plan for all full-time employees.

A: Okay. And I have another question.

B: Certainly.

A: Is the position full-time or part-time?

B: Well, the position you are referring to is only part-time.

A: Only part-time. I see.

B: Are you interested in applying?

A: No, thanks. I need a full-time job right now.

B: Well, thanks for calling.

2.
A: Hello, my name is Michelle Lambert. I'm calling about the ad for a home health aide. Can you tell me a little about the job?

B: Sure. What would you like to know?

A: What kind of qualifications are you looking for?

B: Qualifications? Yes, well, for this particular position, we're looking for someone with at least two years' experience.

A: Two years?

B: Yes, and the applicant also needs to be able to speak Spanish.

A: Ah, okay. . . two years' experience and able to speak Spanish . . . Also, what should I do if I'm interested in applying?

B: You need to complete an application and submit it online.

A: Submit an online application . . got it! Thanks very much.

B: You're welcome.

3.
A: Hello. May I speak to Katie Ruiz?

B: Yes, this is Katie Ruiz.

A: This is Carl Yang. I'm in the Human Resources Department at Greenville Hospital. We received your résumé for the community health worker position. I'd like to schedule you for an interview.

B: That's great.

A: Are you able to come in on Thursday at 10:00 AM?

B: Thursday at 10? Yes, that's fine.

A: Okay. I've got you down for 10 on Thursday.

B: Uhm, may I ask you a couple of questions?

A: Certainly.

B: Does this job require working on the weekends?

A: The weekends? No, we aren't looking for someone to come in on weekends for this particular position.

B: Okay. And, uhm, what is the start date?

A: The start date is April 1st.

B: April 1st?

A: Yes. Are you able to start on April 1st?

B: Sure. No problem.

A: Great. We'll see you Thursday, then.

Lesson 7, Activity 1: Listening Review (page 100)
Part 1: Listen to what is said. When you hear the question, Which is correct?, *listen and choose the correct answer: A, B, or C. Use the Answer Sheet.*

1.
A: What's your dream job?

B: I'd love to work in a hospital.

A: Do you want to be a doctor?

B: No. I'd prefer to be a physician assistant.

Which is correct?
A. The woman wants to be a doctor.
B. The woman wants to be a physician assistant.
C. The woman doesn't want to be a physician assistant.

2.
A: Does the plan cover my dependent?

B: It covers your spouse or domestic partner, and children up to a certain age.

A: I'm divorced, but I have a child. He's 20 years old. Does the plan cover him?

B: No, It only covers children up to the age of 19.

Which is correct?
A. The man has a spouse.
B. The man doesn't have a dependent child.
C. The plan covers the man's son.

3.
A: You pay a $20 co-pay in the Network Plan.

B: Okay. What about the Open Access Plan? Is it the same?

A: No. It's a few dollars more. The Open Access Plan co-pay is $25.

Which is correct?
A. The Open Access Plan co-pay is less than the Network Plan co-pay.
B. The Open Access Plan co-pay is the same as the Network Plan co-pay.
C. The Open Access Plan co-pay is more than the Network Plan co-pay.

4.
A: Can I ask you a few questions about the job?

B: Certainly.

A: Are you looking for someone with both a certificate and two years' experience?

B: No, you just need the certificate. But we are looking for someone with good communication skills.

Which is correct?
  A. The applicant should have a certificate and good communication skills.
  B. The applicant should have a certificate and two years' experience.
  C. The applicant should have two years' experience and be able to communicate in Spanish.

5.
  A: We received your résumé and we'd like you to come in for an interview.
  B: Oh, great!
  A: Are you able to come in on Wednesday at 3?
  B: Oh, I'm afraid I have an appointment tomorrow at 3. How about Thursday?
  A: Thursday would work. Can you come in at 2, then?
  B: Yes. See you then.

Which is correct?
  A. The interview is on Thursday at 2 PM.
  B. The interview is on Friday at 2 PM.
  C. The interview is tomorrow at 3 PM.

Part 2:
You will hear the first part of a conversation. To finish the conversation, listen and choose the correct answer: A, B or C. Use the Answer Sheet.

6.
  A: What do you want to do when you finish school?
  B: I would like to be a teacher.
  A: Really? Why do you want to be a teacher?

  A. I'd rather be a nurse,
  B. I'd prefer to be a gardener.
  C. Because I like working with people.

7.
  A: I have a few questions about the medical benefits.
  B: Sure.
  A: Is my domestic partner covered if I join the Network Plan?

  A. If you join the Network Plan, you can only see Network doctors.
  B. If you join the Network Plan, there's a deductible of $250.
  C. Both plans cover you and your spouse or partner.

8.
  A: I'm trying to figure out which plan is the most economical.
  B: Sure.
  A: So what's my total out-of-pocket cost if I join the Network Plan?

  A. Your out-of-pocket cost is $1,200.
  B. Your co-pay is $20 per visit.
  C. Your deductible is $250.

9.
  A: Hi. I'm calling about the ad for a physician assistant.
  B: Yes. How can I help you?

  A. We're looking for someone with at least two years' experience.
  B. Can you tell me a little about the job?
  C. Thank you for calling.

10.
  A: Do you have at least two years' experience?
  B: Yes, I do.
  A: And are you able to work on weekends?

  A. Yes, I do.
  B. Yes, I am.
  C. No, it isn't.

UNIT 8

Lesson 2, Activity 3: Listen and Write (page 104)
Listen to the conversations. Write the number of the conversation next to the kind of communication.

1.
  A: Mom, can I borrow the car tonight?
  B: Tonight?
  A: Yeah, I've got to get something at the mall.
  B: Sorry. I've got to go to a meeting tonight.

2.
  A: Everybody's talking about Denise's party last weekend. Did you go?
  B: Yeah.
  A: So what did you think of it?
  B: It was fantastic. She had a DJ and the food was great.

3.
  A: Can I help you with anything?
  B: Yes. I could use some help with this photocopying.

4.
  A: I'm so worried, but I just don't know what to do . . .
  B: Why don't you call the clinic and make an appointment?
  A: Okay. That's a good idea.

5.
  A: There you go.
  B: Oh, thank you so much. I don't know what I would have done without your help!
  A: You're very welcome.

6.
  A: Excuse me.
  B: Yes?
  A; Sorry to interrupt, but there's a call for you.
  B: Oh, okay.

Lesson 3, Activity 2: Listen and Write (page 106)
Listen to the conversations. Write M (man) or W (woman) next to the kind of communication.

Conversation 1:
  A: All right. Are there any questions? Does anyone need help?
  B: Uhm, yes, Mr. Pinkley What do you think of my Web page?

A: Let me see, Dina.
B: How do you think I could improve it?
A: Wow, Dina, you did a nice job on this.
B: Thank you.
A: But this part of the page up here looks a little empty.
B: Hmm . . . what should I do?
A: I think you might want to move your photos around a little bit.
B: Oh. . . Yes, that looks much better!

Conversation 2:
A: Hey, Mark, sorry to interrupt your work.
B: Oh, hi, Jennifer. I'm not really working . . .
A: Are you okay? Is anything wrong?
B: Well, now that you ask. . . can you help me with something?
A: Sure.
B: My girlfriend is mad at me. We had a misunderstanding so I wrote her an email. Would you mind looking at it? How does it sound?
A: It sounds fine. I'm sure she'll feel better after she reads this.
B: Oh, gee, thanks. I can't tell you how much I appreciate your help.
A: No problem!

Conversation 3:
A: Arggh! This is hard!
B: Well, did you read the instructions?
A: Yes, but they're so confusing. . . You know, I really could use a little help here. . .
B: Okay. Let me do it.
A: Be my guest.
B: Okay, let's see. . . it says "Add the totals on lines 11 and 12, then . . ." hmm . . .
A: It's hard, isn't it?
B: Hey, I know! Let's pay someone to do our taxes this year!
A: Now you're thinking! That's a great suggestion!

Lesson 4, Activity 3: Listen and Apply (page 109)
Listen to a short presentation. Practice your listening skills while you take notes. Then answer the questions. Compare your answers with a partner.

Do you want to communicate better with your kids? Here are some tips:

First, make the time. Set aside some time to talk. It doesn't have to be a formal meeting. In fact, some of the best discussions happen when you're in the car or making dinner in the kitchen.

Ask your children's opinions. Children love it when someone asks for their opinion. This means that you are taking them seriously. You'll get more information from your kids this way.

Finally, don't interrupt your children when they are speaking, even if you think you know what they are going to say. In a survey, 50 percent of the children said that their parents interrupted them when they were talking. It's always a good idea to give your children extra time to explain things.

Lesson 7, Activity: Listening Review (page 114)

Part 1
First you will hear a question. Next, listen carefully to what is said. You will hear the question again. Then choose the correct answer: A, B, or C. Use the Answer Sheet.

1. What might Mark be saying?
   A: Can you hear what Mark is saying?
   B: No. He's too far away, but he's waving his hand.
   A: Is he saying, "Hello"?
   B: No. He might be saying, "Come here."

What might Mark be saying?
   A. Come here.
   B. I can't hear you.
   C. Hello.

2. What is the woman doing?
   A: As I was saying, . . .
   B: Could I interrupt for a minute, Sam?
   A. Sure. . .
   B. You have a phone call.

What is the woman doing?
   A. asking for help
   B. making a suggestion
   C. interrupting

3. What does the man do?
   A: Hey, that looks heavy!
   B: Yes. I think I could use some help.
   A: Here. Let me help you carry that.
   B: Thanks so much for your help!

What does the man do?
   A. He offers help.
   B. He expresses appreciation.
   C. He asks for an opinion.

4. Who is speaking?
   A: Does anyone need help?
   B: Uhm, yes, Ms. Kim, would you please take a look at my paper?
   A: Sure, Mike.

Who is speaking?
   A. a parent and a child
   B. a doctor and a patient
   C. a teacher and a student

5. What does the woman do?
   A: Can you tell me how to make an international phone call?
   B: Sure. Dial 011, then the country code, . . .
   A: Uh huh . . .
   B: and then the number. Did you get that?
   A: Yes. Thanks.

What does the woman do?
   A. She checks for understanding.
   B. She makes a request.
   C. She asks for feedback.

Part 2

You will hear the first part of a conversation. To finish the conversation, listen and choose the correct answer: A, B, or C. Use the Answer Sheet.

6.

A: What is Jon saying?
B: I don't know, but he's pointing at the table.

A. Then he must be saying, "Wait a minute."
B. Then he must be saying, "Put it on the table."
C. Then he must be saying, "I don't know."

7.

A: Are you ready to go?
B: Just about. What do you think of my new dress?

A. You're welcome.
B. It looks nice.
C. Sure. Go ahead.

8.

A: And this is the living room . . . we painted it ourselves.
B: Wow, you did a lot of work! And it looks wonderful!

A. Thanks!
B. You're welcome!
C. Sure. Go ahead.

9.

A: Now, the last step is to choose "Save" from the pull-down menu.
B: Okay, choose "Save" from the pull-down menu . . .
A: Is that clear?

A. You're welcome.
B. I'd be happy to.
C. Yes. Thanks for your help.

10.

A: Are you okay? Is anything wrong?
B: Actually, yes. I'm having trouble with this assignment. Do you think you can help me?

A. Thank you.
B. Sure. Go ahead.
C. I'd be happy to help.

UNIT 9

Lesson 2, Activity 3: Listen and Write (page 118)
Listen to the news report about what the three branches of government are doing. Write each activity in the correct place in the chart.

A: And now, it's time for our Washington Roundup segment. Jan, what was happening in the nation's capital today?
B: Well, Dave, there was a lot going on in Washington today. In Congress, the House voted on the "English Plus" bill. This bill encourages people to use languages other than English, for example, in education and in public safety information. The House passed the bill, and now it will go to the Senate. In other Washington news, the Supreme

Court made an important decision today on the gun issue—the right to keep or carry a loaded handgun. As you may know, Washington, D.C., does not allow citizens to carry handguns. But today the Supreme Court decided that that law is unconstitutional. Over at the White House, the President vetoed the children's health insurance bill. That's the bill that would provide healthcare to all children. Afterwards, the President met with the press and explained that the bill needed more work to be sure all children would be covered.
A: Thank you, Jan, for a very informative report.

Lesson 3, Activity 2: Listen for General Information (page 120)
Listen to the information about holidays. Write the name of the holiday and check if the holiday celebrates an event or a person.

1.

A: Today, we're going to be discussing the history of some major U.S. holidays. Uhm, okay, to start, does anyone know what holiday is coming up just next week?
B1:Oh, I know.
A: Yes?
B1:It's Memorial Day.
A: Memorial Day. That's right.
B1:Is it next Monday?
A: Exactly. We celebrate Memorial Day on the last Monday in May.
B1:It's *always* the last Monday in May?
A: Right. Now, can anyone tell me what Memorial Day celebrates? No? All right. Memorial Day honors people who died while serving in the United States military. Uhm, yes?
B2:Is that any branch of the military?
A: Yes. It can be the Navy, the Army, the Marines . . .
B2:And does it matter what war they were in?
A: No. It honors people who were in any war. In fact, people first started celebrating Memorial Day after the Civil War, back in the 1800s, but it didn't become an official national holiday until 1967.

2.

A: Okay. Now, what's the next national holiday on the calendar?
B3:Oh, uhm, that would be Independence Day? Uhm, the Fourth of July?
A: Right. Independence Day. Many people also call it the Fourth of July, which is the date we celebrate it, as well.
B3:It's always on July 4th, right?
A: Right. And I'm sure everyone knows what Independence Day celebrates? Uhm, yes?
B4:It celebrates the day that the United States became independent from Great Britain.
A: Right. It actually celebrates an important event in American history.
B4:Wasn't July 4th the day that the war with Great Britain ended?

A: No. Actually, it celebrates the day that Congress approved the Declaration of Independence, July 4th, 1776. Can anyone tell me what the Declaration of Independence said?

B5: It said that we would not be part of Great Britain anymore and that we had the right to have our own government.

A: Right.

3.

A: Okay, now moving through the calendar, can anyone tell me what national holiday we have in September? No one? Okay, It's Labor Day.

B2: When is Labor Day?

A: Labor Day is on the first Monday in September.

B2: It's *always* the first Monday in September?

A: Right. And what does Labor Day celebrate?

B3: Oh, I know!

A: Yes?

B3: It celebrates workers.

A: Right. It celebrates all the people who work hard to keep the country going. That was the original idea when it started back in 1894. Workers were angry, and Congress decided it would be a good idea to celebrate workers . . .

B4: So Congress gave them a day off from work?

A: Exactly. But today, it's actually a day off for everyone.

4.

A: Now, what national holiday do we have at the beginning of the year?

B4: In January?

A: Yes.

B1: Oh, that's Martin Luther King, Jr. Day.

A: And what date is that? No one? Martin Luther King, Jr. Day is always the third Monday.

B1: It's January 18th this year, right?

A: Right. And why do we celebrate this person?

B4: Because King was an important civil rights leader.

A: Right. Martin Luther King, Jr. Day celebrates an important person in U.S. history, a civil rights leader. And what did he do? Yes?

B1: King worked to make sure that everyone had equal rights.

A: Right. And President Reagan signed a law to make it an official holiday in 1983.

5.

A: Okay, we have another national holiday that celebrates an important person. Or I should say, two important people. Anyone?

B2: Is it Presidents' Day?

A: Right.

B4: Is it February 22nd?

A: Well, Presidents' Day is on the third Monday in February.

B4: Oh, like some of those other holidays. . .

A: Right. It's always on the third Monday in February. And who do we celebrate on that day?

B4: Presidents of the United States?

A: Well, most states celebrate George Washington and Abraham Lincoln on Presidents' Day.

B1: Because they were both born in February.

A: That's right. Why is Washington important?

B1: He was the first president of the United Sates.

A: And Lincoln?

B2: He was the 16th president. He ended slavery.

A: Yes.

Lesson 4, Activity 3: Listen and Write (page 123)
Listen to the conversations about voting. Match the conversation with the topic.

1.

A: Traffic between here and Greenville is terrible.

B: I know. There are more and more cars on this road every year.

A: Well, I sure hope Proposition B passes in the election next month.

A: Proposition B? Which one is that?

B: If Proposition B passes, we'll have a high-speed train between here and Greenville.

A: Oh, that's right. That will really help the traffic problem.

B: It'll be good for the environment, too.

A: That's right.

2.

A: Hello. I'm asking people their opinion of Proposition 3. Can I ask how you're going to vote next week?

B: Uhm, sure, but I get all those propositions mixed up. Which one is 3?

A: Well, if you vote "Yes" on Proposition 3, it means you agree to give more money to improve our public schools.

B: But where does the money come from?

A: From taxes.

B: Well, I'm against paying more taxes, so. . .

A: So you'll vote "No" on Proposition 3?

B: That's right. I'm against it.

A: Well, thank you very much.

3.

A: Are you planning on voting next week?

B: I don't know. It's just a city election.

A: Yes, but it's very important. You *should* vote.

B: Why?

A: Because we're going to choose a new mayor.

B: Why is that important?

A: Well, for one thing, the mayor is in charge of our city budget. He or she decides how to spend money on the city.

B: Well, that does sound pretty important.

A: Right. We really need someone who's good with money.

B: You're right. I'll definitely vote next week.

4.

A: What do you think about Patricia Wong?

B: You mean the woman who is running for state senator?

A: Yes.

B: I don't know. I think I like the other guy.

A: Randall Jones? He would be a terrible senator!
B: I disagree. The person we choose will represent us in the state government, so he or she needs to know the kinds of problems we have here.
A: Well, then Patricia Wong would be a great state senator!
B: She doesn't have enough experience.
A: I disagree. I'm voting for Patricia!
B: And I'm voting for Randall!

Lesson 7, Activity 1: Listening Review (page 128)
Part 1:
Listen to what is said. When you hear the question, Which is correct?, listen and choose the correct answer: A, B, or C. Use the Answer Sheet.
1.
A: What was the Senate like?
B: We saw people discussing and voting on a bill.
A: Did they pass the bill?
B: No, they didn't.

Which is correct?
A. The Senate voted on a bill.
B. The House passed a bill.
C. The Senate passed a bill.

2.
A: Congress sent the gun bill to the President today.
B: What happened?
A: He vetoed it.

Which is correct?
A. The President agreed with the bill.
B. The President disagreed with the bill.
C. The President passed the bill.

3.
A: Today the Supreme Court made an important decision.
B: And what was that?
A: It decided that the gun law did not break the rules of the Constitution.

Which is correct?
A. The Supreme Court passed a gun law.
B. The Supreme Court vetoed a gun law.
C. The Supreme Court made a decision about a gun law.

4.
A: What was happening in Washington today, Amy?
B: Well, the President signed two bills and vetoed one bill.

Which is correct?
A. The woman is talking about the executive branch.
B. The woman is talking about the judicial branch.
C. The woman is talking about the legislative branch.

5.
A: We're having a party on Independence Day. Can you come?
B: I'd love to, but I have other plans.

Which is correct?
A. The woman plans to come to the party.
B. The woman plans to have a party.
C. The woman can't come to the party.

Part 2:
First you will hear a question. Next, listen carefully to what is said. You will hear the question again. Then choose the correct answer: A, B, or C. Use the Answer Sheet.
6. What did the man do?
A: What did you do on your trip to Washington?
B: I visited Congress.
A: Did you go to the Senate?
B: No. I went to the House of Representatives.

What did the man do?
A. He visited the House of Representatives.
B. He visited the Senate.
C. He voted in Congress.

7. Which branch of government are they talking about?
A: What does Congress do?
B: It proposes and passes bills.

Which branch of government are they talking about?
A. They're talking about the judicial branch.
B. They're talking about the executive branch.
C. They're talking about the legislative branch.

8. What holiday is next month?
A: Is Presidents' Day next month?
B: No, it's Martin Luther King, Jr. Day.
A: Wasn't he a president?
B: No, he was a civil rights leader.

What holiday is next month?
A. Civil Rights Day
B. Martin Luther King, Jr. Day
C. Presidents' Day

9. What holiday are the people talking about?
A: My favorite holiday is the one in May.
B: Is that because you like to remember people who fought in wars?
A: No. It's because I like to get a day off from work!

What holiday are the people talking about?
A. Labor Day
B. Memorial Day
C. Independence Day

10. What is the man doing on Independence Day?
A: We're having a picnic on Independence Day. Can you come?
B: I'd love to, but I have to work.
A: I didn't think anybody worked on Independence Day!
B: Well, I work at the airport and a lot of people travel on July fourth.

What is the man doing on Independence Day?
  A. He's traveling.
  B. He's working.
  C. He's having a picnic.

UNIT 10

Lesson 2 , Activity 3: Listen and Take Notes (page 132)
Listen to the employees ask for time off. Write the type of leave.

1.
  A: Ms. Jones?
  B: Yes, Robert?
  A: May I speak to you for a moment?
  B: Certainly.
  A: May I have the week of April 4th off?
  B: May I ask why?
  A: Yes. My wife is having a baby
  B: A baby!?! Congratulations!
  A: Thank you.
  B: Of course you can have that week off. I'm sure you'll have a lot to do. And you'll want to get to know the new baby, too!
  A: Thanks.

2.
  A: Oh, Sam, I just wanted to tell you how sorry I was to hear about your grandmother.
  B: Thanks, Sue. She had a long and happy life, but we're going to miss her.
  A: Certainly.
  B: That reminds me—the funeral is next Thursday . . .
  A: Uh-huh . . .
  B: . . . and I was wondering if I could have a few days off.
  A: Let's see . . . next week . . .
  B: Yes, that's right. Since the funeral is in New York, I need some time to fly there.
  A: Okay So Wednesday to Friday?
  B: Yes, that would be great.
  A: That shouldn't be a problem.
  B: Thank you very much, Sue.

3.
  A: Oh, Don?
  B: Yes, Mike?
  A: I have a bit of an emergency this week. . .
  B: What is it?
  A: The babysitter is sick, and my wife's on a business trip.
  B: I see. . .
  A: So there's no one to take care of the kids tomorrow.
  B: Uh-huh. . .
  A: May I take the day off tomorrow?
  B: Sorry, Mike. We need you here.
  A: But. . .
  B: It's too short notice. I don't have any time to find you a replacement now.
  A: I see.

B: I'm afraid you're going to have to deal with the problem some other way.
A: Okay . . .

4.
  A: Mr. Hayes?
  B: Yes, Janette?
  A: I have to have surgery next month.
  B: Oh, my. It's nothing serious, I hope!
  A: No, no. It's not serious. It's just my foot. I'm going to have an operation on my left foot.
  B: I see.
  A: And I'm not supposed to walk for a few days after the surgery.
  B: Uh-huh. . .
  A: So I was wondering if I could take the week of May 14th off.
  B: Hmm, let me see. . . May 14? That shouldn't be a problem.
  A: Thank you very much!
  B: And thank you for asking so far ahead of time. It really helps.

Lesson 3, Activity 2: Listen and Take Notes (page 134)
Listen to the phone calls. Write the information in the chart.

1.
  A: Hello.
  B: Um, hi. This is Dan. Is Rick there?
  A: Let me see . . . Um, hey guys, is Rick here? Um no, he's not here. Do you want to leave a message?
  B: Yes, thanks, Can you tell him that I called?
  A: Okay, Dan, right?
  B: Right. And, um, I'm going to bring his book to class tomorrow.
  A: Dan . . . bring book to class tomorrow . . . Okay, I got it.
  B: Thanks, dude.
  A: No problem.

2.
  A: Speedy Delivery. Robert Jackson's office.
  B: Uh, yes. May I please speak to Mr. Jackson?
  A: He's in a meeting right now. May I take a message?
  B: Yes. Would you tell him that Ann King is calling?
  A: Ann King . . . Yes?
  B: And I'm returning his call.
  A: You're returning his call. . .
  B: Yes. He called me to make an appointment for an interview. . .
  A: Uh-huh . . . And your number is. . . .?
  B: It's 415-555-3489.
  A: 415-555-3489?
  B: That's right.
  A: Okay, I'll have him try you again.
  B: Thank you very much.
  A: You're welcome.

3.
  A: You have reached 858-555-3478. If you'd like to leave a message, please do so after the beep.

B: Uhm, hi, Lara. This is Rob. I've been waiting for the bus for half an hour. I think I'm going to be a few minutes late. Go ahead and buy the tickets and get in line. If you have any questions, call me back. See you soon. Bye-bye.

Lesson 4, Activity 3: Listen and Apply (page 137)
Listen to the conversation and complete the chart.

A: Hey, Ting, can you get our W-2 forms? I'd like to finish our taxes today.
B: Okay. Here they are.
A: Thanks. I'll fill in the form. You can read the information to me.
B: Okay.
A: So, what were your wages, Ting?
B: My wages were 25 thousand 500 dollars.
A: 25 thousand 500 dollars, huh?
B: Yeah, 25 thousand 500.
A: Okay, And how about my wages?
B: Your wages were 24 thousand 950 dollars.
A: 24 thousand 950 dollars? Okay. . . Now, let's see how much was withheld. . .
B: Let me see, Wei. For your salary of 24 thousand 950, 2 thousand 742 dollars was withheld.
A: Is that state or federal?
B: That's 2 thousand 742 dollars withheld for federal taxes.
A: How about you?
B: I had 2 thousand 896 dollars withheld.
A: Okay, you had 2 thousand 896 withheld for federal taxes. How about state taxes?
B: My state withholding was 1 thousand 20 dollars.
A: Okay, you paid 1 thousand 20 dollars in state taxes. What about my state taxes?
B: You paid 1 thousand and 3 dollars.
A: 1 thousand and 3 dollars?
B: Right.
A: Hey, we might get a little bit back! If we get a refund, what should we do with the money?
B: Let's buy a new TV!
A: I don't think we'll get enough for a TV!

Lesson 7, Activity 1: Listening Review (page 142)
Part 1:
First you will hear a question. Next, listen carefully to what is said. You will hear the question again. Then choose the correct answer: A, B, or C. Use the Answer Sheet.

1. Who is the woman?
   A: May I see your boarding pass, please?
   B: My what?
   A: Your boarding pass. I can't let you board the plane until I put it through the ticket reader.
   B: Oh, okay.

Who is the woman?
   A. She's a passenger.
   B. She's an air traffic controller.
   C. She's a gate agent.

2. What equipment is the man using?
   A: Would you please lift up your arms?
   B: I'm afraid I'm going to miss my plane.
   A: It'll just take a second. I'm just going to wave this over your body. There. You can go to your gate now.

What equipment is the man using?
   A. a headset
   B. a metal detector
   C. a ticket reader

3. What kind of leave does the woman want to take?
   A: Uhm, Mr. Bradshaw, may I take off the rest of the day today?
   B: May I ask what for?
   A: My babysitter is sick. There's no one to take care of the kids.
   B: Oh, okay.

What kind of leave does the woman want to take?
   A. maternity leave
   B. medical leave
   C. childcare emergency leave

4. Why does the man want to take time off from work?
   A: Barb, may I take a few days' bereavement leave?
   B: Sure. No problem. I was very sorry to hear about your grandfather.

Why does the man want to take time off from work?
   A. Because someone died.
   B. Because he has jury duty.
   C. Because he's sick.

5. Who called?
   A: Hello. Mark here.
   B: Hi. Is Jean there?
   A: No, she isn't home right now. Can I take a message?
   B: Yes, thanks. Tell her Joe called.

Who called?
   A. Mark
   B. Jean
   C. Joe

Part 2:
Listen to what is said. When you hear the question **Which is correct?**, *listen and choose the correct answer: A, B, or C. Use the Answer Sheet.*

6.
   A: Ms. Richard's office.
   B: Hello. This is Mindy Lee. May I please speak to Ms. Richards?
   A: I'm sorry, she isn't available right now. Would you like to leave a message?
   B: Yes. Would you please tell her to call me at 858-555-9467?

Which is correct?
   A. Ms. Richards left a message.
   B. Mindy Lee left a message.
   C. Mindy Lee isn't available.

7.

Leave a message after the beep.

A: Hi, Rick. This is Sara. I left my English book at home. Can you bring it when you come to school today? I'll meet you in the cafeteria at noon. Thanks!

Which is correct?

A. Rick forgot his book.
B. Sara is coming home at noon.
C. Sara forgot her book.

8.

A: Are you asking to take a week off from work in August?
B: No, in September. And I only need four days. It's for a medical leave.
A: Oh, that should be okay.

Which is correct?

A. The man needs to take a week off in September.
B. The man needs to take four days off in August.
C. The man needs to take four days off in September.

9.

A: Mary, you're back! It's so great to see you!
B: Well, it's good to be back, but I really miss my baby.
A: How old is she now?
B: Just two months.

Which is correct?

A. Mary just came back from a maternity leave.
B. Mary just came back from a paternity leave.
C. Mary just came back from military leave.

10.

A: Hurry! We have to load these quickly. The plane is leaving soon.
B: Don't worry. I'll get the conveyor belt ready.
A: Thanks!

Which is correct?

A. They are ticket agents.
B. They are airport security screeners
C. They are baggage handlers.

VOCABULARY LIST

Numbers in parentheses indicate unit numbers.

abuse (3)
academic counselor (1)
accident (5)
accomplish (1)
account balance (4)
admittance clerk (7)
advance (1)
air conditioning (2)
air traffic controller (10)
aircraft maintenance
    technician (10)
airport security screener (10)
alcohol (3)
alcoholic beverages (6)
allergic (3)
allergy (3)
allow (6)
anonymous (3)
anticipate (8)
appendectomy (3)
appreciate (8)
appreciation (8)
areas (6)
assault (3)
asthma (3)
ATM (4)
available (2)
baggage handler (10)
be in charge of (1)
benefits (7)
bereavement leave (10)
bill (9)
biomedical equipment
    technician (7)
bleeding (5)
boarding passes (10)
body language (8)
bounce a check (4)
bounced check (4)
branch (9)
burn (5)
calcium (3)
cancer (3)
cashier's check (4)
certificate (1)
check card (4)
checking account (4)
check-up (3)
childcare emergency leave (10)
cholesterol (3)
come true (7)
communication style (8)
community center (6)
community health worker (7)
competitive (8)
complain (2)
compliment (8)
congratulate (2)
Congress (9)

consciousness (5)
constitutional (9)
construction site (5)
consumption (6)
continuing education (1)
conveyor belt (10)
co-pay (7)
cover letter (7)
credit card (4)
credit history (2)
crisis (3)
damage (4)
debit card (4)
debt (1)
deductible (7)
deductions (7)
defect (4)
delegate (1)
Democrat (9)
democratic (9)
demonstrator (6)
dependents (7)
diet (3)
direct deposit (4)
disabilities (6)
disease (3)
distinguished (9)
domestic partner (7)
domestic violence (3)
drug abuse (3)
ear plugs (5)
earn (9)
effectively (8)
elevate (5)
elevator (2)
emergency (5)
entrepreneur (1)
equal opportunity (2)
etiquette (10)
evacuate (5)
exceed (6)
executive (9)
expenses (1)
explode (5)
express (8)
expression (8)
fair housing (2)
feedback (8)
financial aid (1)
firearm (6)
first aid (5)
fish (6)
flammable (5)
focus (1)
fracture (5)
fuel truck (10)
gas mileage (4)
gate agent (10)
gauze pad (5)

GED (1)
get to the point (8)
give orders (8)
give up (2)
graffiti (6)
gross pay (7)
ground service equipment
    mechanic (10)
hard hat (5)
hazard (5)
headset (10)
healthcare provider (3)
heat (2)
heat exhaustion (5)
helmet (6)
home health aide (7)
hotline (3)
House of Representatives (9)
illegal (6)
immediately (2)
income taxes (10)
Independence Day (9)
infect (3)
infection (3)
inform (2)
injure (5)
injury (5)
insufficient (4)
insufficient funds (4)
intense (5)
interest (4)
interrupt (8)
interruption (8)
jail (6)
judicial (9)
jury duty (10)
knee pad (6)
lab technician (7)
Labor Day (9)
laundry room (2)
leash (6)
leave (of absence) (10)
legislative (9)
license (6)
life vest (3)
litter (6)
loan (4)
location (2)
loiter (6)
long-term goal (1)
low-fat (3)
make (of car) (4)
make a good impression (10)
make a request (8)
make a suggestion (8)
Martin Luther King Day (9)
maternity leave (10)
mayor (9)
medical leave (10)

medical records specialist (7)
medication (3)
Memorial Day (9)
metal detector (10)
mileage (4)
military leave (10)
minor (5)
model (of car) (4)
naturalization (1)
need attention (7)
neglect (3)
neighborhood (2)
net pay (7)
network (7)
newcomers (6)
nutrition (3)
nutritional (3)
objective (7)
obstacle (7)
occupants (2)
offer (8)
on sale (4)
online banking (4)
open access (7)
open doors (1)
operate (3)
operation (3)
orderly (7)
origin (9)
original receipt (4)
out-of-pocket (7)
overdraft (4)
parent-teacher conference (1)
party (9)
pass a bill (9)
paternity leave (10)
pay by (check, credit) (4)
pay off (1)
period (of coverage) (4)
permit (6)
persuasive (8)
physician assistant (7)
PIN (4)
position (2, 9)
posted (6)
post-operative (3)
premium (7)
prenatal (3)
pre-owned (4)
prepare (1)
prescribe (3)
prescription (3)
present (2)
president (9)
Presidents Day (9)
pressure (5)
preventive care (7)
previous (2)
prioritize (1)

priority (9)
progress visit (3)
prohibit (3)
prohibited (6)
propose a bill (9)
proposition (9)
provide (3)
provider (3)
PTA meeting (1)
quota (9)
rash (3)
reduce (1)
reduced-cost (3)
refer to (10)
referral (3)
refund (4, 10)
registration (9)
rental application (2)
replacement (4)
representative (9)
Republican (9)
request, v. (2)
request, n. (8)
research (8)
responsibilities (1)
résumé (7)
revise (7)
revising (7)

rob (5)
routine (3)
rude (8)
run for (9)
safety equipment (5)
safety glasses (5)
savings account (4)
scaffolding (5)
seatbelt (6)
security (2)
Senate (9)
senator (9)
serve (9)
service charge (4)
shock (5)
short-term goal (1)
speaker of the House (9)
speed (6)
speed bumps (6)
statement (4)
stretch (9)
submerge (5)
suggest (8)
suggestion (8)
sunblock (3)
supervisor (2)
supplement (3)
supply (3)

supporting ideas (8)
Supreme Court (9)
surface (5)
surgery (3)
surgical (3)
swipe (4)
take orders (8)
take time off (10)
team player (10)
teamwork (10)
tech support specialist (7)
thank (2)
the Constitution (9)
the press (9)
ticket agent (10)
ticket reader (10)
tow tractor (10)
toxic (5)
traffic stop (6)
trash (6)
treatment (3)
trespass (6)
trespassing (6)
tutor (1)
universal (9)
unopened (4)
unused (4)
unworn (4)

update (9)
utilities (2)
vacation (10)
valid (4)
vandalism (6)
vest (5)
veto (9)
vice president (9)
vitamin (3)
void (4)
void (4)
volunteer, v. (1)
volunteer, n. (6)
vote for (9)
vote on (9)
wages (10)
warranty (4)
washer and dryer hookup (2)
waste time (1)
weapons (6)
well baby visit (3)
withheld (10)
withhold (10)
witness (5)
working conditions (7)
workmanship (4)
X-ray scanner (10)

IRREGULAR VERBS

Irregular Verbs

Base Form	Simple Past	Past Participle	Base Form	Simple Past	Past Participle
be	was/were	been	keep	kept	kept
become	became	become	know	knew	known
begin	began	begun	leave	left	left
bleed	bled	bled	lend	lent	lent
break	broke	broken	lose	lost	lost
bring	brought	brought	make	made	made
buy	bought	bought	meet	met	met
choose	chose	chosen	pay	paid	paid
come	came	come	put	put	put
cost	cost	cost	read	read	read
cut	cut	cut	ring	rang	rung
do	did	done	run	ran	run
drink	drank	drunk	see	saw	seen
drive	drove	driven	sell	sold	sold
eat	ate	eaten	send	sent	sent
fall	fell	fallen	set	set	set
feel	felt	felt	shake	shook	shaken
fight	fought	fought	shut	shut	shut
find	found	found	sleep	slept	slept
forget	forgot	forgotten	speak	spoke	spoken
fry	fried	fried	speed	sped	sped
get	got	gotten	spend	spent	spent
give	gave	given	take	took	taken
go	went	gone	teach	taught	taught
grow	grew	grown	tell	told	told
have/has	had	had	think	thought	thought
hear	heard	heard	wear	wore	worn
hold	held	held	write	wrote	written
hurt	hurt	hurt			

CREDITS

SKILLS INDEX

ACADEMIC SKILLS